Sports law and policy
in the Europe...

ONE WEEK LOAN

MANCHESTER
UNIVERSITY PRESS

European Policy Research Unit Series

Series Editors: *Simon Bulmer, Peter Humphreys* and *Mick Moran*

The European Policy Research Unit Series aims to provide advanced textbooks and thematic studies of key public policy issues in Europe. They concentrate, in particular, on comparing patterns of national policy content, but pay due attention to the European Union dimension. The thematic studies are guided by the character of the policy issue under examination.

The European Policy Research Unit (EPRU) was set up in 1989 within the University of Manchester's Department of Government to promote research on European politics and public policy. The series is part of EPRU's effort to facilitate intellectual exchange and substantive debate on the key policy issues confronting the European states and the European Union.

Titles in the series also include:

The governance of the Single European Market   Kenneth Armstrong and Simon Bulmer

The politics of health in Europe   Richard Freeman

Immigration and European integration   Andrew Geddes

Mass media and media policy in Western Europe   Peter Humphreys

The regions and the new Europe   Martin Rhodes (ed.)

The rules of integration   Gerald Schneider and Mark Aspinwall

Political economy of financial integration in Europe   Jonathan Story and Ingo Walter

Fifteen into one?   Wolfgang Wessels, Andreas Maurer and Jürgen Mittag

Extending European cooperation   Alasdair R. Young

Regulatory politics in the enlarging European Union   Alasdair Young and Helen Wallace

Sports law and policy in the European Union

Richard Parrish

Manchester University Press
Manchester and New York

distributed exclusively in the USA by Palgrave

Published by Manchester University Press
Oxford Road, Manchester M13 9NR, UK
and Room 400, 175 Fifth Avenue, New York, NY 10010, USA
www.manchesteruniversitypress.co.uk

Distributed exclusively in the USA by
Palgrave, 175 Fifth Avenue, New York,
NY 10010, USA

Distributed exclusively in Canada by
UBC Press, University of British Columbia, 2029 West Mall
Vancouver, BC, Canada V6T 1Z2

British Library Cataloguing-in-Publication Data
A catalogue record for this book is available from the British Library

Library of Congress Cataloging-in-Publication Data applied for

ISBN 0 7190 6606 9 *hardback*
ISBN 0 7190 6607 7 *paperback*

First published 2003

11 10 09 08 07 06 05 04 03   10 9 8 7 6 5 4 3 2 1

Typeset in Sabon
by Servis Filmsetting Ltd., Manchester
Printed in Great Britain
by Biddles Ltd, Guildford and King's Lynn

For Lowell

Contents

Acknowledgements

This book is based partly on a doctoral thesis completed in 2001 at the University of Manchester. In writing 'The Path to a European Union Sports Policy' I received valuable assistance from Professor Simon Bulmer and Professor Peter Humphreys at the University of Manchester and Professor Claudio Radaelli at the University of Bradford. Of course, the views expressed in this text (and any errors) are my own. In addition, I owe special thanks to past and present sports law researchers at the Anglia Polytechnic University. In particular Simon Gardiner and John O'Leary have frequently provided me with an invaluable platform with which to share my ideas. I am also grateful to those members of the EU who shared their thoughts on this matter with me and allowed for the re-production of key documentation.

The final word is of course reserved for my family. Without the support of Berenice this book would never have been completed. Without the interventions of my adorable son Lowell, it would have been completed much sooner! I don't regret a minute. Happy first birthday son.

Introduction

Out groups from Brossell Norman for advocacy walk Mod

Sports Law and Policy in the European Union is a deliberately provocative title. It is not widely accepted that a discrete body of sports law has emerged or is emerging within the European Union (EU) or within national jurisdictions. Furthermore, given that the EU has no legal competence to develop a sports policy, one might ask (as I was by an eminent 'sport and the law' lawyer), 'what the bloody hell has the Common Market got to do with sport?' Browsing through the list of EU activities contained in Article 3 of the EU's Treaty, it is clear that sport has no place in the Treaty. Nevertheless, Article 3 does state that the EU is to establish an area where goods, persons, services and capital can freely circulate and where competition is not distorted. As an activity of undoubted commercial significance, sports bodies must therefore ensure that their activities do not contradict these Treaty provisions. As the European Court of Justice's (ECJ's) ruling in *Bosman* demonstrated, EU law can have a profound impact on sport. Although this brief explanation does not justify the label 'EU sports law', it does explain why there is a relationship between sport and EU law.

The EU's policy involvement in sport extends beyond legal regulation. Article 3 also expresses the EU's desire to expand into more social arenas. Since the 1984 Fontainebleau Summit, the EU has attempted to extend European integration beyond the economic field by establishing a 'people's Europe'. In order to do so the EU intends to use sport to implement a range of social, cultural and educational policy objectives outlined in Article 3. However, the excessive commercialisation of sport combined with legal regulation at EU level threatens to undermine these political objectives. Without more co-ordinated action in the field of sport, EU policy towards sport risks being pulled apart by competing policy tensions.

Traditionally, the sports sector has developed rules which have attempted to maintain a competitive balance between participants. Given the extent of commercialisation in European sport, the maintenance of these rules is considered by many as essential. However, many of these alleged pro-competitive rules have been regarded as anti-competitive by the EU. Again, the policy tension within the EU is evident. On the one hand, the EU has a regulatory policy interest in sport as a result of its commitment to protect the legal foundations of the Single Market. On the other, the EU harbours political policy aspirations for sport, particularly in the field of the people's Europe project. The research agenda concentrates on this policy tension. In particular, this tension has contributed to the development of a more co-ordinated EU sports policy in which these tensions can be reconciled. The glue binding this policy is not however derived from primary or secondary legislation but rather case law. In short, the defining characteristic of EU sports policy is the construction of a discrete area of EU sports law. EU sports law extends beyond the mere application of law to sport, to the construction of a legal approach for dealing with sports disputes which allows both the EU's regulatory and political policy objectives for sport to co-exist within the EU sports policy framework. This research agenda is particularly fascinating because the twin concepts of EU sports law and EU sports policy have emerged in the absence of a Treaty base for sport. They have therefore developed without the engine of legislation. For lawyers and political scientists alike, this poses many interesting questions about the dynamics behind policy change in the EU.

The emergence of a co-ordinated EU sports policy held together by a discrete area of sports law is a new development in the EU. It has its roots in the post-*Bosman* political debate about the future of EU involvement in sport. The theoretical method of investigation employed in this text reflects this political impetus behind the birth of EU sports law and policy. The approach, drawn from policy analysis, stresses the need for 'subsystem analysis'. Within the EU operate numerous policy-specific subsystems, one of which concerns sport. Operating within them are rival advocacy coalitions attempting to steer policy in a direction consistent with their belief system. The identification of the coalitions composition and belief systems is therefore an essential methodological starting point. However, policy changes as a result of the activities of the advocacy coalitions and their success depends on their ability to influence policy in numerous institutional venues. Coalitions who are institutionally well resourced will be able to exploit legislative, budgetary, legal and other venues in order to ensure their belief system prevails.

The sports policy subsystem is composed of two advocacy coalitions. The *Single Market* coalition has a regulatory policy interest in sport. Actors within it seek to ensure the legal foundations of the Single Market are protected. As a significant economic activity, sports rules should comply with EU law. The *socio-cultural* coalition pursues more political policy objectives for sport. In particular the actors within it want the specific characteristics of sport to be recognised in the application of EU law. As such, sport is seen less as an economic activity and more as a social and cultural pursuit. Both coalitions are relatively evenly matched institutionally. This means that they are both able to pursue their respective policy interests in sport in a manner which has the potential to undermine each others fundamental beliefs. For example, the ECJ's ruling in *Bosman* undermined efforts to have sport classified as a social and not commercial pursuit. Given that the member states are closely aligned to the socio-cultural coalition, the coalition possesses the ability to amend the Treaty in order to grant sport an exemption from EU law. For the Single Market coalition, this would set a dangerous precedent and would undermine the legal foundations on which the EU is based. In circumstances where both coalitions possess the ability to undermine each other's fundamental policy beliefs, a learning process within the subsystem takes place. In order to protect their fundamental beliefs, coalitions are prepared to compromise within the secondary aspects of their belief systems. This learning inspired compromise is promoted by a culture of mutual adjustment within the EU.

From within this mediation has emerged a more co-ordinated sports policy. The construction of the *separate territories* approach for dealing with legal disputes involving sport is the defining characteristic of this policy. Separate territories refers to the definition of a territory for sporting autonomy and a territory for legal intervention. By reconciling these two tensions, the EU has facilitated an approach to sports policy which allows the EU's regulatory and political policy interests in sport to co-exist. The future debate over the relationship between sport and the EU will focus on the boundary between the two territories. By developing a particular legal approach to sport which treats sport differently to other sectors, the EU has in effect established a discrete body of sports law in the EU. The field is however very new and the future definition of the territories is potentially confused by many variables. Nevertheless, by following the methodology developed in this text it is suggested that changes in the landscape of the separate territories and hence sports law and policy more generally, will be confined to measures that will not undermine the fundamental beliefs of the two coalitions. Until such time as the institutional balance of power changes within the subsystem, change will be confined to the secondary aspects of the respective belief systems. As is explained later, this clearly has implications for the future of EU sports law and policy.

In writing this book I was mindful of Beloff *et al.*'s warning that 'any book on sports law carries with it the danger that it will contain little more than information' (Beloff *et al.* 1999: 15). I have kept the descriptive passages to what I consider an appropriate and necessary level. In the absence of widespread academic attention on the development of EU sports law and policy, it is important to write a text which pulls together the mass of available information. However, this is not a textbook. Information alone will not advance our understanding of this relatively new field. The theoretical framework alluded to above is my contribution to the next stage of the sports law debate. As an academic subject taught at growing number of universities, sports law needs theoretical underpinning. The search for theory within sports law is a growing yet nascent field. Without it, this rich area of socio-legal study will become stunted.

Whilst the text is designed to be as comprehensive as possible, it is naturally limited in its scope. In particular, I have chosen to separate the issue of doping from the wider sports law/sports policy debate. The future debate on the relationship between sport and the EU will be dominated by the issues of sports law and doping. The two domains naturally collide. For instance in August 2002 the Commission rejected a complaint against the International Olympic Committee by swimmers banned from competition for drug offences.[1] The Commission took the view that the rules on doping did not fall within the scope of the EU's competition rules. Whilst the analysis contained within this text may have implications for the doping debate, I do not wish to claim doping as a central theme of this text.

Notes

1 IP/02/1211, 'Commission Rejects Complaint Against International Olympic Committee by Swimmers Banned from Competitions for Doping', 09/08/02.

1

The birth of EU
sports law and policy

Despite the absence of a Treaty base, the EU currently operates a sports policy. This policy is the product of activity within the EU's sports policy subsystem, a subsystem formed in response to the infamous *Bosman* ruling. Prior to that the EU operated a highly polarised and fragmented sports policy characterised by two conflicting policy approaches to sport. First, the EU took a fleeting regulatory interest in sport. The ECJ and the Competition Policy Directorate intervened in sport to correct free movement and competition restrictions and distortions within the Single Market. These interventions were not however informed by the EU's other main policy strand and as a consequence EU sporting actions were not co-ordinated. The second strand of policy involvement in sport involved the EU pursuing a political interest in sport. In particular, sport was identified as a tool through which the EU could strengthen its image in the minds of Europe's citizens. As the two strands of policy involvement in sport did not relate to one another, a policy tension characterised EU sports policy.

Today, the regulatory and political policy strands of EU involvement in sport relate to one another in a more co-ordinated manner. The construction of the separate territories approach to sport has allowed both policy strands to co-exist within the framework of a more co-ordinated sports policy. The practical effect of separate territories is a shift in the nature of EU regulatory involvement in sport. Single Market regulation has become tempered by socio-cultural regulation. In other words, the EU is moving from a market model of regulation towards one in which the EU recognises the social and cultural characteristics of the sports sector within its regulatory approach. By establishing separate territories of sporting autonomy and judicial intervention, the EU has in effect established a distinct legal approach for dealing with sports-related cases. The recent application of law to the sports sector is deeply influenced by the political values embedded within sports policy. Accordingly, current legal interventions in sport balance the EU's regulatory and political policy interests in sport. The development of the separate territories therefore marks the birth of EU sports law.

EU sports law is therefore a product of the EU's sports policy. The EU lacks the necessary Treaty base to develop a fully fledged common sports policy underpinned with primary and secondary legislative actions. Sports policy is therefore primarily regulatory in nature. It seeks to alter the values which underpin the regulation of sport. In other words, sports policy attempts to balance the classic Single Market regulation of sport with a form of regulation which respects sports social and cultural nature. The clarification of the legal environment allows for the EU's other political policy interests in sport to be pursued without being undermined by Single Market regulatory actions. EU sports policy can then develop through sports integration into a number of socio-cultural policy subsystems such as education, youth and health.

For those seeking to develop a socio-cultural sports policy, the involvement of law is viewed with unease. Sport is an essentially private pursuit which fulfils important social, cultural, educational and physical functions within society. Furthermore, sport and the law are often considered 'separate realms'. In other words, the law operates in a manner totally incompatible with the operation of sport. 'Legal norms are fixed rules which prescribe rights and duties; relationships within the social world of sport are not seen in this way' (Foster 1993: 106). However, sport has never claimed to operate above the law. After all, sport could not operate without law. Rather, it has developed an internal legal structure of its own. On the one hand, this legal system specifies the rules of the game such as the offside law in football. On the other, it also concerns the organisation of the sport. 'Organisational' laws regulate important issues such as access to the competition, the rights of players and the exploitation of broadcasting rights.

Throughout the 1990s sport developed into a significant industry in its own right. The extent of this commercialisation contributed to the 'juridification' of sport, 'where what are intrinsically social relationships between humans within a social field become imbued with legal values and become understood as constituting a legal relationship – social norms become legal norms' (Gardiner *et al.* 1998: 66). Juridification therefore refers to the process through which the general laws of the land penetrate the internal laws of sport. The juridification of sport accelerated interest in the idea of *sport and the law* as an area of legal study. Established general legal principles deriving from, for instance, criminal law, contract law, the law of torts, public law, administrative law, property law, competition law, EU law, company law, fiscal law and human rights law, have been applied to a wide number of sporting contexts including: public order and sport, drugs and sport, safety in sport, disciplinary measures in sport, conduct in sport and wider issues relating to restraint of trade and anti-competitive behaviour in sport.

The extent of the relationship between sport and law has lead some academics to extend their legal analysis beyond the confines of *sport and the law* by identifying a distinct body of *sports law* (Gardiner *et al.* 1998, Beloff *et al.* 1999). As Beloff *et al.* claim, 'the law is now beginning to treat sporting activity, sporting bodies and the resolution of disputes in sport, differently from other activities or bodies. Discrete doctrines are gradually taking shape in the sporting field' (Beloff *et al.* 1999: 3). In other sectors the weight of legislation and case law combined with the development of discrete doctrines has led to the creation of other activity-led fields of law. As Gardiner *et al.* explain:

> labour or employment law is a subject area that has only achieved recent recognition. It has its origins in contract law in the employment context, but no one would doubt that with the plethora of legislation during the post-war era regulating the workplace, it has become a subject area in its own right. Passing through various incarnations such as industrial law, it is now a mature legal subject. (Gardiner et al. 1998: 73)

The concept of sports law is not universally accepted. Grayson argues that:

> no subject exists which jurisprudentially can be called sports law. As a sound bite headline, shorthand description, it has no juridical foundation; for common law and equity create no concept of law exclusively relating to sport. Each area of law applicable to sport does not differ from how it is found in any other social or jurisprudential category. (Grayson 1994: xxxvii)

Critics of sports law argue that cases involving sport are grounded in the well-established fields of law such as contract and tort. Indeed, 'the traditionally minded, purist lawyer, may indeed distrust any activity-led "vertical" field of law, preferring the surer, traditional ground of rule-led "horizontal" law' (Beloff *et al.* 1999: 3).

In recent years, the *sport and the law* versus *sports law* debate has taken on a new dimension. Commercial pressures and the public's desire to see top-class competition has fuelled the internationalisation of sport. To regulate this cross-border activity, sports governing bodies have established rules governing relations between participants. The international and non-governmental character of modern sport has not however ushered in for sport a new form of international autonomy insulated from law. The growth of the EU's Single Market has been central to the internationalisation of sports law. The re-regulation of sport has taken place within the context of the Treaty of Rome's fundamental economic freedoms. As the EU is keen to ensure these freedoms are protected, it has applied the Treaty's free movement principles to a growing number of sports-related cases. The ECJ rulings in *Walrave, Donà, Heylens* and *Bosman* illustrate the growing relationship between sport and the EU. However, the relationship between sport and the EU has a relevance beyond the narrow confines of regulating economic activity within the Single Market. The EU has social and cultural aspirations and sport has been identified by the EU institutions as one of the tools through which these goals can be achieved. Following *Bosman*, political arguments have penetrated the world of sport and EU law. A new approach for dealing with sports cases is emerging in which the EU is establishing the boundaries of judicial penetration in sport – in other words the birth of EU sports law. The construction of EU sports law allows the EU's regulatory and political policy objectives for sport to co-exist within the context of an embryonic EU sports policy.

The observation that a distinct body of law known as sports law is emerging in the EU requires both empirical and theoretical justification. One of the weaknesses of the sports law argument is the lack of theoretical underpinning. Although the literature on the emergence of sports law is descriptively strong, it remains unclear at what point the concept of *sport and the law* loses its relevance and the distinct area of *sports law* emerges. Furthermore, beyond the assertion that commercialisation has driven juridification, little has emerged on the dynamics driving the birth of sports law. Although sports initial linkage to the EU's legal framework was driven by legal/regulatory norms, the emergence of a distinct field of sports law within a wider sports policy has been politically driven. Within the context of the EU, political science and public policy therefore offer a fruitful venue for analysis. Law should not shy away from the insights offered by other disciplines. One of the most refreshing developments in both law and political science has been the interest shown in 'judicial politics'. As Wincott argues, 'somewhat belatedly the Court of Justice is now being subjected to sustained political analysis and taken into account in the general political science literature on European integration' (Wincott 1996:170).

The birth of EU sports law and policy offers both political science and law the opportunity to further develop this research agenda. Although the *politics of sport* is a well-developed area of research, the *politics of sports law* remains largely untouched by political science. As such, political science has been slow in recognising the empirical and theoretical significance of the growth in the EU's sporting activity. It has been law that has colonised this new research terrain. However, law has been equally slow in underpinning its work with theoretical strength, partly because of the practitioner-based focus.

Single market sports regulation: sport and the law 1970–1995

The EU's first excursion into sporting issues occurred in the 1970s. Two ECJ rulings established important principles governing the relationship between sport and the EU. In *Walrave* (1974) and *Donà* (1976) the ECJ established that sport is subject to EU law in so far as it constitutes an economic activity within the meaning of Article 2 of the EEC Treaty, although exemptions from the principle of non-discrimination on the grounds of nationality are permitted but linked with the practise of sport on a non-economic basis.[1] A number of years later in *Heylens*, the ECJ addressed the issue of the recognition of qualifications for sports trainers.[2] However, it was not until the seismic *Bosman* ruling of 1995 that the full implications of previous case law became apparent.[3] In the case, Jean Marc Bosman, a Belgian footballer, successfully challenged UEFA's use of nationality restrictions and the international transfer system.

Walrave, Donà, Heylens and *Bosman* are examples of cases where the subject matter just so happened to be sport. The well-established principles of the free movement of workers and the freedom to provide services simply became applied to sporting contexts. Although the ECJ did make reference to the specific characteristics of sport, particularly in *Bosman*, the principles were applied in a manner irrespective of the subject matter.

The European Commission's attitude towards discriminatory/restrictive practises in sport in the aftermath of *Walrave* and *Donà* was somewhat contradictory. Despite condemning restrictions on player mobility, the Commission's negotiated settlement approach with the sports world initially resulted in sport and competition law operating in separate realms. The Commission appeared keen to avoid confrontation with the sports world. A number of factors altered this position. The ruling in *Bosman* acted as an important watershed. Even though in *Bosman* the ECJ did not address the question of competition law and sport, instead focusing on free movement principles, the Commission used the ruling to justify greater scrutiny of sporting activity. Furthermore, competition law offered individual litigants a more cost-effective venue for redress than the private enforcement route via national courts and the ECJ. The Commission's sports-related competition law caseload swelled considerably following *Bosman*. Finally, the change in the economic status of sport undoubtedly contributed to juridification.

The juridification and commercialisation of sport are parallel developments in Europe. The commercialisation of European sport is one of the major reasons why a relationship between sport and the EU exists at all. Sport in Europe has traditionally operated in an environment dominated by public service television and in a context where the actions of governmental and non-governmental organisations have co-existed. In organisational and competitive terms, European sport has been organised on a 'pyramid' structure. Organisationally, sports clubs support a structure comprising regional federations, national federations and European federations. Competitively, clubs move up and down a pyramid of competition on the basis of promotion and relegation, i.e. merit-based criteria as opposed to economically based criteria. Since the 1980s, this European 'model' of sport has come under sustained pressure due to the television-led commercialisation of sport.[4]

Until the 1980s the regulation of broadcasting was a matter of purely national jurisdiction. In Britain, for example, competition in broadcasting was minimal, often taking the form of a monopoly or a 'comfortable duopoly' (Collins 1994: 146). At the beginning of the 1980s there were very few commercial television broadcasters in Europe, yet by the early 1990s there were 58 (Collins 1994: 146). Technology-driven changes in the field of trans-frontier satellite broadcasting altered the nature of broadcasting in Europe (Collins 1994, Humphreys 1996). With a trend in the 1980s towards the deregulation of national broadcasting markets, new forms of international regulation concerning the new 'Europeanised' broadcasting market took shape. In particular the EU emerged as the key new regulatory actor. The new broadcasting opportunities offered by new technology such as satellite broadcasting greatly benefited the sports sector in Europe. Football in particular was able to sell the broadcasting rights to events to the new wave of commercial operators who had embraced the new technology. As most of these new operators were financed on a subscription basis, revenues were higher than from the public sector broadcasters. This allowed the sports sector in Europe to maximise profits by selling rights to the highest bidder. However, sport's new found wealth merely confirmed the operation of the sports sector in Europe as an economic activity subject to supranational regulation. Nowhere are these above developments better illustrated than in modern European football.

In 1996 Rupert Murdoch, Chairman of News International and leading pioneer of satellite television in Britain remarked, 'we have the long-term rights in most countries to major sporting events and we will be doing in Asia what we intend to do elsewhere in the world, that is, use sports as a battering ram and a lead offering in all our pay television operations'.[5] For broadcasters, sport is an ideal lead-offering, due to its popularity. The new commercial operators have recognised this. Murdoch added, 'sport absolutely overpowers film and everything else in the entertainment genre and football, of all sports, is number one' (*World Soccer* 1997).

The introduction of new broadcasting technology greatly changed the English football broadcasting market. In the 1987–1988 season the rights for live league football were sold for £3.1 million (Spink and Morris 2000: 167). In 1988, British Satellite Broadcasting (BSB) challenged the 'comfortable duopoly' of the BBC and ITV by negotiating a four-year deal with ITV worth £11 million per season. Having contributed more financially, ITV acquired the exclusive sole rights to league football for the four-year period and by 1991 were broadcasting 18 live matches per season. Evidence therefore suggests that in the UK market up until 1992 with the creation of the Premier League, broadcasters dominated the relationship with the football sector. A number of factors served to redress the balance. First, the football authorities saw the potential benefits of maximising income through the introduction and maturation of a new player, BSkyB. As Parry remarked, 'two is a cartel and three is a market' (Parry 1996: 21). Second, football required wholesale modernisation both on and off the pitch. On the pitch

top British players were increasingly moving to foreign clubs with no recip-
rocal flow. This led to fears that the national team would suffer and clubs
would not prosper in European competitions. Off the pitch, in the aftermath
of the Hillsborough disaster, the Taylor report imposed a large financial
burden on clubs by requiring ground modernisation.

In 1992, the newly formed Premier League negotiated a broadcasting contract from a position significantly stronger than in previous years. The deal
finally concluded was with the BBC and BSkyB and was worth £214 million
over five years, a significant rise from the previous ITV deal. BSkyB held the
exclusive rights to screen live Premier League matches whilst the BBC could
screen highlights. Under the terms of the contract, every team was to be
broadcast at least once a season. The total number of live games to be broadcast was 60 per season. This compared to 54 in the five years of ITV/BBC
coverage. By 1996, the cost of football rights once again rose sharply. The
Premier League signed a new £743 million four-year agreement with BSkyB
and the BBC with BSkyB contributing £670 million. As more broadcasters
entered the bidding process so the cost of football rights rose. The launch of
digital and cable television services towards the end of the 1990s further
increased competition in the rights sector and provided a platform for the
development for pay-per-view football. The presence of NTL and ITV
Digital in the bidding process for the re-negotiation of the 1996 agreement
saw the total value of the rights rise to £1.1 billion for three years, with
BSkyB paying £720 million to broadcast English Premiership games for a
three-year period.

The broadcasting sector and sport have therefore revolutionised each
other. 'This marriage between sport and television is one made in heaven'
(Griffith-Jones 1997: 289). That was until the collapse of ITV Digital. ITV
Digital went into administration and returned its broadcasting licence following the signing in 2000 of the £315 million contract to broadcast lower
league games in England. In July 2002, BSkyB and the Football League
signed a £95 million contract to broadcast Football League games for a four-
year period, an amount considerably less than ITV Digital agreed to pay in
2000 to broadcast the games over three years. This left the Football League
with a considerable shortfall in revenue. The Football League sued Carlton
Communications and Granada Media arguing that they guaranteed the
liabilities of ITV Digital. In *Carlton Communications PLC and Granada
Media plc* v. *Football League* (2002), the court rejected the Football Leagues
claim by finding that the contract between the parties contained no such
guarantee.[6] The resulting recession within the English Football league illustrates the extent to which football relies on broadcasting.

The finances of top-flight football in England and across Europe are not
as precarious. The continued mass appeal of top-flight football has resulted
in many clubs becoming listed on the stock market. Clubs across Europe are
also entering into agreements with media companies. In Italy for instance

media companies own a share or control AC Milan, Fiorentina, Lazio, Parma and Roma. In Britain, media companies own a stake in Manchester United, Leeds United, Sunderland, Chelsea, Manchester City (all BSkyB), Newcastle United, Aston Villa and Middlesborough (NTL) and Liverpool (Granada). A similar picture is emerging in Europe's other major leagues. The eleventh edition of the 'Deloitte and Touche Annual Review of Football Finances' shows that the income of top-flight European football clubs continues to grow. In 2000/2001 the English Premiership operating profits increased by 51 per cent to £81 million (134 euros). However, the report found that only the top-flight English and German leagues consistently make an operating profit with broadcasting remaining the single largest source of income for the main leagues in Europe. Despite the difficulties experienced by the English Football League, the report remains positive about the future financial wealth of top-flight football in Europe. New commercial opportunities in the new media remain untapped and the tide appears to have turned regarding cost control in football. In this connection the report argues, 'there is now a remarkable convergence of views across Europe and a real window of opportunity to address the issues around football's cost base'.[7] In particular salary capping is top of many clubs agendas (see Chapter 5).

The politicisation of Single Market sports regulation 1995–1999

The commercialisation of sport in Europe was therefore an essential pre-requisite for international juridification. Although *Walrave and Donà* had established the potential for sport to be linked to the EU's legal framework, the Commission had not completed juridification by applying the EU's competition laws to sport. Following *Bosman*, the Commission was compelled to respond. The initial post-*Bosman* relationship between EU competition law and sport was characterised by considerable confusion and great legal uncertainty. Usually acting on a complaint, the Competition Policy Directorate launched a series of high-profile investigations into the operation of sport in Europe. These investigations have included examinations into re-structured transfer systems, competition between sporting federations, rules preventing the multiple ownership of sporting clubs, rules preventing club re-location, the operation of Formula One motor-racing, ticketing arrangements for major sporting events and restrictive practices in the sale and purchase of broadcasting rights and the transmission of sporting events. The extent to which the EU only appeared to acknowledge sports economic potential resulted in the EU attracting considerable criticism from those who thought this approach paid insufficient attention to sports social and cultural significance. The EU's Single Market regulatory approach to sport therefore became politicised.

The relationship between sport and politics is not unique to the EU. The nation state has traditionally pursued a political interest in sport. Work on the relationship between sport and the nation state has been subject to numerous studies (Allison 1986, 1993, Cashmore 1996, Houlihan 1997, Greenfield and Osborn 2001). Distilling the main themes from these works, it is possible to identify four main explanations as to why there is a relationship between sport and public policy.

The first broad explanation concerns the use of sport as an instrument of domestic policy in a political system. Governments have used sport as a means through which particular policy objectives can be achieved. Within this category, a number of themes are evident. First, governments have used sport as a means of social integration and control. Governments have used sport as a means of assimilating recent immigrants and of reconciling sectarian, cultural or political differences (Houlihan 1997: 107). Governments have actively promoted sporting activities as a means through which social tensions can be reduced. Not only has sport the potential to tackle the 'problem' of excessive leisure time, it can also promote discipline and self esteem. For example, In Britain the Thatcher government used sport as a means to implement its social policy objectives following urban unrest in the early 1980s. Leisure expenditure was targeted in favour of specific social groups and urban areas. Monnington explains that this policy was a continuation of an approach adopted by the previous Labour government, 'but the significant difference now was that justification swung away from provision "as need" in support of welfare principles to provision "as a means"; a means to maintain public order' (Monnington 1992: 144). The regeneration of urban areas through sporting provision allows governments to address more than just social issues. Sport can also be used as a locomotive for economic development and health promotion.

The second explanation concerns the use of sport as an instrument of foreign policy. Sport has traditionally been employed as a means of international protest and boycott. Since the overtly political Berlin Games of 1936, all Olympics have been contested in a political context and boycotts are a common feature. For the first post-war games held in London in 1948, Germany, Italy and Japan were all excluded. The Netherlands, Egypt, Iraq and Spain boycotted the 1956 games in protest at the Anglo-French invasion of Suez. South Africa was suspended from the Olympic movement in 1964 and expelled in 1970, a fate shared by Rhodesia (now Zimbabwe) in 1972 having unilaterally left the Commonwealth. In 1976, 20 African nations boycotted the Montreal Olympics in protest at New Zealand's participation.[8] The USA boycotted the 1980 Moscow Olympics and most Soviet bloc countries reciprocated by boycotting the Los Angeles Games in 1984. In 1988, Cuba and North Korea boycotted the Seoul Games in protest over South Koreas refusal to share events with North Korea. In addition to protest, sport has also been used as an instrument for promoting a country's international prestige and image. Government's calculate that they will benefit domestically from a positive external image.

The third explanation concerns the indirect and often unintentional nature of state involvement in sport as a consequence of state policy rather than an instrument of state policy. Although generally disinterested in sport, other than as a means of social control, the activities of Margaret Thatcher's Conservative government in the 1980s had a profound impact on the sports sector. Monnington remarked that 'sport has experienced the consequences of "Thatcherism"' (Monnington 1992: 148). The reform programme of Thatcher, which included compulsory competitive tendering, local management of schools, the opting out of schools from local authority control and more generally local authority restructuring and national curriculum reform, all have had a significant impact on the operation of sport in the UK. Compulsory competitive tendering effectively privatised many publicly owned leisure facilities and forced local authorities to adopt market-based practices for leisure provision. As Monnington reminds us, 'sport is affected in these instances as a consequence of policy, rather than being used as an instrument of policy implementation' (Monnington 1992: 149).

A final theme straddling all of the above explanations concerns an essential pre-requisite for the success of any political system – legitimacy. Sport can be of enormous symbolic benefit to politicians and political systems. Sport can give politics a human face and can reconnect the politician with their constituency. The size and quality of the national stadium reflects the importance of the state itself. Participation, if not success in international competitions such as the Olympics is a defining characteristic of nationhood. Political systems need to be held together by more than the glue of economics, they need to be socially constructed. The EU has acknowledged this problem. Whilst the elitist and bureaucratic path to integration in the 1950s and 1960s created the 'new Europe', the lack of popular involvement in the project failed to create 'new Europeans'. The crisis of European integration in the 1970s contributed to the birth of the people's Europe agenda in the mid-1980s.[9] The failure of the people's Europe agenda to establish itself resulted in widespread public opposition to the Maastricht Treaty. The Danes rejected the Treaty in a referendum and over 49 per cent of French voters rejected it. The British government was forced to call a vote of no confidence to pass the Maastricht Bill through Parliament. In short, the lack of popular support for integration was limiting the ability of governments and the EU more generally to realise their political policy objectives. The sense of remoteness from the EU felt by many of Europe's citizens therefore needed political attention.

The essentially economic approach to sport adopted by the EU sat uncomfortably with the general theme of a people's Europe. Through *Bosman* the EU became associated with emancipating very rich footballers, thus making them even richer. The EU was seen as a venue through which the full commercial potential of sport could be exploited at the expense of the real values of the game. As such, the EU was not reconnecting itself with its citizens, it was taking the people's game further away from them. A body of opinion emerged within the EU seeking to give the socio-cultural and integrationist qualities of sport a higher priority and for sport to be afforded a higher level of protection from EU law. The European Parliament emerged as an important venue through which such ideas were discussed. Both the 1994 'Larive report' on the European Community and Sport and the 1997 'Pack report' on the 'Role of the European Union in the Field of Sport' demonstrated a desire to balance the economic regulation of sport with the promotion of sports socio-cultural and integrationist qualities.[10] Furthermore, the Parliament has been successful in inserting an amendment into the second Television Without Frontiers Directive (TWF) in 1997, guaranteeing public viewing access to major sporting events on television.[11]

Sport also received the attention of the member states. Following *Bosman*, calls intensified for sport to be granted a legal base within the European Treaty. The proponents of such a move hoped that a legally based Article for sport would limit what was perceived as the insensitive application of EU law to sport whilst granting the EU a legal base to develop a socio-cultural common sports policy. Despite the strength of support, the Heads of State and Government meeting in Amsterdam in June 1997 decided only to attach a non-binding Declaration on Sport to the Amsterdam Treaty which called on the institutions of the EU to recognise sports social significance.[12] Although the Declaration disappointed those who wished to see a legal competence for sport established within the Treaty, the Declaration is significant in that by implicitly criticising *Bosman* it has served to politicise *sport and the law* in the EU. Member states have followed up the Declaration by releasing important political guidelines on sport and the EU in the form of Presidency Conclusions. In this connection, the member states confirmed their determination to see the regulation of sport balanced by a socio-cultural agenda at Vienna (December 1998), Paderborn (June 1999), Helsinki (December 1999) and during the Portuguese (first half of 2000) and French (second half of 2000) Presidencies of the Council of the European Union.

The Commission's institutional response to the Amsterdam Declaration came throughout 1998 and 1999. The Education and Culture Directorate (then known as DG X) published series of papers on sport. 'The Development and Prospects for Community Action in the Field of Sport' and 'The European Model of Sport' stressed the multi-dimensional nature of sport and established dialogue with the sports world.[13] Attached to the 'The European Model of Sport' document was a questionnaire designed to canvass opinion on the future direction of the EU's involvement in sport. The findings of this exercise were used by the Commission to prepare the first EU conference on sport held in Greece in May 1999. The conclusions of the Conference were then used by the Commission to prepare a report, at the European Council's request, on an approach to safeguarding current sports structures and maintaining the social function of sport within the EU framework. The report was submitted to the December 1999 Helsinki European Council. At the heart of the 'new approach' embodied in the Helsinki report is a framework for applying EU law to sport. The report claims that 'this new approach involves preserving the traditional values of sport, while at the same time assimilating a changing economic and legal environment'.[14] The Helsinki report therefore represents the EU's first attempt to co-ordinate the Single Market and socio-cultural policy strands of its involvement in sport. In essence, the report establishes an embryonic EU sports policy. However, it is a policy which is curiously unattached to the Treaty. In the absence of specific primary and secondary sports legislation, the glue binding the policy strands together is sports law.

Socio-cultural sports regulation: the birth of EU sports law 1999

The assertion by Beloff *et al.* that a discrete area of sports law exists is supported by their observation that the English courts have established the parameters of judicial intervention in sport.

> The cornerstone of what could be called the founding principles of sports law is the definition of respective territories of the courts and the bodies which govern sport. The courts in England and elsewhere have firmly established a region of autonomy for decision making bodies in sport, a region which – unless the reasons for doing so are compelling – the courts decline to intervene. Equally firmly they have charted the outer limits of that region and insisted that those limits be observed by the decision makers in sport, on pain of judicial intervention. (Beloff *et al.* 1999: 4)

Beloff *et al.* note that the 'courts in England and elsewhere' have established these territories. Although it is unclear exactly what 'elsewhere' refers to, it is argued in this text that similar territories are beginning to appear in the EU. Of course, placing too much distance between the English legal system and that of the EU would be misleading. EU law is supreme and can carry direct effect and direct applicability. In other words, EU law takes precedent over national law where the two come into conflict (supremacy) and EU law can take legal effect into the national legal systems without the need for national implementation measures (direct applicability) whilst giving rise to rights or obligations on which individuals may rely before their national courts (direct effect). Furthermore, Article 234 of the Treaty creates an organic link between the two systems by providing for a preliminary reference procedure for national courts to seek clarification from the ECJ on matters concerning the interpretation and validity of EU law. Clearly therefore this distinction between national patterns of sports law and EU sports law is somewhat artificial. Nevertheless, the EU is not a state in the classic mould of nation states. As an organisation it blurs the boundaries between the executive, legislative and judiciary. The Commission for instance possesses quasi-judicial powers in relation to the operation of competition law.

The ECJ works under the threat of sanction from the European Council. Furthermore, the EU is a curious hybrid of political, bureaucratic and legal styles and cultures. It is, in short, a system without direct comparison in Europe. As a source of English sports law, EU sports law therefore merits separate attention.

EU sports law was born out of the post-*Bosman* political discussions on the future of sport in the EU. It is an essential component of modern EU sports policy. Accordingly, it is a very recent development. The argument that a distinct area of EU sports law has emerged therefore risks the challenge that this is a premature claim. Soft law is included within the definition of EU sports law. Soft law refers to rules of conduct which in principle have no legally binding force but which nevertheless may have a significant effect on policy and legal developments. Soft law refers to non-binding measures adopted by the EU institutions such as Treaty Declarations, Presidency Conclusions, political guidelines and Commission orientation papers, comfort letters and notices.

The use of soft law stems from the peculiarities of the EU's system of law and governance. The EU is obviously a multi-national organisation. The size, complexity and diversity of the EU results in protracted decision making at the best of times. In the absence of unanimity, member states often favour the use of soft law when they are unable to agree upon binding measures but nevertheless wish to place political pressure on the EU institutions for a change in policy direction. As such, soft law can be employed by the member states as an implied threat of taking further harder measures unless EU institutions change their approach. Soft law has therefore offered important guidance as to the interpretation and scope of the application of EU law. The Amsterdam Declaration is increasingly a frequently sourced reference in Commission competition law cases and ECJ cases. The Commission (in this context the Competition Policy Directorate) also favours the use of soft law. Politically, the Commission must be sensitive not only to the interests of the member states, but also to the requirements of business operating in the Single Market. Soft law is therefore often used as the politically pragmatic option. The voluntary notification system used in competition law also lends itself to the use of soft law. Furthermore those seeking clearance often favour informal negotiated settlements. The Commission is also hampered by resource limitations which results in the use of administrative rather than judicial measures to resolve cases. In addition, it is not uncommon for soft law to be used as quasi-legal justification by EU institutions for the development of policy initiatives. Again, the Amsterdam Declaration on Sport has informed much of the EU's recent sports-related activity. Soft law has therefore characterised much of the development of EU sports law. The lack of a formal Treaty base to take 'harder' measures in sport clearly also necessitates the use of soft law.

The Commission's first formal post-Amsterdam review of the application of competition rules to sport came in a policy paper in February 1999.[15] In the paper the Competition Policy Directorate made a distinction between purely sporting situations which are not covered by the scope of competition law and wholly commercial situations to which Treaty provisions will apply. Even though the distinction between sporting rules and commercial rules is problematic, the Commission recognised that even concerning commercial rules the particular characteristics of sport must be taken into account. The paper represents the first attempt to establish the respective territories of sporting autonomy and judicial intervention. Through Commission case law, attempts have been made to further define these territories. The Commission's recognition of the specificity of sport has been demonstrated in cases concerning the collective sale of sports broadcasting rights, collective purchasing agreements, restrictions on the cross-border transmission of sport, ticketing arrangements, issues concerning the maintenance of the single structure model of sport, multiple club ownership, club relocation, the operation of Formula One motor racing, the granting of state aid to sport and the operation of the international transfer system for players.[16] Whilst the Commission has closed some of the above cases through formal decisions, in many instances it has relied on informal negotiated settlements and other soft law measures.

The absence of black letter law in the field of sport is on the one hand understandable. 'Sporting bodies continue to argue that, while competition law is generally an adequate mechanism for regulating normal markets, it can often be too crude to be applied to markets touched upon by sport, because sport operates under different market conditions to other sectors' (Kinsella and Daly 2001: 7). The use of informal soft law measures can therefore be defended on the grounds of flexibility and sensitivity to the concerns of sport. As such, the use of soft law represents a distinct quasi-legal approach in its own right. Of course, soft law poses a number of problems. Although sport favours the negotiated settlement approach, the lack of clear precedents leaves the regulatory environment as confusing as ever. The adoption of harder measures would arguably benefit sport through the establishment of legally binding respective territories of sports autonomy and legal intervention. The Commission's proposal to increasingly share the burden of applying competition law (including the exemption procedure) with national regulatory bodies and courts rests on the assumption that sufficient case law has been acquired to facilitate this decentralisation.[17] As Kinsella and Daly observe, the lack of harder measures adopted by the Commission in the field of sport means that this case law experience has not yet been acquired (Kinsella and Daly 2001: 13). Given the lack of hard sports law and the general vagueness of Article 81, the future of the competition law component of the separate territories is uncertain.

The recent activities of the ECJ further illustrate the extent to which political arguments have permeated traditionally legal domains. The ECJ's sports-related rulings in *Deliège* and *Lehtonen* further develop the concept of respective territories.[18] Although in *Walrave*, *Donà* and *Bosman* the ECJ recognised the special characteristics of sport thus acknowledging the distinction between economic and social activities, the rulings essentially attempted to extend the scope the of the free movement principle. By contrast, *Deliège* and *Lehtonen* established sports specific limitations (albeit limited ones) on the scope of the principle of free movement. It is worth noting that in *Deliège* and *Lehtonen* the ECJ took the somewhat unusual step of referring to the Amsterdam Treaty's Declaration on Sport.

The impact of this soft law Declaration has therefore been significant. The member states have subsequently declined the invitation made by the Parliament and representatives of the sports world to harden the Declaration into a Treaty Article or protocol for sport. Meeting during the Nice Summit in December 2000, the member states did however re-visit the Declaration in light of the on-going discussion between the Commission and FIFA/UEFA on the re-modelling of the international transfer system. The Nice Declaration on Sport (released as a Presidency Conclusion) represents the member states contribution to the debate on the birth of EU sports law as part of a wider EU sports policy. Whilst the Amsterdam Declaration ran to just 58 words, the Nice Declaration was over 1,000 words. The significant passage read,

> even though not having any direct powers in this area, the Community must, in its action under the various Treaty provisions, take account of the social, educational and cultural functions inherent in sport and making it special, in order that the code of ethics and the solidarity essential to the preservation of its social role may be respected and nurtured.[19]

Without formally granting sport a Treaty base, the above passage in effect launches an informal member state commitment to launch an EU sports policy in which the construction of EU sports law is the defining characteristic.

Conclusions

The birth of EU sports law is essential to the viability of a EU sports policy which is not legally rooted to the Treaty. EU sports law allows the EU's regulatory interest in sport to co-exist with its other political sporting objectives. The birth of EU sports law and policy is further promoted by the arena in which the debate on sport is taking place in the EU. A sports policy subsystem has emerged in the EU composed of coalitions of actors attempting to steer sports policy in a direction consistent with their belief system. The Single Market advocacy coalition pursues a regulatory policy interest in sport. It stresses the economic significance of sport. Sport and law therefore collide whenever sport is practiced as an economic activity. The activities of the Single Market coalition established the Single Market model of sports regulation in the EU. The socio-cultural advocacy coalition has, by contrast, pursued a more socio-cultural and educational policy interest in sport. Sport should therefore be treated differently to other economic sectors before the law. Furthermore, sport should be much more closely integrated into the EU's system in order to enhance the prospects of achieving a people's Europe. The activities of the socio-cultural coalition have shifted the nature of the EU's regulatory involvement in sport towards a socio-cultural model. The birth of EU sports law has taken place within the context of this socio-legal and essentially political discussion between advocacy coalitions over the direction of sports policy. The development of sports law is an approach favoured by both coalitions as it allows them to protect their fundamental belief systems.

Chapter 2 explores the theoretical basis for this claim. As politics is considered to be the mid-wife in the birth of EU sports law, the approach favoured is drawn from political science/public policy. Policy subsystems and advocacy coalitions are considered key arenas in which policy change takes place. Yet, in order to appreciate the dynamics of policy change it is important to locate the work of advocacy coalitions within an institutional context. The institutional resources at a coalition's disposal have a consequential impact on its ability to shape law and policy in the EU.

Chapter 3 analyses the operation of the sports policy subsystem by examining the composition of the two central advocacy coalitions and by specifying the institutional powers they have at their disposal. Unable to influence policy in one venue, a strongly resourced coalition will be able to go 'venue shopping' in order to try its luck in others. The control of venues by advocacy coalitions is problematic in the EU. The contemporary EU is a multi-level organisation. Treaty change has altered the balance of power between the EU institutions. As such, the EU is now considered a paradise for the agenda setter. Even subsystems traditionally dominated by legal and technocratic norms are no longer insulated from wider political and public policy concerns.

Chapter 4 begins the review of the legal context of sports relationship with the EU. The ECJ rulings in *Walrave*, *Donà*, *Heylens*, *Bosman*, *Deliège* and *Lehtonen* receive particular attention. The chapter traces the development of ECJ jurisprudence from the initial application of general EU legal principles such as the right to free movement to the emergence of a more distinct area of EU sports law.

Chapter 5 continues the case law analysis by examining the relationship between sport and EU competition law. The method of disposing of its sports-related caseload tells us much about the Commission's approach. Faced with administrative and political pressures, the Commission has sought to establish an approach for dealing with sport which differs from the general approach to market regulation.

Chapter 6 explores the political context of sports relationship with the EU. A combination of sport's popularity among Europe's public and the EU's wider political/public policy objectives for sport has served to politicise the sports policy subsystem. Previously dominated by legal norms, the subsystem has become penetrated by political arguments over the direction of sports policy. The peculiar multi-level nature of the EU combined with the public law nature of the EU's legal system allows for the expression of wider public-interest justifications for *prima facie* restrictive sports rules. In other words, the EU and its legal system exists for reasons other than simply to resolve disputes between sports economic stakeholders. The 'state', defined broadly to include the EU institutions, has interests in this field as well. However, just as the EU's institutional structure can act to promote agenda expansion, so it can frustrate and constrain actors. The birth of sports law has not been legislatively driven as the EU has no Treaty base to develop sports legislation. The non-legislative politicisation of law has therefore been at the heart of the socio-cultural coalition's approach. The use of soft law as a counterweight to the unavailability of legislation has therefore been a preferred tactic.

Chapter 7 examines the future of EU sports law and policy. The future is as open ended as it has ever been. The claims of predictive breakthroughs traditionally perpetuated in political science is rejected. Nevertheless, by establishing the analytical methodology employed in this text it is possible to make some conditional assumptions on the future of sports law and policy in the EU.

Notes

1 Case 36/74, *Walrave and Koch* v. *Association Union Cycliste Internationale* [1974] ECR 1405. Case 13/76, *Donà* v. *Mantero* [1976] ECR 1333.
2 Case 222/86, *UNECTEF* v. *Heylens* [1987] ECR 4097.
3 Case C-415/93, *Union Royale Belge Sociétés de Football Association and others* v. *Bosman* [1995] ECR I-4291.
4 See 'The European Model of Sport', Consultation Document of DG X, 1998.
5 Address by Rupert Murdoch to News Corporation AGM in Adelaide, 15/10/96.
6 *Carlton Communications PLC and Granada Media plc* v. *Football League* [2002] EWHC 1650, QBD Commercial Court, Langley J, 1 August.
7 For a summary of the report see *Sports Law Bulletin*, 5 (4) July/August 2002.
8 Despite world opinion, New Zealand maintained sporting links with South Africa.
9 COM (84) 446 Final, 'A People's Europe', Reports from the *ad hoc* Committee.
10 A3-0326/94/ Part A (27/4/94) Part B (29/4/94), 'Report on the European Community and Sport', Rapporteur: Mrs J. Larive. A4-0197/97, 'Report on the Role of the European Union in the Field of Sport' (28/5/97), Rapporteur: Mrs D. Pack.
11 Article 3a Directive 97/36/EC.

12 Declaration 29, Treaty of Amsterdam amending the Treaty on European Union, the Treaties establishing the European Communities and certain related Acts, 1997.

13 'Developments and Prospects for Community Activity in the Field of Sport', Commission Staff Working Paper, Directorate General X, 29/09/98 and 'The European Model of Sport', Consultation Document of DG X. 1998.

14 Com (1999) 644, 'Report from the Commission to the European Council with a View to Safeguarding Sports Structures and Maintaining the Social Significance of Sport within the Community Framework', The Helsinki report on sport', 1/12/99.

15 DN: IP/99/133, 'Commission Debates Application of Its Competition Rules to Sport', 24/02/99.

16 For a review of these cases see Chapter 5.

17 COM (2000) 582 Final, 'Proposal for a Council Regulation on the Implementation of the Rules on Competition Laid Down in Articles 81 and 82 of the Treaty and Amending Regulations' (EEC) No. 1017/68, (EEC) No. 2988/74, (EEC) No. 4056/86 and (EEC) No. 3975/87. ('Regulation Implementing Articles 81 and 82 of the Treaty'), 27/09/00.

18 Joined cases C-51/96 and C-191/97, *Deliège* v. *Asbl Ligue Francophone de Judo and others* [2000] ECR I-2549. Case C-176/96, *Jyri Lehtonen and Castors Canada Dry Namur-Braine* v. *Fédération Royale des Sociétés de Basketball and Ligue Belge-Belgische Liga* [2000] ECR I-2681.

19 Declaration on the Specific Characteristics of Sport and its Social Function in Europe, of Which Account Should be Taken in Implementing Common Policies, Presidency Conclusions, Nice European Council Meeting, 7, 8, 9 December 2000.

2

Towards a theory of
EU sports law and policy

Traditionally in Britain, sports law has not been a theorised area of study. To some extent this unsatisfactory state of affairs still persists despite the teaching of sports law as an academic discipline on a growing number of University programmes. Sports law programmes are run by the Anglia Polytechnic University, Kings College, the Manchester Metropolitan University and the University of Westminster. The reporting and analysis of sports law is improving. Since 1993 the British Association for Sport and the Law based at the Manchester Metropolitan University has published the *Sport and the Law Journal*. Since then a growing number of journals have contributed to the reporting and analysis of sports law. Among the main publications are the *Sports Law Bulletin, Sports Law Administration and Practice Journal* and the *International Sports Law Review*. The maturation of sports law as an academic discipline is also reflected in the growing volume of academic texts on the subject. In addition to Grayson's seminal *Sport and the Law* (1994), recent additions to the sports law catalogue include, Gardiner *et al.*'s *Sports Law* (1998, 2001), Beloff *et al.*'s *Sports Law* (1999), Caiger and Gardiner's *Professional Sport in the European Union: Regulation and Re-regulation* (2000), Greenfield and Osbourne's *Law and Sport in Contemporary Europe* (2000), McArdle's *From Boot Money to Bosman: Football, Society and the Law* (2000), O'Leary's *Drugs and Doping in Sport: Socio-Legal Perspectives* (2000) and Greenfield and Osbourne's *Regulating Football* (2001). Others do exist and more are planned.

The expansion in this interest shown to sports law has undoubtedly served to theoretically strengthen the discipline. Nevertheless, much of the attention on sports law has been written by practitioners with practitioners in mind. Whilst this has underpinned sports law with insightful legal analysis, the academic discipline of sports law remains theoretically fragile. As Gardiner explains, 'what is now needed is increased examination of why law is involved increasingly in sport – a legal theory of sports law' (Gardiner 1997: 12). Furthermore, as Beloff *et al.* recognise, sports law is 'a field which has yet to be subjected to thorough treatment from a theoretical perspective' (Beloff *et al.* 1999: 15).

The theorised field of sports law is however far from barren. Given the apparent relationship between the commercialisation of the sports sector and juridification, the emerging dominant theoretical approach has concerned regulation (for a review of the literature see Gardiner *et al.* 2001). Foster's presentation of a typology of different models for regulating sport proves particularly useful when examining EU involvement in sport (Foster 2000b). Foster examines five models of sports regulation. The first is the *pure market model* in which sport is seen purely as a business, subject to the same type of regulation experienced by other businesses. Although an essentially non-interventionist model, the actors within sport are seen as economically maximising individuals and as such the normal form of regulation is through the market and the predominant legal instrument is regulation. The danger with the free market approach is that sporting competition will be eliminated as the weaker participants struggle to compete with the strong. With the *defective market model* of regulation, competition law can be employed to ensure monopoly does not result from the market approach. The *consumer welfare model* addresses other limitations of the pure market model. Regulation can protect the rights of the disadvantaged within sport. Foster notes that historically fans and players have had limited economic power against their clubs. This model gives these groups legislative protection from sporting federations. The *natural monopoly model* assumes that sport is organised as a natural monopoly and that statutorily backed regulation is required in order to regulate its activities. Due to the existence of monopoly, competition law is viewed as an inappropriate regulatory tool. Finally, Foster identifies the *socio-cultural model* in which sporting values are considered more important than profit. The social and cultural significance of sport and indeed sports autonomy is protected from commercial pressures. Clearly the commercialisation of sport has implications for the adoption of such a regulatory approach to sport. The maximisation of profit by sports bodies is arguably as important as the protection of the socio-cultural aspects of sport. Foster argues a form of 'supervised self-government' may reconcile these commercial and sporting interests (Foster 2000b: 269).

Foster's typology has implications for the analysis of EU involvement in sport. Lowi's classification of policy types – regulatory, redistributive and distributive policies – has been adapted for use within the EU by Pollack (Pollack 1994). Pollack argues that the EU pursues policy involvement in each of these areas. As Pinder acknowledges, due to the EU's constitutional predisposition for negative integration, the forces of regulation are strong in the EU (Pinder 1993). Furthermore, as the EU lacks a Treaty base to develop a legally rooted common sports policy, it has emerged as a EU competence as a regulatory policy. Nevertheless, as Hix indicates, regulatory policy *but with communication with external authorities (ie Commission), they can gain field expertise*

making can involve more than removal of barriers to trade (Hix 1999: 215). Such 'de-regulatory' policy making is often accompanied by 're-regulatory' policy making in which regulation is underpinned with policy values. EU environmental policy is one example of the interplay between regulation and values. As Bell and McGillivray explain,

> it is an inescapable fact that environmental law and environmental lawyers do not operate within a value-free vacuum . . . . environmental law is for the real world, where political, social, scientific and economic factors influence the way that law works in practice. Thus, when environmental rules are placed into a practical context there is a need to be aware that law is not some stand-alone monolith which can be interpreted in isolation from external issues, in particular values. (Bell and McGillivray 2000: 28)

Consequently, it is not uncommon for regulatory policies to become penetrated by political and other values.

Foster poses (and answers) a number of important questions in relation to the regulation of sport. First, why regulate? The commercialisation of sport, the unequal power distribution within sport and the monopolistic structure of sport all point to reasons why sports should be regulated. Second, who is to be regulated – the clubs or the governing bodies? Third, what kind of regulation is preferred? Foster argues that sporting self-regulation can be justified on three grounds. First, sport is best placed to regulate its own activities due to the specialism it has acquired. Second, the cost of regulation is borne by sport itself. It is therefore cheaper. Third, self-regulation is likely to produce better compliance. The case against self-regulation essentially concerns public interest arguments. First, sporting structures are undemocratic and do not evenly distribute power to all stakeholders. Regulation has the potential to address many problems in sport such as excessive commercialisation. Governing bodies have been unwilling or unable to tackle these wider public interest issues. A related concern is the lack of accountability and the absence of good practice in sport. Regulation can impose good governance on sport, a claim which fundamentally challenges the 'sport knows best' argument for self-regulation (Foster 2000b: 270–280).

SPORTING SELF-REGULATION

really?

These arguments are equally as applicable in the context of the EU as they are in national jurisdictions. Traditionally a distinction has been made between regulation and law. In other words, as Foster argues, 'law is seen as adjudicating between different private interests and regulation as protecting the public interest against private self interest' (Foster 2000b: 277). This distinction loses its relevance in the context of the EU. Both competition law and the law of the four freedoms are heavily influenced by both private and public interest concerns.[1] In the absence of a Treaty base for sport denying the EU the opportunity to pass sports legislation, law has become an essential component of the EU's regulatory policy interest in sport.

Flowing from Foster's analysis is an additional question relevant to regulation at the EU level. Beyond the questions of why regulate, who is to be regulated and what kind of regulation is preferred is a potentially more problematic question. Why has the regulation of sport changed in the EU? The review of EU activity in sport conducted in Chapter 1 indicates the extent to which the nature of the EU's regulatory approach has changed. A review of pre-1999 case law in the EU locates the EU's regulatory involvement in sport towards the 'market' end of Foster's spectrum – in other words Single Market regulation predominated as the EU employed free movement principles and competition law to correct market failures and distortions. The commercialisation of sport was used to justify this approach. Yet, the EU pursues political policy interests in sport which extend beyond the issue of market regulation. The EU has a political interest in the social and cultural dimensions of sport. The activities of the socio-cultural advocacy coalition have been successful in changing the nature of regulation to locate it more towards the 'socio-cultural' end of Foster's regulatory spectrum – socio-cultural regulation. This begs an obvious question. How do regulatory policies change in the EU? The methodology employed to answer this question is applicable for understanding why policies change at all in the EU.

These questions go to the heart of the debate on European integration theory. In the context of this text, the questions are, how has the EU developed a sports policy in the absence of a Treaty Article for sport and what drives sports policy change? Central to these questions is the further issue of why the content of EU sports policy has been dominated by the development of sport law? The short answer is that sports law has emerged as a tactic to enable the EU's competing policy has objectives for sport to co-exist. In the absence of guiding legislation, sports law provides stability and the necessary legal certainty for the EU to continue to pursue a regulatory interest in sport without undermining its socio-cultural policy objectives for sport. It is argued below that policy analysis can be employed as a tool for theoretically strengthening the sports law argument.

The literature on European integration falls, very broadly, into one of two categories. The roots of integration theory lie in the post-war attention paid to the EU as an emerging political state. Political science and international relations theory filled the theoretical void by attempting to understand the motivations for establishing the new political system (the transactionalist/communications approach) and the aspirations for its development (federalism and functionalism). As the EU evolved, intergovernmentalism and neo-functionalism emerged as the dominant paradigms, explaining both the nature of the organisation and predicting the future of integration. Both approaches focused particularly on the major constitutional decisions to have shaped the EU. However, 'it is important to focus, not simply on the process through which major institutional change takes place in the EU, but also on the day to day functioning of the EU as a polity' (Cram 1996). As such, a body of literature drawn from comparative politics and policy analysis has emerged which examines the governance of the EU. Therefore, whilst intergovernmentalism and neo-functionalism attempt to explain the *process of integration,* approaches drawn from policy analysis focus their attention on the *politics of governance.* ⌐Essentially Europeanization⌐

Sport is not unique in becoming linked to the operation of the Single Market in the absence of a Treaty base. At its inception the EU lacked a cultural, media, education and environmental policy. Today, the EU has extensive involvement in these and other important policy sectors. How does the EU acquire an interest in these areas despite the lack of a Treaty base? What processes are at work that give rise to the development of distinct areas of law such as environmental law? Essentially, what is being examined is 'task expansion'. Pollack offers a definition. 'By task expansion I mean (a) the initial expansion of the Community agenda to include new policy areas and (b) the subsequent development and growth of substantive policies in each of these new policy areas' (Pollack 1994: 96).

This two-stage process has been evident in the development of sport as a EU competence. Initially, general legal principles were applied to sport thus giving sport a EU dimension. The ECJ rulings in *Walrave, Donà, Heylens* and *Bosman* stemmed from the general application of law of the four freedoms. Post-*Bosman* sports case law has taken place within the context of a political debate concerning the substantive development of sport as an area of competence. Evidence indicates that the ECJ and the Competition Directorate are increasingly recognising the specificity of sport in their case law. The shift in the regulatory approach to sport has given rise to a distinct area of jurisprudence known as EU sports law.

The birth of EU sports law has wider implications. As an emerging federation the EU is involving itself in a growing range of policy sectors, some of which are extra-constitutional – they lack a formal Treaty base. This challenges the assumption that the EU is not omni-competent or cannot become omni-competent without huge Treaty reform. Of course the EU may not wish to become omni-competent in its truest sense, but in an environment where consensual decision making over Treaty reform is becoming increasingly laboured (particularly with the prospect of enlargement), now is an opportune time for researchers to (re)examine 'creeping competence' (Pollack 1994, 2000).

It is the contention of this chapter that approaches focusing on the *process of integration* are ill equipped to deal with the complexities of modern EU governance. The arguments forwarded by intergovernmentalists and neo-functionalists are reviewed in the first section of the chapter. The favoured approach is drawn from the body of literature examining the *politics of governance.* The second section reviews this literature and establishes the analytical framework of the book.

The process of integration

Intergovernmentalism

For intergovernmentalists, state actors control policy evolution in the EU. Far from diminishing the influence of the nation state, European integration is resisted by the 'obstinate' state (Hoffmann 1964, 1966), strengthens the nation state (Milward 1992) or it depends on inter-state bargains (Moravcsik 1991, 1993).

Hoffmann's obstinate nation state restricted itself to uncontroversial economic integration. Although observable in some sectors, such as welfare, Hoffmann saw the neo-functional concept of spillover as being empirically flawed (see below). Rather than embarking on positive integrative steps, the EU found it easier to follow the negative integration route of removing obstacles to trade. Perversely for Hoffmann, the success of spillover is likely to be its undoing since 'the more each partner has already obtained through past measures – the less he will be incited to make new concessions in anticipation of further gains' (Hoffmann 1965: 85). Furthermore, the more integration progresses from the economic field (*low politics*) to the political field (*high politics*) the greater the chance of failure. In the realm of high politics nation states were not prepared to be compensated for their losses by gains in other areas. Instead, the nation recoils from these difficult decisions preferring instead the tried and tested nation state approach in which uncertainty is perceived to be minimised. Hoffmann's observations in this connection are supported empirically by two events, the failure of the European Defence Community in 1954 and the Luxembourg Crisis of 1965/1966. In both cases the Community failed to break new ground because integration had tried to break out of the narrow confines of economic integration. For Hoffmann therefore spillover is limited in its applicability and once applied outside its boundaries becomes no more than an act of faith.

Milward's historical intergovernmental account of European integration does not begin with the assumption that European integration has been an altogether modest affair (Milward 1992, Milward *et al.* 1993). Instead, he asserts that the institutional and constitutional development of the EU was not an attempt to erode the nation state, and as such a move to be resisted, but an attempt at strengthening it. Milward argues that the EU became an external support system for Europe's nations, creating a new political consensus capable of rescuing the nation state but requiring a limited transfer of sovereignty. The policy competencies acquired by the Community reflected the desire by Europe's nations to underpin and stabilise the consensus on which the European nation was rebuilt. The motivation for the post-war rescue of the nation state was therefore *economic*, but within that framework existed the greatest *political* barrier to this rescue – the German question. Milward suggests that European integration developed at the intersection between these two ambitions. By examining this intersection, Milward explains how national policy became internationalised, a clear acceptance by Europe's nations that the rescue of the nation state could not be achieved within traditional national borders. As such Milward attempts to re-assert the role of the historian within explanations for post-war European integration. In effect, Milward accuses political science and integration theorists as having been unmasked by history. Empirically the work of Deutsch, Haas, Lindberg and Lipgens is flawed because central to their diverse theses is the assumption that the nation state is being superseded by a new form of governance promoted by increased communications (Deutsch), spillover (Haas and Lindberg) or a federally directed change in political consciousness spurred by the war (Lipgens).

Moravcsik's accounts of European integration focus on the preferences and power of the member states. Moravcsik refined his earlier work on intergovernmental institutionalism by adding to his theory of interstate bargaining an explicit theory of national preference formation grounded in liberal theories of international interdependence (Moravcsik 1991, 1993). Moravcsik employs these two theoretical approaches to test his claim that European integration depends on macro-level interstate bargains negotiated by member states with the aim of managing economic interdependence. Moravcsik treats the key intergovernmental players as essentially rational actors seeking to maximise their rationally conceived interests, constrained by domestic societal forces and the international environment. Moravcsik employs a liberal theory of state–society interaction and national preference formation to explain how governments define interests. He then employs an intergovernmental theory of interstate strategic interaction to account for the bargain which takes place between member states in order to realise those interests. The political outcomes of these intergovernmental bargains reflect the preferences and bargaining power of the various member states. Moravcsik sees the supranational institutions as having little influence in shaping these outcomes. Rather, institutions in the EU are used to facilitate intergovernmental bargains and improve decision-making efficiency.

Moravcsik's rejection of neo-functionalism is two-fold. Empirically, neo-functionalism has mis-predicted the course of European integration. The emphasis on functional and political spillover has been misguided. Functional linkages can only sporadically be detected, fundamentally calling into question the gradual and automatic nature of integration. Indeed, events such as the 1965 Luxembourg crisis and resulting compromise of 1966 have demonstrated the resilience of the nation state in the process of integration. Rather than the smooth process outlined by neo-functionalists, European integration has proceeded in fits and starts through intergovernmental bargains that have set the agenda for 'an intervening period of consolidation' (Moravcsik 1993: 475). Similarly, Moravcsik sees the concept of political spillover as flawed. He sees the autonomous influence of supranational officials as increasing 'slowly and unevenly, if at all' (Moravcsik 1993: 476). Second, Moravcsik makes a theoretical criticism of neo-functionalism. Rather than employing general theories of international political economy, neo-functionalists attempted to explain European integration as a unique process. As a result, neo-functionalism lost the benefit of comparability and testability.

Neo-functionalism
From a neo-functional perspective, policy evolution in the EU is functionally determined and supranational actors play a key role in defining policy alternatives. Two strands of neo-functional thought are relevant in this respect – functional and political spillover. From Ernst Haas's early neo-functional work in *The Uniting of Europe* to more contemporary revisions, the concept of functional spillover has been an enduring centrepiece of neo-functional theory (Haas 1957). The content, timing and nature of this functional spillover has been questioned yet it continues to be employed by integration theorists as an intervening variable between functional action and European political integration, a dynamic absent in Mitrany's functionalist account (Mitrany 1943 [1966]). Functional integration is essentially economic in nature. It refers to the build up of pressure created by incomplete integration by modern interdependent economies.

The focus on the economic rationale for integration in the face of mounting international pressures is a strand of neo-functional thought similar in conception to other theoretical accounts of regional integration. Moravcsik, a leading critic of neo-functionalism remarked, 'the focus on economic interests may still be viable. It remains plausible for example, to argue that integration is a distinctive policy response of modern welfare states to rising economic interdependence' (Moravcsik 1993: 476).

Despite the similarity, neo-functionalism remains clearly distinct from the intergovernmentalist camp in that neo-functionalism de-emphasises state capabilities in the regional integration process. Furthermore, the economic rationale for integration as developed by neo-functionalists was seen as merely one dynamic in the integration process, the others being political and societal factors (see political spillover). For the neo-functionalist, the economic decision to integrate one sector creates pressures for further sectoral integration. Only by following this incremental logic can the policy maker ensure the maintenance of the gains achieved by the initial decision to integrate. The decision to harmonise coal and steel policy in Europe in 1952 for example, created pressures for further sectoral integration in functionally linked areas. The realisation of the benefits of the European Coal and Steel Community (ECSC) necessitated a wider, more general level of economic integration as embodied in the 1957 Treaty of Rome. As Haas explained, 'policies made pursuant to an initial task can only be made real if the task itself is expanded, as reflected in the compromises made among the states interested in the task' (Haas 1961). From this perspective, incremental task expansion becomes a necessity as a half way house between integration and sovereignty would be unsustainable. Clearly, therefore, neo-functionalists see this as a crucial dynamic, perpetuating task expansion as 'problems in one area will raise problems or require solutions in another' (Muttimer 1989).

In its original form, functional spillover was portrayed as a theoretical breakthrough, a plausible explanatory and predictive account of how European integration would become self-sustaining. In essence functional spillover was regarded as automatic and essentially inevitable, 'sector integration . . . begets its own impetus toward extension to the entire economy even in the absence of specific group demands and their attendant ideologies' (Haas 1957: 297). These alleged self-sustaining properties of European integration have however never been universally accepted as representing reality. Even though occasional functional linkages could still be detected, progress has been patchy and far from smooth. By 1961, Haas had called into question his original expectation concerning the inevitability of spillover. Instead he argued, 'functional contexts are autonomous. Integrative forces that flow from one kind of activity do not necessarily infect other activities, even if carried out by the same organisation' (Haas 1961). The experience of the 1965 Luxembourg crisis followed by the retrenchment of the 1970s forced neo-functionalists into even greater retreat. Less than 20 years after commenting on the unsustainability of a 'half-way house' between integration and sovereignty, Haas, in 1976, described the EU as exactly this (Haas 1976).

In addition to functional spillover, neo-functionalists also identified a complementary process, political spillover. 'Political spillover, in short, consists of a convergence of the expectations and interests of national elites in response to the activities of the supranational institutions' (Cram 1997: 16). At the supranational institutional level, political spillover is promoted by the independent, autonomous and essentially creative actions of the European Commission, Parliament and the ECJ. From this perspective, political behaviour and policy outcomes in the EU are shaped endogenously through a process of supranational institutional creativity. The Commission, Parliament and ECJ can detach themselves from tight member state supervision to expand the policy remit of the EU. This might be achieved through the exploitation of institutional powers, the exaggerated interpretation of Community goals, the seizing upon of crises to expand policy, the creative use of brokering or a combination of all of these backed up by considerable personal skill on the part of leading figures. For Haas, this institutional ingredient is central to neo-functional theory: 'the existence of political institutions capable of translating ideologies into law is the cornerstone of the definition' (Haas 1957).

Haas also identified a societal dimension to European integration. Acting as agents of European integration, supranational institutions promote dialogue between the central authority and relevant interest groups. As more sectoral areas are brought under supranational control within the regional integration process, so traditionally nationally centred belief systems would change. 'As time went by, these interest groups would come to appreciate the benefits of integration, and thereby transfer their demands, expectations and loyalties from national governments to a new centre, thereby becoming an important force in favour of further integration' (Pollack 1994: 99).

Haas's example of shifting societal expectations was drawn from the experience of the ECSC which was viewed with scepticism by most industrial groups in 1951 yet by 1955 became the focus for demands for more supranational powers. Good experience of integration therefore breeds familiarity, trust and crucially demands for more action. The task of the supranational institutions is to develop channels of communication facilitating this bottom-up demand shift and ultimately translate such demands into legislative (or indeed judicial) action, thus expanding the institutional and policy remit of the Community. The supranational institutions thus provide the home for shifting societal demands.

As with functional spillover, the concept of political spillover has also been re-examined. Haas, drawing on the work of Lindberg and Scheingold (1970, 1971) explained how different integration outcomes are likely. Lindberg and Scheingold identified three such possible outcomes, 'the fulfilment of a postulated task on the part of practices and/or institutions created for integrative purposes, the retraction of such a task (i.e. disintegration) and the extension of such a task into spheres of action not previously anticipated by the actors' (Lindberg and Scheingold 1971).

The 'crisis' of neo-functionalism in the 1970s and early 1980s became replaced by renewed theoretical optimism with the launch of the Single European Market project. Clearly, however, any revised concept of functional and political spillover would have to take into account the role of key actors in shaping political outcomes. In particular, the failing of early neo-functionalism lay in it de-emphasising state actors. As such, although a move towards some kind of supranational political integration could be detected, the process was unpredictable, depending in large part on the calculations of self interest made by the member states. From an internal perspective the relationship between the Single European Act, the Maastricht Treaty and the Amsterdam Treaty can be functionally examined. Externally however the collapse of Communism and the re-unification of Germany point to an equally persuasive set of dynamics. The danger is that spillover becomes a term conceptually stretched over a set of events to which the concept may or may not be applicable. 'Spillover, then, is rather like a mirage; it is there if you want it to be' (O'Neill 1996: 129).

Implications for EU sports law and policy
Largely absent from the analytical foundations of intergovernmentalism and neo-functionalism has been a focus on the role of the ECJ in the integration

process. This gap in the literature became populated throughout the 1990s (see for instance Burley and Mattli 1993, Volcansek 1992, Weiler 1993, Garrett and Weingast 1993, Wincott 1996; also see Chapter 4 where a more comprehensive review of legal approaches is conducted).

Burley and Mattli's classic neo-functional analysis of the role of the ECJ places heavy emphasis on the cultivation of integration by the Court. The ECJ has constitutionalised the Treaty through a process in which law has spilled over from purely economic sectors to new spheres. Making the observation that the law governing the free movement of workers spilled over into the sphere of sport via *Bosman* is, on the face of it, appealing. Furthermore, the ECJ's rejection of member state submissions supporting the maintenance of the transfer system appears to further undermine the intergovernmentalist argument on state supremacy.

By contrast, intergovernmentalism rejects the idea of a Court able to engineer integration in a manner inconsistent with member state preferences. The member states power of sanction over the Court has the effect of reigning in the ECJ's judicially active impulses. Occasionally governments may be prepared to accept short-term losses in order to secure wider long-term gains. The 'defeat' in *Bosman*, can therefore be viewed in this light. In other words, even though the ruling was unpopular within national capitals, it did not fundamentally undermine member state interests. Indeed, by strengthening the principle of the freedom of movement, the ruling was in fact consistent with the member states wider interests.

Given the depth of theoretical and empirical material provided by intergovernmentalism and neo-functionalism, why not employ these tools to examine the birth of EU sports law and policy? Two central reasons have already been discussed above, namely the level (macro in nature) and insularity of the approaches. However, taking each approach in turn, further related weaknesses are evident.

First, intergovernmental analyses of policy evolution overstate the importance of state actors within the EU whilst under-estimating their commitment to achieve 'positive' integration. Clearly, the member states are important to the development of policy in the EU but they do not monopolise the process. The EU is far more multi-layered and complex than intergovernmentalists claim (Marks *et al.* 1996). As such, an approach is needed that can capture the real nature of EU subsystemic, systemic and supersystemic governance (Peterson 1995). Indeed, when tracing the emergence of a *de facto* EU sports policy, member state involvement at the Amsterdam Summit represents only the tip of the iceberg and the first formal involvement of the member states. Since Amsterdam, the member states have become more active. If a post-Amsterdam snapshot of sports policy development were to be taken covering the period 1998–2000, an intergovernmental analysis may become more appealing. However, this would be to exclude an analysis of the messy development of sports policy prior to member state involvement. Accordingly, an approach is required that not only captures the real nature of EU governance, but also adopts an historical, not snapshot approach. Intergovernmentalism may therefore have some value in accounting for policy 'decision', but it is more limited in terms of explaining 'agenda setting' and 'issue definition' (Hogwood and Gunn 1984). At best, state actors are merely one (albeit powerful) policy advocate within any given policy subsystem.

If intergovernmentalism is of limited applicability, what of neo-functionalism? It has already been noted that Burley and Mattli's neo-functional analysis of legal integration provides potential insights into the birth of EU sports law. Furthermore, Pollack's neo-functional analysis of task expansion in the field of regulatory policies is also useful in forging a link between the operation of the EU's Single Market and the development of new policies. In relation to regulatory policies, Pollack argues that the initial decision to establish a common market set in motion a dynamic process of functional spillover in relation to regulatory policies. He argues, 'the existence, timing and content of Community regulatory policies are explicable primarily in terms of functional spillover from the common market' (Pollack 1994: 118). As Pierson argues, the huge range of closely related policy sectors in which the EU involves itself increases the likelihood of new policy sectors being drawn into the regional integration process as an unintended consequence of activity in related fields (Pierson 1996). Functional spillover can therefore develop out of 'high issue density' (Pierson 1996: 139). The proximity of sport to many of the fundamental economic activities of the EU therefore increases the potential of sport being caught within the scope of the law of the four freedoms. For example, Article 42 (ex 51) relating to the adoption of measures in the field of social security necessary to provide for freedom of movement for workers has provided the basis for functional spillover into education policy. In particular, in the mid 1970s, the Commission launched an action programme aimed at facilitating the movement of migrant workers. This resulted in a Council Directive in July 1977 on the education of children of Community migrant workers.

It may be that neo-functionalism only possesses descriptive qualities. The concepts of functional and political spillover are contestable. The notion that functional spillover is automatic is empirically flawed. Although spillover is a useful tool to describe the linkages between policy sectors, it struggles to account for the dynamics driving the connections. Political spillover is also questionable. Neo-functionalism de-emphasises the important role played by state actors. As demonstrated by the Amsterdam and Nice Declarations on sport, the member states have been influential in establishing a EU sports policy. In this connection, neo-functionalism over-emphasises the autonomy of supranational players. The relationship between the ECJ and the Competition Directorate has been influential in linking sport to the EU's legal framework but their role cannot be divorced from the wider political context within which they operate. As such, political spillover, although not totally dismissed, is uneven at best. It is clear that individual litigants have been important in bringing sports-related cases before the ECJ and Competition Directorate, however there is little evidence suggesting that this form of bottom-up litigation has been encouraged by EU officials. Indeed, given the increasing caseload of the under-resourced Competition Directorate, it is unlikely Commission officials would want to increase their caseload further. Rather than characterising bottom-up litigation as political spillover, it can be better characterised as legal opportunism.

What lessons need to be drawn when constructing an analytical toolkit for examining the birth of EU sports law and policy? First, an approach is needed that is best able to capture the real nature of EU governance. The EU is becoming a more flexible and multi-layered organisation than intergovernmentalists and neo-functionalists recognise. As such, policy-shaping and making capabilities are dispersed and not monopolised. In addition, the traditional forums for agreeing policy, such as Council/European Council meetings are becoming less dominant as alternative venues for policy development emerge. An intergovernmental decision to grant a policy Treaty status rarely signals the birth of a new policy. Rather, such a move usually formalises pre-existing developments, even if these developments have taken place outside the context of the Treaty. As such, an analytical toolkit must be able to capture the role of these alternative policy and institutional venues and the role played by key policy advocates within them. If no one actor dominates, how are conflicting approaches to policy managed within the formal and informal institutional structure?

The second feature the analytical toolkit needs to capture is an historical approach to understanding policy change. A snapshot of European integration is unlikely to capture the true nature of policy change. Nor is an approach that attempts to scientifically map out integration likely to capture the differences between different policies. Rather, what is required is a methodology for analysing European integration rather than a grand theory, in particular a methodology that examines policy change over time.

The third feature required is an approach that cuts across the insularity of intergovernmentalism and neo-functionalism. State actors and non-state actors are both central to policy evolution. Analysing interstate bargains must remain central to the methodology but must be properly located within the context of a multi-layered EU. In addition, spillover need not necessarily be discarded, rather spillover needs similarly placing in correct context. Constitutive politics or key events, such as a change in the economic status of a sector, can spark spillover. Spillover may also be generated by high issue density or may be encouraged as policy advocates exploit a growing number of institutional venues. However, the inexorable logic of spillover is rejected.

The politics of governance

Given the limitations of the political science approaches reviewed above, the researcher must step outside this toolkit for studying European integration and turn to an approach that examines the governance of the EU. This research agenda is more modest. Rather than explaining the big picture of European integration, studying the governance of the EU illuminates the day-to-day detail of integration. In this connection, researchers usually turn to *either* an actor-based *or* an institutions-based approach. The approach adopted in this text attempts to bridge the two whilst acknowledging the useful but limited insights offered by intergovernmentalism and neo-functionalism. As such, to address the need to examine the role of key actors, the study employs the Advocacy Coalition Framework (Sabatier 1988, 1991, 1998). In order to capture the crucial role played by institutions, the study uses new institutionalism (March and Olsen 1984, 1989, Armstrong and Bulmer 1998). Alone, the Advocacy Coalition Framework fails to recognise the importance of political institutions in policy evolution. Hence the need to take an 'institutional turn' (Jessop 1990, 2000). However, alone, new institutionalism fails to capture the nature of competition between rival policy advocates. Taken together, they both add theoretical depth to the important yet largely descriptive findings of multi-level governance (Marks *et al.* 1996).

Multi-level governance

An essential starting point for this research agenda is an acceptance that the EU can be characterised as a multi-level organisation. As explained above, macro theories of European integration have traditionally tended to over-state or under-state the role played by intergovernmental and supranational actors. By seeing decisional 'power' as dispersed within the EU's policy process we can explain a growing phenomena in the EU, best described as a 'control deficit'. Given a sharing of competencies in decision making, one set of actors, be they intergovernmental or supranational, find it more difficult to control policy development in the EU. Due to a changing institutional balance of power promoted by recent Treaty changes, policy advocates find themselves able to exploit a growing number of institutional venues to shape policy. However, this fragmentation of policy 'influence' need not necessarily lead to analytical fragmentation. A review of multi-level governance (MLG) provides the starting point to illustrate this argument.

The MLG school of thought provides an alternative account of European integration to that of intergovernmentalism and neo-functionalism. The empirical, if not theoretical, strength of MLG lies in the recognition that member states remain the key actors in the process of European integration but increasingly share policy-making competence across multiple levels of government, including sub-national and supranational. In explaining why member states no longer monopolise European level policy making, Marks, Hooghe and Blank make three assumptions (Marks *et al.* 1996: 346). First, decision making in the EU is shared by actors at different levels rather than being monopolised by the member states. Second, individual member state control is diminished by collective decision making in the European Council and Council of Ministers. Third, political arenas are interconnected rather than nested. As such, the state does not act as a gatekeeper between domestic and supranational politics.

Marks *et al.* use these assumptions as the basis on which to answer the central intergovernmental criticism of why member states would tolerate a slippage in their control. Two broad responses are supplied. First, multi-level governance assumes that the maintenance of sovereignty is just one goal of many for member states. As such, it is not inconceivable that this goal might be sacrificed for the attainment of other goals such as efficient policy provision. The costs of such an action may be felt by the member state but may be offset by the expected benefits, be they economic or political. In addition, life in an electoral marketplace means that member states may tolerate losses in their control if these losses only manifest themselves in the long run. For politicians, the short-term gains are prized whilst long-term costs are discounted (Marks *et al.* 1996: 349).

Second, member states may use the EU as a shield to insulate themselves from domestic criticism. Furthermore, a member state may accept a loss of control if that is the price that must be paid in order to control the actions of other member states. The strict regulatory ethos of the Single European Market programme reflects the mistrust between member states. Finally, member states may also accept a loss of control in order to limit future reform attempts once they have left office. This ensures a degree of permanence for their original architecture (Marks *et al.* 1996: 349–350).

Marks *et al.* go beyond explaining the logic of shifting decision making to supranational institutions to explain why this would entail a loss of individual and collective member state control. The most obvious constraint on individual member state control is the use of qualified majority voting (QMV) in the Council, even though consensual decision making remains a popular informal institutional device (Marks *et al.* 1996: 350–352). The ability of member states to control supranational institutions collectively is also constrained. The chief opportunity for member states to assert themselves in the policy-making process comes with the negotiation and signing of new Treaties. Although unanimity is the rule, member states do not start with a clean slate. Collectively, unanimity can act as a barrier to policy and institutional reform and even where agreement is possible the ratification process can act as a constraint. Furthermore, the mapping out of the rules of the game can lead to considerable discretion on the part of the supranational institutions as to how to operationalise these general principles. Day-to-day EU governance is therefore an arena intergovernmentalists tend to ignore.

One of the reasons for this is that intergovernmentalists assume the principal–agent theory will guarantee that if the agents (supranational institutions) are operationalising Treaty principles in a manner undesired by the principals (member states), then the latter will simply replace or reform the agent (Marks *et al.* 1996: 352–354).

Marks *et al.* provide four reasons why the principal–agent theory might not necessarily hold. The first constraint on the ability of the principal to control the agent stems from 'the multiplicity of principals'. The existence of 15 principals with different agendas, constrained by unanimous voting, means altering the agent is not straightforward. Indeed, this scenario can further strengthen the agent due to the nature of the Treaties negotiated under these constraints. Disagreements between principals can lead to ambiguous Treaties that reflect compromise and sensitivity. This allows for a diverse and creative interpretation of the Treaty by the agents, whose delegated task is to operationalise the Treaty principles (Marks *et al.* 1996: 354).

A second constraint stems from 'informational asymmetries', the privileged access to information supranational institutions enjoy. Being involved extensively in day-to-day EU governance gives the supranational institutions an advantage over intergovernmental actors in terms of expertise and access to information. The European Commission in particular benefits from wide-scale consultation with interest groups, a process Commission officials attempt to develop and consolidate whenever possible. A superior knowledge of EU processes can allow the supranational institutions to distance themselves from tight member state supervision (Marks *et al.* 1996: 355).

A third constraint limiting the validity of the principal–agent theory results from the use of 'detailed regulation as a response to mutual mistrust.' In cases where member states cannot trust each other to adhere to the rules, for instance in relation to the granting of state aid, rigid regulation of a highly detailed nature tends to be the response. Under these conditions, the Commission and the ECJ have a particularly crucial role to play in developing and overseeing this regulation. In effect, the member states allow themselves to be locked into a particular institutional and policy design because they mistrust one another (Marks *et al.* 1996: 355).

A final constraint is the emphasis on 'unintended consequences'. Member state rationality is bounded by time, resources, knowledge, multiple values, precedent and organisational limitations (Hogwood and Gunn 1984: 50). Stripped of the ability to continually scan policy horizons, assessing the likely consequences of individual and collective action, member states are forced to gamble with the possibility of unintended consequences. European integration can develop as a result of unintended consequences, especially if supranational actors seize upon them to develop integration and their own remit. Furthermore, if policy or institutional powers develop as a result of unanticipated consequences, member states may be constrained in their ability to limit the impact due to the above reasons. Because of the existence of unanticipated consequences, decision making in the EU tends to be incremental. Although this incrementalism may reflect an increased ability of the member states to learn from previous experience, incrementalism can result in a form of path dependence that insulates supranational actors from member state control (Marks *et al.* 1996: 355–356).

Marks *et al.* examine four stages of the EU's policy process – policy initiation, decision making, implementation and adjudication – in order to draw three main conclusions regarding the applicability of multi-level governance. First, the member states share decision-making authority with supranational actors. Second, member states are individually and collectively constrained in EU decision making. Third, sub-national interests are active at the European level as well as in the national arena. At all levels of EU decision making, competence is shared. The Commission has a powerful, although not dominant role in policy initiation. The Council shares decision making with the European Parliament in some cases and is constrained by QMV. The implementation of policy is shared and highly restrictive regulatory policies often restrict member state control. In terms of adjudication, the judicial activism of the ECJ, backed up by the Commission and national courts, questions the validity of the principal–agent theory (Marks *et al.* 1996: 356–371).

Multi-level governance provides the descriptive context within which policy evolves. Decision making and influencing capabilities are shared by actors across numerous levels resulting in no one set of actors dominating. As such the EU is a paradise for those wishing to influence policy. As Peters argues,

> agenda setting in the EU is significantly different from that process as it is practised in most national political systems. In particular . . . the existence of a number of points of access, of a large number of influential policy advocates, and of a wide range of policy options that have been legitimised in one or more of the constituent political systems makes agenda setting substantially easier than in most other environments. (Peters 1996: 62)

Agenda setting, issue definition and agenda expansion
Pollack's definition of task expansion as '(a) the initial expansion of the Community agenda to include new policy areas and (b) the subsequent development and growth of substantive policies in each of these new policy areas' (Pollack 1994: 96) implies new policies in the EU emerge as a result of a two-stage process. First, an issue emerges on to the agenda (agenda setting) then it is subsequently defined and developed (issue definition). For the purposes of this work the 'agenda' is taken to mean the list of subjects the EU is capable of pursuing an interest in. It refers to a set of issues or problems to which EU officials may have paid some attention, but no policy or set of policies has yet emerged (Kingdon 1995: 3). The term issue definition is taken to mean,

the process by which an issue (problem, opportunity, or trend), having been recognised as such and placed on the public policy agenda, is perceived by various interested parties; further explored, articulated and possibly quantified; and in some but not all cases, given an authoritative or at least provisionally acceptable definition in terms of its likely causes, components, and consequences. (Hogwood and Gunn 1984)

The definition of an issue also implies some action. Usually, this will be in the form of a policy decision. By distinguishing the systemic agenda from the institutional agenda, Cobb and Elder have made an important contribution to the task expansion debate (Cobb and Elder 1972). The systemic agenda is composed of 'all issues that are commonly perceived by members of the political community as meriting public attention and involving matters within the legitimate jurisdiction of existing governmental authority' (Cobb and Elder 1972: 85). By contrast, the institutional agenda is 'that set of items explicitly up for the active consideration of authoritative decision makers' (Cobb and Elder 1972: 86). A clear similarity exists between the notion of the systemic agenda and the agenda setting stage of the EU's policy process and between the institutional agenda and the issue definition stage.

Accordingly, task expansion refers to (1) the movement of an issue on to the EU's systemic agenda and (2) the movement of the issue from the systemic agenda on to the institutional agenda for definition and development. From a pluralist perspective, agenda setting and issue definition can be explained in terms of open competition between interested groups. Functionalist accounts of the political system devised by writers such as Easton, and Almond and Powell, tended to stress how inputs were converted into outputs in the political 'system' in a rational, non-discriminatory manner (Easton 1965, Almond and Powell 1988). In his New Haven survey, Dahl found no evidence of a ruling elite (Dahl 1961). Indeed observing New Haven, Polsby concluded that, 'in each issue area different actors appeared, their roles were different and the kinds of alternatives which they had to chose among were different' (Polsby 1993: 15). The 'openness and neutrality' (Parsons 1995: 125) of agenda setting from this pluralist perspective has more recently been called into question by writers observing how access to the political agenda is controlled.

An early and influential critic of the pluralist perspective was provided by E. E Schattschneider in the *Semi-Sovereign People* (Schattschneider 1960). Schattschneider examined how conflict can escalate beyond the original confines of the dispute leaving those originally involved with little or no influence over unfolding events. Agendas therefore have the potential for expansion, yet crucially, for Schattschneider, agendas are controlled and structured by those players (pressure groups, parties or institutions) best able to control this expansion. Whilst the weaker groups seek to expand conflict by recruiting new participants to its support, the stronger side will

Eg. Fifpro ← *may not want to topple *not necessarily topple but use
involve are of (predicted alternative strategies to topple winners
potential implications of ← as a bargaining tool for greater influence
adopting such a strategy in key (contentious) areas of policy

Towards a theory of EU sports law and policy 41

normally seek to suppress conflict. Whereas the 'strong' may seek to restrict participation by adopting narrow technical or procedural definitions of alternatives, the 'weak' may try and link issues to major themes. Accordingly, the same issue may either be 'routine and procedural' or it may 'go to the heart of democracy'.

Schattschneider's work highlights the distinction between agenda setting and issue definition (alternatives). For Schattschneider, 'the definition of alternatives is the supreme instrument of power', and 'he who determines what politics is about runs the country, because the definition of alternatives is the choice of conflicts' (Schattschneider 1960: 69). Indeed, once an issue is on an agenda, the way it is subsequently defined may escalate the conflict. As Rochefort and Cobb explain, 'the outside audience does not enter the fray randomly or in equal proportion for the competing sides. Rather, the uninterested become engaged in response to the way participants portray their struggle' (Rochefort and Cobb 1994: 5). Although Schattschneider's work focuses on how issues are controlled in the policy process whereas this work examines the openness of EU public policy, his focus on conflict expansion is particularly useful. Schattschneider argued that the 'losers' in the policy process would adopt strategies to topple the 'winners'. Such strategies would involve appealing to those currently not involved in the debate. In such circumstances, Sabatier argued that 'losers' would construct 'coalitions of convenience' (Sabatier 1998: 119). Schattschneider's focus on conflict expansion is broadly accepted in this study, although the nature of this is expansion is queried. Within more open, 'multi-level' political systems the researcher must examine the role multiple institutional venues play in the strategies of those wishing to escalate the agenda. Before this can examined an examination of the nature of the agenda is first required.

Systemic agenda setting

Before an issue is considered on the institutional agenda, it first must have been on the systemic agenda. How does an issue expand to such an extent where governmental action is seen as necessary? For Hogwood and Gunn an issue, especially a new one, will be more likely to reach the systemic agenda if one or more of the following circumstances apply. First, the issue has reached crisis proportions and can no longer be ignored. Second, the issue has reached particularity (for example acid rain). Third, the issue has an emotive or human-interest angle that attracts media attention. Fourth, the issue seems likely to have a wide impact (for example health scares). Fifth, the issue raises questions about power and legitimacy in society. Finally, the issue is fashionable in some way which is difficult to explain but easy to recognise (for example inner-city crime) (Hogwood and Gunn 1984). However, these factors do not guarantee access to the public policy agenda. In order to explain this, Hogwood and Gunn argue that the actions of key players need examining. In particular these include, the agenda setters (organised interests, protest groups, party leaders, influentials) and the gatekeepers of the mass media such as newspaper editors and television producers.

Cobb and Elder identify numerous reasons accounting for why an issue may reach a political system's systemic agenda (Cobb and Elder 1972). First, an issue may be well defined. Second, it may possess social significance. Third, it may have a long-term relevance. Fourth, it may be relatively non-technical. Finally, the issue may lack a clear precedent. Like Schattschneider, Cobb and Elder argue that agendas are structured by certain players. Strategies for controlling issue expansion include group strategies and issue strategies. Group strategies may involve the discrediting or co-option of leaders, whilst issue strategies may involve the use of symbols. If a conflict is made sufficiently prominent (most likely with the assistance of the media), access to the formal institutional decision-making process will be facilitated (Richardson and Jordan 1979: Chapter 4). For both Schattschneider and Cobb and Elder, agenda setting is therefore concerned with how conflict is managed, more specifically how conflict is either suppressed or expanded.

Hogwood and Gunn's approach implies systemic agenda setting is externally determined. In other words social, economic and political forces external to the political system compel governments to act. Without rejecting the significance of such forces, is it possible also to identify a set of internal dynamics shaping systemic agenda setting? Paul Pierson's study of the evolution of EU social policy makes an important implicit contribution to the study of systemic agenda setting (Pierson 1996). Employing an historical institutionalist analysis (although in places resembling a more rational choice strand in institutional thought) Pierson examines how *unanticipated consequences* and *high-issue density* in the EU may result in the emergence of new issues. Pierson notes that growing issue density has two consequences. First, it generates 'overload' (Pierson 1996: 137). Overload greatly complicates EU decision making for the member states. In such circumstances, member states are more likely to delegate responsibility to supranational actors. Member state 'grip' over an issue may therefore slip. Second, issue density promotes spillover. Due to the huge range of policy issues in which the EU pursues an interest, new policy issues may be unintentionally drawn into the regional integration process, thus giving that issue a EU dimension. Externally generated factors may increase the potential for this to occur. For instance a change in the 'image' of the issue may serve to give it a EU dimension.

Institutional agenda setting

External and internal forces may pull an issue on to the systemic agenda. The interplay between these two forces may also prove influential in moving the issue on to the EU's institutional agenda for active definition and policy decision. For example high-issue density in the EU may create a 'latent' regulatory environment for a particular industry operating within the Single Market. The regulatory environment may be latent due to the underdeveloped economic status of that industry. In such circumstances the issue will remain on the systemic agenda. However, an externally generated change in the economic status of the industry may activate regulatory interest from the EU. Accordingly, the issue is dragged on to the institutional agenda in a particular form. Pinder argues that in the EU the 'free trade ideology is firmly built into the system, but the planning ethic is no more than a possibility for the future' (Pinder 1968: 98). Although undoubtedly the balance has shifted, the force of the four fundamental freedoms remains strong. The movement of an issue from the systemic to institutional agenda will often therefore be promoted by the logic of negative integration (Pinder 1968). New policy issues are therefore frequently introduced on to the EU's institutional agenda with definition bias. For example legal/regulatory norms held together the sports policy subsystem.

The manner in which an issue reaches the institutional agenda is significant for policy definition and for eventual policy outcomes. It is no great insight into EU policy making to observe that individuals and groups 'frame' issues differently. Those who were instrumental in an issue reaching the agenda may feel their definition is most appropriate. Others may be drawn into the policy process at the issue definition stage in protest at the original definition. As Rochefort and Cobb suggest, 'the uninterested become engaged in response to the way participants portray their struggle' (Rochefort and Cobb 1994: 5). As the post-Maastricht EU has attempted to develop a more social and cultural dimension within the spirit of Adonnino (see Chapter 1), so subsystems dominated by legal and technocratic norms and values are becoming penetrated by broader political arguments. The politicisation of law and regulation has occurred in a wide range of policy subsystems including the single currency, tax policy and media ownership policy (Radaelli 1999a). The sports policy subsystem has witnessed similar politicisation. Issue definition is therefore greatly influenced by value judgements, but with value judgements comes conflict. However, rather than being an obstacle to policy evolution in the institutional agenda-setting stage, conflict can represent an important resource (Harcourt 1998). In this connection, Sabatier's work on competition between policy advocates within policy subsystems is important.

An actor-based analysis: the advocacy coalition framework

For those wishing to explain policy evolution/agenda escalation in the EU, Sabatier's Advocacy Coalition Framework (ACF) provides an excellent starting point (Sabatier 1988, 1991, 1998). Sabatier's focus on the dynamics of non-incremental policy change has important implications for those seeking to explain a similar phenomena–task expansion. Although not applied to the EU, the ACF's focus on competing advocacy coalitions

within policy subsystems effectively captures the real nature of EU governance. Sabatier begins his analysis of policy change by examining the growth
of public policy (air pollution) environmental programmes in the United
States (Sabatier 1988). Sabatier notes that, in the 1950s federal programmes were very limited, yet only a decade later federal expenditures had
risen more than 20-fold and by 1970 Washington had instituted a massive
regulatory programme designed to improve air quality. Despite this
clamour, progress in combating air pollution in the 1970s was slow as other
issues such as energy prices emerged and as the technical and political difficulties of action became known. Sabatier's approach to understanding
such change is based on three basic premises. First, that in order to fully
understand the process of policy change a period of at least ten years should
be examined. Second, throughout this period a focus on 'policy subsystems'
can help explain policy change. Third, public policies or programmes can
be conceptualised in the same manner as belief systems, i.e. as sets of value
priorities and causal assumptions about how to realise them (Sabatier
1988: 131).

First, on time span, Sabatier argues that policy change is the result of
cumulative effects. For example, as new findings and ideas are fed into the
policy process, so policy gradually changes. Indeed it often takes considerable time to implement and evaluate policy once agreed. In short, 'policy
analysis has a long-term 'enlightenment' function. Policy analysis gradually
alters the arguments surrounding policy problems' (Parsons 1995: 195).

On the second premise, Sabatier views the policy process as comprising
more than the 'iron triangle' of administrative agencies, legislative committees and interest groups at a single level of government policy (Sabatier 1988:
131). For Sabatier, the 'policy subsystem' will involve many more actors at
various levels of government such as interest groups, bureaucrats, academics, politicians, think tanks and journalists. These actors generate and
exchange ideas in relation to policy problems. Subsystems tend to be autonomous due to their specialised nature yet they may involve a large number
of actors who are involved in dealing with a problem. For example, Sabatier
identifies ten sets of actors involved in the US air pollution control subsystem. These include the governmental bodies, consumer groups, environmental groups, manufacturers groups, academics and researchers and
journalists. In the case of acid rain, other countries become involved in the
subsystem. These groups are termed 'advocacy coalitions'.

Finally, on belief systems, Sabatier argues that within subsystems lie 'value
priorities, perceptions of important causal relationships, perceptions of
world states, perceptions of the efficacy of policy instruments' (Sabatier
1988: 132). Given that individuals attempt to translate their beliefs into
public policy, it becomes clear that beliefs can play an important role in
structuring politics. Beliefs are also important because actors are attracted
to one another on the basis of shared beliefs. As Sabatier explains,

actors can be aggregated into a number of advocacy coalitions composed of people from various organisations who share a set of normative and causal beliefs and who often act in concert. At any particular point in time, each coalition adopts a strategy(s) envisaging one or more institutional innovations which it feels will further its objectives. (Sabatier 1988: 133)

Therefore, for Sabatier, operating within an organisation such as the EU are numerous *policy subsystems*. A subsystem consists of various actors who are seeking to influence policy. Operating within policy subsystems are competing *advocacy coalitions*, each composed of a group of like-minded individuals seeking to re-direct policy in line with their particular *belief system*. Beliefs within an advocacy coalition are organised hierarchically. At the highest level, fundamental ideological beliefs form the *deep core*. At the next level, *policy core* beliefs comprise fundamental policy positions and strategies for attaining core values. Sabatier describes policy core beliefs as the 'fundamental glue' of coalitions (Sabatier 1998: 103). At the base of the hierarchy lie a range of narrower concerns such as implementing decisions and policy preferences known as the *secondary aspects* of a coalition's belief system. Changes in beliefs are more likely to occur in the *secondary aspects* of a belief system. The empirical although not normative elements of the belief system within the *policy core* are subject to change through learning over a period of time, whilst beliefs in the *policy core* remain resistant to change.

Advocacy coalitions attempt to translate their beliefs into public policy through the use of *guidance instruments* such as changes in rules, budgets, personnel or information (Sabatier 1998: 104). *Policy brokers* attempt to mediate between conflicting coalitions within a policy subsystem. Policy outputs result from this interaction between competing advocacy coalitions. However, for Sabatier policy making within subsystems is affected by external factors and the internal structure of policy subsystems. Sabatier's approach for examining external factors affecting policy change within subsystems distinguishes between (1) parameters that are relatively stable over decades and (2) those aspects of the system that are susceptible to significant fluctuations over the course of a few years and thus serve as major stimuli to policy change (Sabatier 1988: 143).

The relatively stable parameters (both internal and external to policy subsystem) include:

- *Basic attributes of the problem area (or 'good'):* Institutional policy options are affected by the issue under consideration. Some issues lend themselves to governmental regulation whilst others can be left to the market.
- *Basic distribution of natural resources:* A focus on this can help us explain why during the 1970s the USA could encourage utilities to switch from oil to coal whilst the coal-deprived French turned to nuclear power.

- *Fundamental cultural values and social structure:* It is apparent that due to prevailing cultural values and norms that some policy options are not feasible at a given time. Similarly the social structures structure access to politics. Change in these areas is likely to take considerable time.
- *Basic legal structure:* The constitutional structure of a political system affects both policy change and policy-oriented learning (see below). Basic legal norms tend to be resistant to change thus minimising policy change in this area. Policy-oriented learning can be affected if the policy style of a system is closed preventing learning from taking place.

The dynamic (system) events (external to policy subsystem) include:

- *Changes in socio-economic conditions and technology:* Public opinion can affect policy change as it did with environmental policy in the 1970s. Major events also have a profound impact on policy. Sabatier notes that the Arab oil boycott of 1973–1974 contributed to calls for a relaxation of car pollution controls, even from groups previously supportive of such efforts.
- *Changes in systemic governing coalitions:* It is clear that with changes of government come changes in policy approaches.
- *Policy decisions and impacts from other subsystems:* Sabatier notes that policy subsystems are only partially autonomous. The argument advanced here echoes the logic of functional integration. Sectors cannot be integrated in sectoral isolation. Coal and steel production, for example, cannot be isolated from energy policy, which cannot be isolated from transport policy and so on.

For Sabatier, the internal structure of a policy subsystem is particularly important. This is why Sabatier extended the definition of a subsystem to include journalists, analysts, researchers and other important players. Sabatier makes five observations relating to the internal structure of policy subsystems. First, although members of policy subsystems may be easily identified, it is also important to identify the 'latent' constituency. If this constituency can be activated and brought into the subsystem, this may have a significant effect on policy change.

Second, new policy subsystems are capable of emerging, particularly if actors are dissatisfied at either the way the issue is being defined or by the neglect of an issue. Sabatier notes that in the USA a food safety subsystem emerged from the agriculture subsystem due to the *laissez-faire* approach to food safety within it.

Third, subsystems usually contain a large number of diverse actors. Methodologically, Sabatier notes that some way of categorising different interests is required. Sabatier points out that within the US air pollution subsystem in the 1970s two sets of *advocacy coalitions* could be identified, the 'Clean Air Coalition' and the 'Economic Feasibility Coalition' (Sabatier

*' could potentially explore this avenue in conjunction with the diverse and potentially conflicting nature of preferences, politics and practices (+ participants)

Towards a theory of EU sports law and policy 47

1988: 140–141). Advocacy coalitions may be diverse but they do share a particular belief system. For instance, the Clean Air Coalition shared a belief (amongst others) in the primacy of human health over economic development. The Economic Feasibility Coalition believed that a balance between the two should be struck. These shared beliefs 'glue' subsystems together. — prevent fluctuations Usually within a policy subsystem, only between two and four advocacy coalitions exist. This is because in order to gain prominence, coalitions need to be made. Fewer coalitions may be expected to survive as a subsystem matures and coalitions are formed. Some actors may not be aligned to an advocacy coalition. These may include actors such as academics who may be able to offer some expertise or actors known as 'policy brokers'. 'Policy brokers' attempt to find compromises between the positions advocated by coalitions. These brokers may be civil servants, elected officials or courts. Policy brokers are not necessarily neutral.

Fourth, the key objective of an advocacy coalition is to translate their beliefs into public policy. Clearly advocacy coalitions seek to steer policy in a direction compatible with their belief system. However, having a belief system does not guarantee influence. The ability of an advocacy coalition to influence policy depends on resources. Such resources include money, expertise, number of supporters and legal authority.

Fifth, belief systems within advocacy coalitions are hierarchical. Fundamental norms and beliefs form the *deep core*. Within the *policy core* are found fundamental policy positions and strategies for attaining core values. Finally, instrumental decisions and information searches necessary to implement the policy core, forms the *secondary aspects*. Change is more likely to occur in the secondary aspects than it is in the policy core or in the deep core. Changes at the level of the policy core are due to factors such as changes in macro-economic conditions, changes in fundamental cultural values and social structure or new systemic governing coalitions. Change takes place at the secondary level as a result of 'policy-oriented learning' between advocacy coalitions. Policy-oriented learning is a form of learning which leads actors to make alterations to their thought patterns or behavioural intentions as a result of past experience. Sabatier argues that, 'policy-oriented learning across belief systems is most likely when there exists a forum which is (a) prestigious enough to force professionals from different coalitions to participate and (b) dominated by professional norms' (Sabatier 1988: 156).

Richardson sees this trend as emerging in the EU. For example the EU has a history of establishing forums, such as the environmental or consumer forum to bring together a wide spectrum of interests to discuss policy evolution (Richardson 1996: 18). This has also been the case with sport. The European Commission has established dialogue with European sporting interests through the establishment of the European Sports Forum. In addition a European Conference on Sport, organised by the Commission, was held in Greece in May 1999. Such occasions are designed to force debate among professionals in an attempt to achieve some convergence of views regarding the nature of the problem and thus the content of the policy solution.

In summary, Sabatier identifies a number of factors affecting the development of policy within a subsystem. First, policy subsystems are affected by significant perturbations external to the subsystem. Sabatier identifies two such forces, both of which provide constraints and opportunities for subsystem actors. On the one hand, 'relatively stable' factors such as the basic constitutional structure, socio-cultural values and natural resources of a political system are unlikely to radically change even in the face of coalition strategies (Sabatier 1998: 102). Similarly, 'external events' such as major changes in socio-economic conditions, changes in public opinion, changes in the systemic governing coalition and policy decisions and impacts from other subsystems are likely to significantly affect policy subsystems. Although significant, Sabatier views such external forces as insufficient to cause changes in the policy core attributes of a governmental programme.

Second, external 'perturbations' provide opportunities for *policy entrepreneurs* to exploit. Such entrepreneurs wish to change policy in some way.

Third, policy change may stem from competition between coalitions. Although external perturbations may result in conditions which lead to the replacement of one dominant coalition by another, a more likely scenario is that a minority coalition increases in importance to such an extent that it can exploit a window of opportunity to challenge the dominant coalition. Usually, the minority coalition lacks the (legislative) resources to push for the adoption of its policy objectives. Under such circumstances the coalition will develop *coalitions of convenience* with other groups (Sabatier 1998: 119).

Fourth, compromise rather than conflict may lead to policy change. Sabatier notes that 'in situations in which all major coalitions view a continuation of the current situation as unacceptable, they may be willing to enter negotiations in the hope of finding a compromise that is viewed by everyone as superior to the status quo' (Sabatier 1998: 119). Under such circumstances a power-sharing arrangement will be established.

Fifth, the ACF contends that policy change can also result from a learning process described as *policy-oriented learning*. This learning process across belief systems is likely to be facilitated by the establishment of a professional forum (Sabatier 1998: 106).

The ACF is not the only actor-based approach able to capture the role played by key policy advocates within the process of policy change. Kingdon uses the concept of a 'stream' to explain the processes involved in agenda setting. Occasionally, the streams align to allow a 'policy window' to open. Policy change takes place within this window (Kingdon 1995). Alternatively, other researchers have employed network analysis to explain policy change (Rhodes 1988). A policy network implies a symbiotic relationship between an interest group(s) and the public policy maker(s). A network is the arena for mediation and bargaining between the two. Networks are policy specific. Policy networks are a useful tool for understanding issue definition in the EU, particularly if we distinguish between policy communities and issue networks. Policy communities tend to have a stable membership, are highly insular and have strong resource dependencies. An issue network by contrast has fluid membership, is highly permeable and possesses weak dependencies (Rhodes 1988, Peterson 1995). Within the context of the EU several policy networks may be in operation, some resembling policy communities, others issue networks. A related realm to that of policy networks is the idea of epistemic communities. Such communities are essentially knowledge based (actual or perceived) and are comprised of experts. Being thus composed, epistemic communities are highly influential and seen as legitimate.

Kingdon's main contribution is his focus on the power of ideas and on how solutions 'search' for problems rather than on pressure and influence. Hence given certain propitious conditions, solutions within an organisation are joined to problems. The opening of a policy window increases the likelihood that the 'solution' will be adopted. Although appealing, Kingdon's work suffers from two flaws. First, he puts 'too much distance between the policy and the political stream' (Sabatier 1991: 151). He therefore de-emphasises the crucial role played by competing policy advocates and as such his work lacks an advocacy analysis. Sabatier's ACF is an attempt to view Kingdon's 'streams' as more closely related. Second, Kingdon's work lacks an institutional analysis. Kingdon does note that 'institutions, constitutions, procedures, governmental structures, and government officials themselves affect the political, social, and economic system as much as the other way around' (Kingdon 1995: 229). Furthermore, Kingdon notes that 'federalism also enhances possibilities for innovation – if a new idea isn't possible in one venue, it might be possible in another, and entrepreneurs can shop around for the most favourable venue' (Kingdon 1995: 230). Kingdon is correct in his analysis, even though his brand of institutionalism merely examines the constraints institutions place on individuals. However, like Sabatier who also briefly notes the importance of institutions, it is not clear why Kingdon does not explicitly attach an institutional analysis to his actor-based analysis of policy change.

Policy networks and epistemic communities are useful for analysing policy change in the EU as they act as a mechanism to order and describe the range of actors involved in the policy process and describe the relationship between them. However, Sabatier's ACF performs this function even better. Furthermore, policy networks suffer from a number of flaws. Network analysis places too much emphasis on pressure and influence within the policy process and not enough on the power of ideas and belief systems. Sabatier's work addresses this. Furthermore, are policy subsystems characterised by stable and symbiotic relationships between policy makers and advocates, a particular feature of the policy communities approach? Even the looser conception of issue networks and epistemic communities fail to capture the true nature of competition between advocates of which decision makers form a part. Finally, network analyses pay insufficient attention to the exploitation of institutional venues for the 'outsider'/'losing' advocacy coalitions. Network analysis may prove useful for accounting for the reconciliation/mediation that often takes place between rival coalitions, but even here network analysis lacks an important institutional dimension.

There is in effect much similarity between the actor-based approaches reviewed above. Although the language differs they all seek to move away from an old institutional analysis and relocate their analysis on the individual. Sabatier's framework is preferred because it best captures the real nature of competition between rival advocacy coalitions operating within the context of policy subsystems, a particularly pronounced feature of EU governance.

Despite the strength of Sabatier's work, the ACF is not without its critics. The key criticism is that the ACF pays insufficient attention to the problem of collective action. Schlager notes that although the ACF (and indeed work on policy communities and policy networks) has shed considerable light on the dynamics of policy change, it has tended to ignore this problem of collective action (Schlager 1995). The ACF has proved useful in explaining the structure of coalitions, the importance of coalition competition in sparking policy change and the role of policy-oriented learning, yet it does not explain 'why actors holding similar beliefs form coalitions to collectively press their goals, how coalitions maintain themselves over time, or the strategies coalitions adopt to pursue policy goals' (Schlager 1995: 244). Furthermore, Olson questions why actors with shared interests will act together when a 'rational' course of action would be to free-ride on the back of the actions of others who would bear the cost of action (Olson 1971). However, this may prove an unanswerable question given that all action, even those determined by particular incentives, involves the payment of some costs from which others will benefit (Marwell and Oliver 1993). Olson's other contention – that successful collective action is more likely where small groups will be strongly motivated to act – may however have relevance to the EU and have implications for explaining the dynamics of coalition action (Peterson and Bomberg 1999: 27).

For the ACF to assume increased relevance to the EU, the issue of coalition strategies must be addressed. The multi-level institutional structure of the EU described above has profound implications for actor strategy. The ACF is strong on providing 'external' reasons for policy change within a subsystem but considerably weaker on integrating the activities of advocacy coalitions into the explanation of policy change. In other words, 'for coalitions to take their rightful place in the policy process requires an explanation of action' (Schlager 1995: 248). The actor selectivity inherent in institutional design is crucial to this action.

An institutional analysis: belief systems and political institutions
How can the crucial issue of coalition action be addressed? As Schlager
notes, 'if the ACF is to better account for action, the institutional structure
and characteristics of the situation in which coalitions form and act need to
be better specified. The institutional setting which both constrains and promotes action must be further developed' (Schlager 1995: 259).

In essence therefore Sabatier's work, like other actor-based approaches,
lacks an institutional analysis. The correct deployment of such an analysis
can provide that crucial missing ingredient in Sabatier's work: the explanation of action. Sabatier notes that the ACF's 'ability to deal with complex situations and its model of the individual derived from psychology make it
attractive to scholars looking for an alternative to the institutional rational
choice models currently dominating much of policy scholarship' (Sabatier
1998: 122).

However, Sabatier also notes that actors are driven by a more complex set
of factors than rational calculations of self-interest. In particular, he claims
that 'actors suffer from a variety of cognitive biases and constraints'
(Sabatier 1998: 109). First, in the face of time and psychological constraints,
actors resort to 'satisficing' (Hogwood and Gunn 1984: 50) or guideline
behaviour consistent with their general belief system, particularly in the
policy core. Furthermore, 'actors' perceptions are strongly filtered by their
pre-existing normative and other beliefs' (Sabatier 1998: 109). Although
Sabatier notes that 'financial resources and institutional rules are critical'
(Sabatier 1998: 117), the ACF does not attempt to fully examine the relationship between satisficing behaviour, pre-existing beliefs and institutions.
Through a closer examination of the influence exerted by political institutions on policy subsystems it is possible to identify institutions as not only
constraining subsystems but also structuring belief systems, strategies and
policy outputs within them. Without an institutional analysis of policy
change and development it becomes tempting merely to emphasise how the
political agenda is 'pushed and pulled' around by societal, economic or political forces (Kingdon 1995: 229). Implicit in this approach is an assumption
that political institutions are merely neutral arenas in which these forces are
played out. However, as Baumgartner and Jones remind us, policy advocates
seek to influence agenda setting and issue definition within 'institutional
venues' (Baumgartner and Jones 1991: 1045). Institutional venues may
affect social, economic and political forces as much as these forces affect
institutional venues. Kingdon notes that examples of both state autonomy
and the state as a reflection of society can be found in cases of agenda setting
(Kingdon 1995: 230). Sabatier's actor-based framework should not therefore be seen as an alternative to institutional analyses, but as complimentary.

The benefits of actor-based institutionalism are increasingly being recognised within political science. In *The Games Real Actors Play*, Scharpf develops an explicit brand of actor-centred institutionalism in which institutions

are portrayed as creating opportunity structures and constraints for purposeful and resourceful actors to navigate within (Scharpf 1997). Similarly, Kiser and Ostrom claim that individual action in the policy process is a function of both the attributes (values and resources) of the individual and the attributes of the decision situation of which the prevailing institutional make-up is central (Kiser and Ostrom 1982). Moe's structural choice approach examines the effect political institutions have on the choices coalition's make in their attempts to re-direct public policy (Moe 1990). Schlager seeks to integrate both the institutional analysis and development framework and the structural choice approach into Sabatier's ACF in order to address the issue of coalition formation and action (Schlager 1995). Furthermore, Fenger and Klok seek to strengthen further Schlager's contribution to the ACF by examining the interdependencies between actors (Fenger and Klok 2001). Additionally, Mintrom and Vergari suggest in the policy entrepreneurs model that policy changes as a result of the actions of policy entrepreneurs who do not treat institutional configurations as fixed but as malleable (Mintrom and Vergari 1996).

In the context of the EU, Pollack similarly recognises the importance of institutional configurations. He argues that member states created EU institutions for particular self-serving reasons and allowed for certain procedural mechanisms such as QMV and decision-making delegation to supranational actors in order to facilitate progress towards their rationally conceived preferences (Pollack 1996). However, reform of institutions, once created, may be difficult to achieve by the member states. First, member states may regard the uncertainty of reform and the transaction costs associated with reform as being an unacceptably high price to pay. Second, the institutions themselves may be resistant to reform and may be shielded by institutional procedures such as unanimity requirements. Although reform is not impossible, Pollack suggests it is infrequent, leading to a state of 'punctuated equilibrium', long periods of stability followed by infrequent (Treaty) change (Pollack 1996: 438). When change (integrative or disintegrative) is negotiated, it is likely to be infrequent and, due to the constraints previously described, unlikely to be major. A path-dependent process of integration is likely to result because change will be greatly affected by existing institutions and institutional decision-making rules.

In effect Pollack is describing a process whereby institutions and policies become locked-in. Pollack identifies two brands of lock-in. The first has been developed by Scharpf who identified two conditions, intergovernmentalism combined with unanimity that result in the 'joint decision trap', a condition resulting in institutions and policies becoming entrenched despite pressures for reform (Scharpf 1988). For the second lock-in, Pollack dips into Pierson's historical institutionalist account of micro-level lock-ins (Pierson 1996) (see below). Thus institutions and policies can become locked-in from above (Scharpf) and from above and below (Pierson).

The work of Baumgartner and Jones also has implications for the ACF (Baumgartner and Jones 1991). Their work is important because their methodology also asserts the importance of examining both actors and institutions. Baumgartner and Jones analyse how public policy often evolves through long periods of stability, punctuated by short bursts of rapid change. Rather than applying different analytical tools to explain the continuity and change of public policy, Baumgartner and Jones retain analytical cohesion by arguing that a single process can explain both periods of extreme change and short bursts of rapid change (Baumgartner and Jones 1991: 1044–1045). Baumgartner and Jones argue that this single process comprises the *policy image* and the *institutional venues* of policy action. The policy image describes the 'interaction of beliefs and values concerning a particular policy' whilst the institutional venues refers to the 'venues of policy action' (Baumgartner and Jones 1991: 1045). The choice of institutional venue is clearly important for with it inevitably comes the ability to shape policy in a direction compatible with an advocate's belief system. However, even though an issue may emerge on the public policy agenda with definition bias, alternative institutional venues often exist 'that can serve as avenues of appeal for the disaffected' (Baumgartner and Jones 1991: 1045). This focus adds clarity to actor-based approaches that seek to explain agenda expansion. As Baumgartner and Jones stress, 'as venues change, images may change as well; as the image of a policy changes, venue changes become more likely' (Baumgartner and Jones 1991: 1047).

Although Baumgartner and Jones do not examine the policy process of the EU, their methodology is applicable for studying EU policy evolution. Within the context of the EU it is important to examine the influence of key actors, be they intergovernmental or supranational players. Yet to complete the investigation into agenda setting and issue definition, it is also necessary to examine the role of these institutional venues. Institutional venues may affect social, economic and political forces as much as these forces affect institutional venues. An analysis of agenda setting and issue definition would therefore be incomplete without some examination of the importance of institutions. This is particularly important when investigating institutional venues in the EU.

It has traditionally been assumed that the EU is very receptive to the ideas of lobbyists and that these groups were capable of manipulating the EU's agenda. Accordingly, agenda setting in the EU was considered externally generated. This analysis may be valid, but it ignores the influence of the institutions of the EU. Not only do the institutions mould and even structure lobbying activities, but institutions pursue their own agendas as well. Political institutions may well 'talk up' a problem in order to see movement of that issue on to the institutional agenda in preparation for action. For example, in order to ensure the success of the White Paper on the EU's institutional agenda, Delors exaggerated the extent of economic decline in Europe. This would, he believed increase the chances of member state approval (Sandholtz and Zysman 1989). Furthermore, as the EU is a very open system, agenda control is made problematic. If policy advocates fail to make progress in one institutional venue, they may go 'venue shopping' and attempt to influence policy in another. The ability of policy advocates to expand the definition of a policy beyond its original confines is greatly enhanced by this openness.

The focus on the role of political institutions in shaping policy is the concern of new institutionalism, an approach that attempts to 'bring the state back in' to policy analysis. Rather than simply concentrating on the formal administrative, legal and political dimension of institutions, a characteristic of *old* institutionalism, *new* institutionalism widens the definition of an institution. Although still accommodating the formal rules, procedures and practices of institutions, new institutionalism also highlights the importance of informal arenas such as informal rules, norms, symbols, beliefs and codes of conduct. New institutionalism therefore better reflects the 'real' culture of institutions than its 'old' variant (March and Olsen 1989).

New institutionalism is useful in the study of European integration because it can help explain not only policy and institutional inertia, but also change. As such it does not represent a macro-theory attempting to scientifically map out future integration. Rather, new institutionalism attempts to re-focus methodology by bringing institutional factors back into the analysis of European integration. In essence, therefore, new institutionalism asserts that *institutions matter* (Armstrong and Bulmer 1998: 50). From within the broad scope of new institutionalism can be distilled two institutionalist categories relevant to the debate about policy and institutional change and inertia in the EU. The main difference between rational choice institutionalism and historical institutionalism is the emphasis they place on the deterministic effect of institutions on political outcomes.

The rational choice element in this category of new institutionalism derives from the emphasis of the importance of utility-maximising individuals with clear intentions within the policy process. The institutionalist element emphasises the importance of institutions in affecting and constraining an individual's choice within that process. Armstrong and Bulmer describe rational choice institutionalism as being at the *thin* end of institutionalism, as institutions and their rules only modify an essentially rational choice model of politics (Armstrong and Bulmer 1998: 53).

At the 'thicker' end of institutionalism lies historical institutionalism. Historical institutionalists ascribe a greater role for institutions within the policy process. Rather than simply constraining individual action, institutions, as defined in the broadest sense encompassing formal and informal practices, can shape and determine individual preferences. As such, historical institutionalism stresses how policy evolution is structured by prevailing institutional configurations and norms. Furthermore, institutions structure access to the political process, thus further influencing policy evolution

(Armstrong and Bulmer 1998: 52–60). In short, institutional configurations and norms can create a *governance regime* capable of structuring a policy debate and hence policy development and evolution. Two studies employing an historical institutionalist analysis have added depth to our understanding of systemic and institutional agenda setting. Pierson's analysis of the development of EU social policy examines the historical development of EU institutions and how prevailing institutional norms and configurations contribute to path-dependent policy evolution (Pierson 1996). Bulmer's study of the governance of the Single European Market similarly employs an historical institutional analysis. However, rather than examining how institutional features constrain actors, Bulmer examines how prevailing institutional norms and configurations structure policy debate within the EU (Bulmer 1998).

Taking an institutional (wrong) turn?
The danger with the above approach lies in falling into the trap of placing too much distance between state and society whilst claiming to do the opposite. The actor/institutions methodology employed in this text does not simply assert that *both* actors and institutions matter. To do so risks bracketing off the role of actors or institutions and focusing the analysis accordingly. A methodology which does this can hardly claim to integrate both actor-based and institutions-based approaches. In other words, the actor-based and institutions-based components should closely relate to one another. Alone the ACF is unable to capture the crucial role played by the formal and informal institutional decision-making context. As such, the researcher needs to take an 'institutional turn' (Jessop 2000). However, does the reliance on new institutionalism represent an institutional wrong turn? An institutional turn refers to, 'the more or less consistent elaboration of the intuition, hypothesis, or discovery that institutions matter in one or more theoretical, empirical, or practical contexts where their existence and/or relevance had previously been overlooked, denied or ignored' (Jessop 2000: 1).

According to Jessop, academics usually take one of three institutional turns. Those taking a *thematic turn* simply acknowledge that institutions are important. Those taking a *methodological turn* may acknowledge that an institutional analysis is an essential starting point for research but in addition chose to examine other variables. Those taking an *ontological turn* assert that institutions 'are the primary axis of collective life and social order' (Jessop 2000: 4). Lying at the 'thicker' end of new institutionalism, historical institutionalism can be interpreted as an ontological institutional turn.

Making some kind of institutional turn is crucial to understanding task expansion in the EU. The complex multi-level structure of the EU provides opportunities for actors to exploit. Institutional design privileges one set of actors and their strategies over another. However, to take an ontological institutional turn would in effect downplay the role of key policy actors in the process of policy change. Although institutions affect the strategies of actors through the actor selectivity inherent in their design, actors 'have some freedom of manoeuvre more or less skilfully and reflexively to choose a path of action' (Jessop 2000: 10). This is particularly pronounced in the EU.

Consequently, the researcher needs to develop a methodology capable of recognising the importance of formal and informal institutional configurations on policy development, without over-emphasising path dependence, whilst recognising that actors in the EU possess significant room for tactical manoeuvre. Jessop's strategic relational approach (SRA) provides some guidance for those wishing to explore the role of actors in the policy process but who want to make an institutional 'turn' (Jessop 1990, 2000). Applying the SRA to the task expansion debate in the EU would involve examining how the institutional structure privileges certain actors whilst also examining how actors 'take account of this differential privileging through strategic context analysis when choosing a course of action' (Jessop 2000: 9). In other words institutional design is important but so also is how actors respond to this. Actors may for instance attempt to influence policy in venues in which they are privileged or they may adopt 'reflexive' strategies in which case they adapt in order to take advantage of the channels of access that institutions provide. In other words the methodology developed in this chapter seeks to analyse actors and institutions in terms of how they relate to each other rather than placing too much distance between them.

· Conclusions

Approaches attempting to explain the *process of integration* (including the legal variants) struggle to capture the nature of day-to-day EU governance. As such, the analytical framework employed in this text is drawn from approaches examining the *politics of governance*. This methodology has been developed in three stages. First, it is important to characterise the EU as a multi-level organisation. Decision-making capabilities are shared rather than monopolised. This institutional description establishes the context within which policy change takes place. Policy evolution and change within this multi-level organisation takes place through a two-stage process, best defined by Pollack as involving the initial expansion of the EU's agenda to include new policy areas and the subsequent substantive development of these policies. As Cobb and Elder remind us, this means that an issue must first appear on the systemic agenda before being actively considered on the institutional agenda. Elite writers such Schattschneider argue that conflict can lead to agenda expansion but this expansion is controlled by elites. However, because of the multi-level nature of governance in the EU, agenda control is more problematic. The initial definition of an issue on the institutional agenda may take place with heavy definitional bias due to the venue within which the issue is considered. Many policy subsystems (including sport) are initially heavily influenced by legal and technocratic norms due to the constitutional predominance of negative integration. However, as Rochefort and Cobb remind us, others will be drawn into the issue definition stage in protest at the initial definition. Frequently this involves the weaker advocacy coalition attempting to re-define an issue by penetrating the subsystem with political argument. In a multi-level organisation, if they are unsuccessful in one venue they will go 'venue shopping'.

The second stage in the construction of the approach analyses the crucial role played by competing policy advocates working within policy subsystems. Although a range of actor-based approaches could be employed for the purposes of this analysis, Sabatier's Advocacy Coalition Framework sits most comfortably with the conception of EU governance employed in this study. According to Sabatier policy evolves as a result of competition between rival policy advocates. Advocates seek to steer policy in a direction consistent with their belief system. The focus on the power of ideas as opposed to the power of pressure and influence is an important contribution but alone is insufficient to fully account for the real nature of policy change in the EU. The third stage in the construction of the approach seeks to confront this 'reality'.

This third stage involves linking the strategies of key policy advocates to the prevailing institutional structure of the organisation in question. This involves taking a methodological as opposed to an ontological *institutional turn*. To give Sabatier's work relevance to the EU and to address the issue of how to explain coalition action, the taking of such an institutional turn is crucial. However, the finding that 'institutions matter' in the context of coalition action refers to more than just the observation that key institutions are players (actors) in the game. One should not confuse *institutions* with *actors*. To do so would negate the need to build into Sabatier's framework an institutional theory. The institutional characteristics of the EU's policy process and political system, such as the existence of a multi-layered and multi-venue EU structure, have profound effects on the dynamics of policy change. The elaboration of these characteristics is crucial if Schlager's criticism concerning the explanation for coalition action within the ACF is to be addressed. In this connection, the work of Baumgartner and Jones is important because it alerts us to the relationship between policy image and institutional venue. In 'open' political systems such as the EU, policy subsystems can be challenged by actors exploiting other institutional venues. The venue in which a policy is discussed will have a significant impact on how the policy is disposed of in terms of outputs. To add analytical depth to the work of Baumgartner and Jones, this study employs new institutionalism as an essential institutional ingredient. Institutions, defined in the widest sense, constrain and empower actors whilst also actively shaping and even determining actor strategies. As such the brand of institutionalism employed throughout this book has a strong actor-based component which sits at the intersection of rational choice institutionalism and historical institutionalism. Without an institutional analysis of policy change and development it becomes tempting merely to emphasise how the political agenda is pushed and pulled around by societal, economic or political forces. As such, political institutions cannot merely be seen as neutral arenas in which these forces are played out.

The interplay between actors and institutions creates policy-specific governance regimes within policy subsystems. In order to operationalise the analytical methodology, these governance regimes need identifying. This involves identifying the range of actors involved in the subsystem, identifying their prevailing belief system and calculating the institutional resources they have at their disposal. By doing so the researcher can assess the viability of coalition strategies and therefore allow for assumptions to be made concerning the future direction of policy within the subsystem. It therefore becomes clear why macro approaches have limited utility in this respect. The analytical methodology employed is not designed to be a predictive tool, it simply allows the researcher to identify possible future policy directions. The predictive quality of the approach is limited by the possibility of perturbations external to the subsystem. External perturbations cannot easily be built into the methodology. For example, the change in the economic status of sport throughout the 1990s proved crucial in forging a link between sport and EU law. A dramatic slump in the economic status of sport or a sudden (although unlikely) fall in the public's interest in sport would, for example, limit the political salience of the issue.

Although governance regimes differ between policy subsystems, they are likely to share certain systemic qualities. First, they are influenced by the constitutional structure of the EU. Treaties not only determine the institutional balance of power within subsystems, they also shape the working logic of integration. For example, embedded within the Treaty of Rome is a commitment to advance both economic integration and socio-cultural/political integration. Such a commitment has resulted in the emergence of competing advocacy coalitions seeking to direct policy in either a market-based or socially based direction. The institutional balance between these advocacy coalitions varies according to institutional power. As Pinder remarked observing the EU in the 1960s, the 'free trade ideology is firmly built into the system, but the planning ethic is no more than a possibility for the future' (Pinder 1968: 98). Since then, the institutional balance has shifted. The Parliament has for example acquired enhanced powers over legislation and the budget. Furthermore, the Single Market has been completed and since Maastricht the planning ethic is more deeply ingrained. Accordingly, socio-political arguments advanced by advocacy coalition's within subsystems previously dominated by legal and technocratic norms have strengthened over time.

Second, they are likely to be influenced by ECJ jurisprudence and the quasi-judicial role played by the Competition Policy Directorate. In particular, Court rulings frequently establish important legal principles guiding the development of policy. In this connection, it is possible to identify a relationship between judicial and legislative/policy processes. However, just as policy initiatives are influenced by judicial or quasi-judicial actions, so the activities of the ECJ and Commission can be influenced by political activity.

Third, governance regimes are likely to be influenced by soft law. Political declarations of intent, although not legally binding, do shape policy evolution and do provide institutional actors with some guidance. In addition, the office of Council Presidency allows member states to push individual agendas. Continuity is ensured by the troika system but agendas can expand as the incumbent continues the predecessor's agenda whilst also developing their own.

Fourth, deeply ingrained within the EU's general approach to policy development is a desire to mediate between conflicting positions. This reflects the complex multi-dimensional and multi-national nature of EU decision making. Through a learning process over time, the EU has developed a range of mediating tools and practises. As Sabatier reminds us, 'in situations in which all major coalitions view a continuation of the current situation as unacceptable, they may be willing to enter negotiations in the hope of finding a compromise that is viewed by everyone as superior to the status quo' (Sabatier 1998: 119). However, mediation will only take place where competing advocacy coalitions are relatively evenly matched or the activities of one coalition do not directly pose a threat to the deep and policy core belief system of the rival coalition. If an advocacy coalition has monopolistic or near monopolistic control over policy evolution, it is unlikely they will mediate. In situations where one coalition is institutionally underprivileged mediation is unlikely unless that coalition can form a coalition of convenience with other groups. Where two coalitions seek to influence policy through a variety of tactics and institutional venues, policy coherence is lost. Under such circumstances policy brokers will seek to mediate between coalitions.

Finally, governance regimes are likely to be influenced by major developments both internal and external to the subsystem. A change in the institutional balance of power prompted by a Treaty change has the potential to fundamentally alter the institutional resources available to actors. External changes also affect subsystems. For example, the collapse of communism greatly affected the content and timing of the Maastricht Treaty. Similarly, the Danish rejection of Maastricht in a referendum affected the nature of the subsequent Amsterdam Treaty. Both Treaties fundamentally altered the balance of power within numerous policy subsystems.

On the face of it the above framework appears disproportionately over-size in order to explain the apparently straightforward question of why EU policy towards sport has changed? However, the shifting focus of regulatory attention away from a Single Market model of sports regulation towards a socio-cultural model raises many complex issues concerning the dynamics of policy change in the EU. In particular, in the absence of a specific legislative framework for sport, the interplay between the formal arena of law and the informal arena of political pressure and conflicting value systems becomes an important focus for analysis. How does theory capture this interplay? This is a far more complex question. The remaining chapters of the text analyse the shifting focus of EU sports policy in light of these theoretical insights. The next chapter analyses the composition of the sports policy sub-system – an essential methodological starting point for understanding sports policy change in the EU.

Note

1   The four freedoms are the free movement of goods, services, labour and capital.

3

The sports policy subsystem

Sabatier's Advocacy Coalition Framework (ACF) proves a useful starting point for those wishing to conceptualise the EU as comprising a myriad of policy subsystems. Operating within these subsystems is a wide range of actors who attempt to steer policy in a direction compatible with their belief system. Sabatier's broad concept of subsystem actors stresses the political nature of subsystem activity. Sabatier defines a policy subsystem as a 'set of actors who are involved in dealing with a policy problem' (Sabatier 1988: 138). The policy 'problem' under investigation is the relationship between sport and the EU. Sabatier notes that 'the most likely reason for the emergence of new subsystems is that a group of actors become dissatisfied enough with the neglect of a particular problem by existing subsystems to form their own' (Sabatier 1988: 138). The emergence in the EU and national capitals of consumer-based subsystems in relation to agricultural produce developed out of the failure of the agricultural subsystem to fully address consumer concerns over food safety. Similarly, a subsystem may also emerge as new actors become involved in issue definition in protest at how actors in another subsystem define the policy (Rochefort and Cobb 1994). Both Sabatier's and Rochefort and Cobb's explanations are clearly related and both are evident in relation to the emergence of a EU sports policy subsystem.

Prior to the ruling in *Bosman*, sport was associated with a wide range of policy subsystems, many of them underpinned with economic and legal values. No clearly identifiable sports policy subsystem existed. A growing body of opinion recognised that these subsystems were inappropriate for dealing with the particular characteristics of sport. Whilst those subsystems dealing with general market regulation were appropriate for most economic sectors, sport was considered different. The traditional rules of market competition did not apply to sport. The ruling in *Bosman* confirmed the view of many who believed that sport needed to be dealt with on its own merits. This was a particularly pressing issue as sport was beginning to develop into a significant economic sector. The potential for sport to be unsympathetically treated within such economic subsystems was therefore increased. It was perceived that the consequence of operating in multiple (economic) venues was the gradual erosion of sports autonomy and fundamental values. In particular, *Bosman* contributed to the emergence of a sports policy subsystem as advocates unhappy at the explicit economic definition of sport adopted in the ruling emerged as a more co-ordinated force.

Consequently, following *Bosman*, a more holistic approach to sport began to be discussed in a more co-ordinated forum. EU sports policy developed within this context. Within this nascent subsystem two advocacy coalitions emerged. Whilst the Single Market coalition define much sport economically, the socio-cultural coalition, composed of a diverse body of opinion, stress the importance of balancing this economic approach with one that recognises the socio-cultural and integrationist qualities of sport. Each coalition attempts to steer subsystem activity in a manner consistent with their belief system. Their success in achieving this depends on the institutional resources they can draw on.

This chapter examines these themes in four sections. The first section reviews the pre-*Bosman* environment where no sports subsystem operated. The second, analyses the emergence and composition of the post-*Bosman* subsystem. The belief systems of the two advocacy coalitions are examined. The third section explores the institutional resources at the coalitions disposal. Where each coalition possesses and can yield sufficient institutional resources to fundamentally challenge the deep and policy core belief system of their rival, the conditions for coalition mediation have been met. In essence therefore, coalitions are prepared to compromise the secondary features of the belief system in order to protect their fundamental beliefs. The final section provides concluding comment.

The pre-Bosman *environment*

Prior to the emergence of a post-*Bosman* sports policy subsystem in the EU, sporting issues were discussed in a range of other subsystems. A 1995 study on 'The Impact of European Union Activities on Sport' conducted by Coopers and Lybrand for DG X of the European Commission, reviewed EU involvement in the sports sector (Coopers and Lybrand 1995). The study detailed the extensive involvement of the EU institutions in sport whilst also conveying the lack of a co-ordinated policy approach. The study did however reveal a growing institutional awareness of this problem and illustrated moves designed to confront this fragmentation through the growth of a range of sporting institutions (see below). The lack of a Treaty competence to develop a common sports policy did however act as an obstacle to a more co-ordinated approach to sports policy.

Prior to *Bosman*, sporting issues were discussed in connection with a wide range of policies. The first of these areas concerns the right of free movement for workers/the self-employed within the Single Market. Since the signing of the Treaty of Rome and the subsequent piecing together of secondary legislation, players, coaches, instructors and even fans have rights of free movement guaranteed by EU law. *Walrave, Donà, Heylens* and various disputes concerning, for example, the operation of ski instructors, illustrate the relationship between sport and issues of free movement. Clearly EU provisions on the right of establishment and the right to provide services have similar consequences for sport. Beyond the issue of worker/self-employed mobility, the Commission has also sought to establish a free market in insurance, sponsorship, advertising and broadcasting services. Sporting activities became linked to these subsystems through such issues as tobacco advertising in sport and the development of the Television Without Frontiers project.

A second arena in which sporting issues emerged concerned the principle of the free movement of goods. EU legislation in this field has had an impact on a range of sports-related activities including: the cross-border transportation of sports equipment, the standardisation of equipment specifications, the commercial exploitation of the Olympic Symbol, the production and marketing of sports food, footwear labelling, quantitative restrictions on sport footwear and certification, testing and technical requirements.

The third economic venue which sport became linked to concerned the application of EU competition law. Following the ruling in *Bosman*, this issue emerged as one of the most extensive areas of EU involvement in sport. However, this relationship did have a pre-*Bosman* history. The main Commission investigations into the compatibility between EU competition law and sporting rules have centred on the sale and purchase of broadcasting rights, the trans-frontier broadcasting of sports events, product endorsement, rules relating to competition between federations, ticketing arrangements for sports events, rules relating to transfers and restrictions placed on foreign players, restrictive trading practices, anti-dumping measures and state aid to sports organisations.

In addition to these essentially economic/legal venues, sport was also linked to a range of socio-economic and cultural policies. Sport was discussed as a health, safety and ethics issue. In this connection, anti-doping measures are of greatest significance. Although more systematic anti-doping measures have been agreed post *Bosman*, doping issues were on the agenda in 1990 when a Council Resolution examined measures to combat doping within the structure already established by the Council of Europe.[1] The EU has also been involved in sports in related measures designed to promote health, training, the protection of young people at work and spectator safety. From this activity emerged the development of EU funding initiatives for sports. Funding for sports-related projects were financed through a variety of mechanisms including the generic structural fund and education and training programmes and the more specific Eurathlon programme. Launched in 1994, the Eurathlon programme was designed to promote increased communications between European citizens, thus contributing to increased solidarity between different nationalities. The EU also made funds

PRE- BOSMAN

available to promote the sporting participation of those with disabilities. Activity in these socio-cultural fields is therefore closely related to the people's Europe project formally launched in 1985.

Finally, a range of other policy initiatives in the EU had an impact on sport. For example, legislation covering the use of horses, dogs and pigeons has been passed by the Council of Ministers. Furthermore, the 1985 Environmental Impact Assessment Directive (in force 1988) compels those developing sporting infrastructure to take into consideration the environmental effects of the event.[2] In particular, the construction of ski lifts, cable cars, yacht marinas, racing circuits and test tracks are specifically covered by the Directive. In 1991 a European Parliament report criticised the preparations for the French Albertville Games for ignoring the provisions of the Directive (Coopers and Lybrand 1995: 108). Water sports have also taken note of the provisions of a Directive designed to conserve natural habitats and wild fauna and flora.[3] Finally, sport was affected by EU monetary and fiscal policy. Before the launch of the euro, the European Currency Unit (ECU) could be used by the organisers of European sports events rather than the US Dollar for money flows from one member state to another. Prize money could also be paid in ECU. To a lesser extent EU secondary legislation on fiscal policy (particularly on tax exemptions) has affected sport.

From within these 'areas', it is possible to identify a range of specific policy subsystems where sporting issues are considered. In the pre-*Bosman* era, sport was therefore linked to a wide range of subsystems including: free movement of workers policy, competition and industrial policy, audio-visual policy and media policy, doping and drugs policy, public health policy, youth policy, education and training policy, employment policy, environmental policy and equal opportunities policy.

The post-Bosman *sports policy subsystem*

A growing body of opinion within and outside the EU recognised that the frequency in which sport was being discussed within the EU necessitated the adoption of a more co-ordinated approach. Essentially, sporting issues were being discussed within two types of subsystem. Socio-cultural subsystems discussed sport within the context of the people's Europe theme. Single Market subsystems discussed sport in terms of market regulation. Dissatisfaction was felt by some advocates who thought that sport was receiving an inappropriate and insensitive hearing within the Single Market subsystems. These market-based subsystems were not the appropriate venue within which the social significance of sport could receive proper attention. After all, competition in the sports sector differed from competition in others sectors in that the objective of participants is not to eliminate opposition. For many, the ECJ ruling in *Bosman* confirmed the inappropriateness of discussing sport in such venues. For those more committed to sport's social

TWO SUBSYSTEMS FOR A MORE COORDINATED EU APROACH

*so sport not formally distinguished or
coloured by either system explicitly
co-ordinated approach not so co-ordinated*

significance, sporting activities needed to be extracted from the disparate subsystems and an independent sports subsystem needed creating.

The task of identifying the internal structure of the subsystem is problematic. Reviewing participant lists at Commission organised sports conferences such as the May 1999 EU Conference on Sport or the annual meeting of the European Sports Forum provides one method. These lists tend to reflect the more active involvement of socio-cultural actors. This coalition is active due to their desire to challenge the prevailing economic definition of sport. The onus is therefore on them to assert themselves in as many institutional venues as possible. Less obvious are members of the Single Market advocacy coalition. As many members of this coalition do not pursue a specific sports-related agenda, their involvement in the coalition is discrete.

Table 1 (overleaf) summaries the composition and institutional resources of the sports policy subsystem.

The Single Market advocacy coalition

The Single Market advocacy coalition within the sports policy subsystem is primarily composed of the Competition Policy Directorate and the ECJ. Secondary members may enter the coalition depending on the topic under consideration. This includes legal and commercial interests. Lawyers have been active in promoting the EU as an avenue for litigation. Members of commercial broadcasters such as commercial television and radio broadcasters and commercial sports bodies are also associated with the Single Market coalition. Commercial interests can use EU law as a means through which the full commercial potential of sport can be exploited. For example, commercial operations in the field of broadcasting require the EU to lift restrictions on market access. Some sports organisations also require free market conditions in order maximise income by freely negotiating with all market providers. In this connection, it is not therefore unusual for some actors to operate in both advocacy coalitions. For example, a sports federation may align itself to the Single Market coalition over an issue such as Article 3a of the Television Without Frontiers Directive whilst operating alongside the socio-cultural coalition over the desire to maintain restrictions on player mobility. Furthermore, the Parliament – considered a leading socio-cultural actor – has consistently called for restrictions on player mobility in European sport to be lifted. The composition of the Single Market coalition is therefore fluid and complex. Nevertheless, certain features of the belief system can be identified.

Deep core beliefs   A belief in the primacy of negative integration is central to the deep core belief system of the Single Market coalition. The promotion and protection the four fundamental freedoms enshrined in the Treaty is central.

*in the area of the international system there has been no observable
domestic, subnational or global actor influencing the EU's position. Only
FIFpro acted with the EU (unsuccessfully) to give base study expertise which
the Commission lacked.*

Table 1 The sports policy subsystem

Single Market coalition	Socio-cultural coalition
Belief system	**Belief system**
Deep core beliefs: A belief in the primacy of negative integration. The promotion and protection of the four fundamental freedoms. No deep core assumptions on sports policy.	*Deep core beliefs:* The promotion of positive integration. Successful European integration rests on an effective balance being struck between economic forces and socio-cultural (and political) forces. Not all members share these assumptions concerning European integration (see moderate and minimalist members below).
Policy core beliefs: Sport is subject to EU law when practised as an economic activity. No general exemption from EU law can be permitted.	*Policy core beliefs:* Acknowledgment that sport is not above the law. Nevertheless, sport possesses social and cultural characteristics which merit a soft touch application of law.
Secondary aspects: Scope for compromise with socio-cultural coalition. Generally the Single Market model of sports regulation is preferred although sensitive to the need for socio-cultural integration.	*Secondary aspects:* Belief in the socio-cultural model of sports regulation. Differences over the precise relationship between sport and the EU exist, indicating that the coalition is a 'coalition of convenience'.
Actors	**Actors**
Pragmatic Single Market regulators: Competition Policy Directorate and the ECJ are primary actors. European Parliament Committee on Legal Affairs and Citizens Rights is secondary actor. Although sport is viewed as a significant economic activity and both the Commission and ECJ have sought to uphold the four freedoms, both actors have acknowledged the socio-cultural dimension of sport. Scope therefore exists for sport's unique characteristics to be taken into account in the application of law as long as the deep and policy core beliefs of the Single Market coalition are not undermined.	*Maximalists:* Strong supporter of People's Europe concept. Support Treaty inclusion for sport in order to (1) protect sports rules from EU law and (2) develop common sport policy (with legal and budgetary base). Strong support within European Parliament (particularly Party of European Socialists) and elements within Education and Culture DG. Support from EU Governments (excluding Britain, Denmark and Sweden). In the absence of Treaty base the maximalists demonstrate commitment to the socio-cultural dimension of sport by seeking to use sport to strengthen subsystems such as education, health, youth, social exclusion and media. In absence of unanimous support from member states to include sport in the Treaty, soft law is preferred tactic. Wide range of European sports bodies broadly share this agenda as it clarifies the legal environment and allows them to compete equally with other sectors for funding.
Ultra Single Market regulators: Elements within legal profession. Commercial interests seeking to maximise sports 'real' market potential. Sport is primarily an economic activity to be regulated in the same manner as any other.	

Moderates: EU should not challenge the autonomy of the European sports sector. Decisions affecting the sports world are best taken by the sports bodies themselves. Moderates support closer links between sport and the Treaty in order to protect sport from EU law (sports protocol rather than Article preferred). Little interest in common sports policy with legal and budgetary base. Clarification of legal environment a priority. Tactical differences exist. Sports bodies of significant economic size are members (UEFA, FIA).

Minimalists: Support the modest use of sport to implement certain EU policy goals and support attempts to limit the application of EU law to sport. However, cautious of extending EU influence in sport further. Do not favour granting sport a Treaty base (either protocol or Article). Belief in subsidiarity and national cultural diversity. Christian Democratic politicians and MEP's generally hold this view. British Conservative forces employ subsidiarity as a vehicle to retain national control over policy areas. The governments of the UK, Denmark and Sweden resist calls for Treaty incorporation for sport. Belief that sufficient flexibility within the EU exists to recognise the specificity of sport. Soft law preferred tactic.

Institutional venues

Competition Policy DG and ECJ have strong and insulated role in acting as the guardian of the EU's legal framework. Individual litigants support this through the provisions of directly effective law, Article 234 and complaints procedure with the Commission. ECJ and the Commission are sensitive to prevailing political context. Resource limitations of Competition Policy DG.

Institutional venues

Right of sporting 'initiative' in Education & Culture DG; EP's legislative, scrutiny and budgetary powers; primary and secondary law-making functions of member states; soft law including Treaty Declarations, Presidency Conclusions, political guidelines, Commission policy papers; Council Presidency agenda setting; the use of formal forums/conferences; the strength of positive (socio-cultural) integration post-SEM; exploitation of related policy subsystems.

Policy core beliefs   Neither the deep or policy core belief system of the Single Market coalition contains core assumptions about sports policy specifically. The fundamental objective concerns protection of the EU's four freedoms. As such, the policy core belief system goes no further than stressing that sport is subject to EU law when practised as an economic activity and that no general exemption from EU law can be permitted. Sport must abide by the fundamentals of EU primary and secondary legislation.

Secondary aspects   It is within the secondary aspects of the coalitions belief system that flexibility exists. Generally the Single Market coalition favour the Single Market model of sports regulation, although flexibility within the secondary aspects of the belief system exists. The Competition Policy Directorate and the ECJ are pragmatic Single Market regulators in relation to sport. Although sport is viewed as a significant economic activity and both the Commission and ECJ have sought to uphold the four freedoms, both actors have acknowledged the socio-cultural dimension of sport. Scope therefore exists for sports unique characteristics to be taken into account in the application of law as long as the deep and policy core beliefs of the Single Market coalition are not being undermined. On policy specific issues, ultra Single Market regulators have consistently argued since *Bosman* that sport should be treated as any other economic activity within the Single Market. Elements within the legal profession have articulated this thought although this is an anecdotal claim.[4]

The socio-cultural advocacy coalition

The composition of the socio-cultural advocacy coalition is complex. Three key actors operate at the EU institutional level. First, the European Parliament has strong socio-cultural tradition. The Parliament is keenly supportive of the people's Europe agenda. However, as described above, the Parliament has been a critic of restrictions on player mobility imposed by sports-organising bodies. Second, the mandate of the Education and Culture Directorate also closely aligns it to the people's Europe project. Finally, the member states working through the European Council, the Council Presidency and informal Sports Councils have emerged as the most significant addition to the socio-cultural coalition.

Other actors operating within the subsystem include: (1) sports bodies, federations, confederations and associations; (2) government-related bodies responsible for sport in the EU, EFTA and applicant countries, including the 'quango' equivalent; (3) National Olympic Committees and related bodies; (4) public service television and radio interests; (5) campaigns such as equality issues in sport; and (6) the Council of Europe.

Deep core beliefs   Whilst the belief in the primacy of negative integration forms the deep core belief system of the Single Market coalition, central to

x positive-negative integration ovals

the belief system of the socio-cultural coalition is a concern for the promotion of positive integration. Whilst negative integration is not rejected by the coalition, successful European integration rests on an effective balance being struck between economic forces and socio-cultural (and political) forces. Although a strong force within the socio-cultural coalition, not all members of the coalition share a concern for the promotion of European integration (see below).

Policy core beliefs　The socio-cultural coalition acknowledges that sport is not above the law. Nevertheless, sport possesses social and cultural characteristics which merit a soft touch application of law.

Secondary aspects　A unifying theme within the coalition is for the socio-cultural model of sports regulation to be more widely employed, although differences over the precise relationship between sport and the EU exist. These differences in the secondary aspects of the coalition's belief system suggest that the socio-cultural coalition is a 'coalition of convenience' (Sabatier 1998: 119). Within the socio-cultural coalition exist three broad schools of thought.

The *maximalists* consist of those EU institutional actors who are supportive of attempts to establish a people's Europe in the EU and recognise the futility of attempting to establish one merely through the force of economic integration. They support the inclusion of sport within the Treaty. Not only would such an Article for sport limit the application of EU law to the sports sector, it would also act as the basis for the development of a socio-culturally based common sports policy with a legally based budgetary line. The Party of European Socialists (PES) within the Parliament generally holds this view (Henry and Mathews 1998: 5). However, on the issue of limiting the application of EU law to sport, this agenda may conflict with their traditional concern for protecting citizens' rights in the Single Market. As such, the maximalists have indicated that a balance should be struck between removing restrictive practices in European sport and harnessing the socio-cultural features of sport for pro-integrative purposes. Their sporting belief system stresses the important social function sport performs in people's lives and as such important sporting events should be broadcast on free-to-air television. Members of the Parliamentary Committee on Culture, Youth, the Media and Sport are strongly associated with the maximalists, although a moderate element is also evident. In addition, the Education and Culture DG has a strong maximalist agenda running through it. As one of the smaller DG's, Education and Culture would benefit politically from expanded EU involvement in sport. The EU governments (excluding Britain, Denmark and Sweden) also support Treaty inclusion for sport. In the absence of such a legal base, the maximalists seek to strengthen the role of sport within subsystems such as the education, health, youth, social exclusion and media subsystems. In the absence of a legal base, soft law is the preferred tactic to limit the application of law to sport. A wide range of European sports bodies are supportive of the maximalist agenda. A Treaty base for sport would not only help clarify the legal environment in which they operate, it would also allow them to tap into a new budgetary line for sports funding. Organisations such as the European Non Governmental Sports Organisation (ENGSO) have traditionally favoured an Article for sport as a means through which sporting autonomy could be safeguarded and EU funding opportunities secured.

Not all sports bodies support the maximalists' agenda. The *moderates* include those members of sports bodies such as sporting federations, confederations, associations, campaign groups and National and European Olympic Committees who do not wish to see the EU further extend its influence in sport but who do want the legal environment clarifying. This encompasses organisations such as UEFA. The sporting belief system of these actors stress that EU law and the EU institutions should not challenge the autonomy of the European sports sector and that decisions affecting the sports world are best taken by the sports bodies themselves. This autonomy refers not only to issues concerning the 'rules of the game' but also to commercial issues. As such, the moderates tend to argue that the collective sale of television rights should be maintained and sports federations should be free to realise the full value of sports rights by negotiating with a range of broadcasters, both terrestrial and satellite/cable. Members of public service television and radio broadcasters do not share this aim. The moderates support measures to protect sport from EU involvement through the incorporation of sport into the EU Treaty through a protocol for sport. This would have the effect of insulating sport from EU law by placing a legal requirement on the EU institutions to recognise the specificity of sport within its legal framework. UEFA support the protocol approach as a method of safeguarding current sports rules without further extending supranational involvement in sport. In the absence of a protocol, the moderates support the use of soft law to achieve these aims. For instance a strengthened Declaration (along the lines of the Nice Declaration) would establish political guidelines for EU involvement in sport.

The *minimalists* share the idea that sport is a social activity as well as an economic activity. They support the modest use of sport to implement certain EU policy goals and support attempts to limit the application of EU law to sport. However, the minimalists are generally cautious of extending EU influence in sport further. In particular, they do not favour granting sport a Treaty base (either through an Article for sport or a protocol). The minimalists are particularly attached to the concept of subsidiarity. The application of this principle naturally limits EU involvement in sport as national cultural diversity is prized above pan European cultural issues. Christian

Democratic politicians and MEP's generally hold this view. British Conservative forces employ subsidiarity as a vehicle to retain national control over policy areas (Henry and Matthews 1998: 5). The governments of the UK, Denmark and Sweden resist calls for Treaty incorporation for sport. Successive British governments have retained a generally consistent view that the EU has no competence to involve itself in sport. The British government hold the view that sufficient flexibility exists within the EU's legal framework to recognise the specificity of sport. Some sports bodies such as the English Sports Council expressed the view that EU involvement in sport runs the risk of inefficiently duplicating the role of national sports councils thus undermining their autonomy (Henry and Matthews 1998: 14).

The identification of the above two advocacy coalitions forms an essential component of Sabatier's methodology. Other than the effect of external perturbations on the subsystem, Sabatier argues that competition between rival advocacy coalitions within the subsystem can generate policy change. He suggests that usually one coalition dominates, although in some instances *Why?* compromise takes place and governmental programmes are built through an accommodation between rival coalitions (Sabatier 1988: 148). Compromise is an important feature within the EU. As a multi-national organisation encompassing many political, administrative and cultural strands, compromise is essential. Although the main actors are partisan, they are not blindly so. To be so would undermine the initial reason for international co-operation. Compromise and mutual adjustment between advocacy coalitions is only likely where the coalitions are both institutionally privileged. In other words, the conditions for compromise are met only if both *Good* advocacy coalitions possess the ability to take measures which would fundamentally undermine the deep and policy core beliefs of their rival. Sabatier's work on the role of policy-oriented learning, policy brokers and the role of professional forums tells us much about the dynamics of coalition compromise (Sabatier 1988: 156). If only one coalition possessed such *non-judged* institutional resources, it would dominate the subsystem. Under such circumstances, the rival would need to expand the range of venues within which it operates in order to mount a successful challenge. Frequently this entails attempting to politicise the debate and draw actors into the subsystem who were previously latent.

PRE-EMPTIVE DOMESTICATION TO CONTROL THE ADAPTIVE PRESSURES OF MISFIT by domesticating or reducing it

Institutional venues

With any brand of actor-centred institutionalism comes the problem of how to define actors and institutions. The EU 'institutions' are actors within the sports policy subsystem. They seek to steer policy in a direction consistent with their belief system. This insight does not however amount to an institutional analysis. The institutional element of the actor-centred institutionalist approach developed in this book derives from an analysis of the formal and informal institutional characteristics such institutional actors bring to the subsystem. Without such an analysis, it becomes tempting merely to point out that institutions have an effect on the strategies of actors. As Sabatier notes, although belief systems will determine the direction in which an advocacy coalition will seek to move a governmental programme, its ability to do so will be critically dependent upon its resources (Sabatier 1988: 143). Institutions and institutional venues are one such critical resource. Institutions constrain and empower actors operating within subsystems. The range of institutional venues open to advocates wishing to influence EU involvement in sport is sizeable but highly dispersed. Sporting issues are discussed in nearly all the Directorate Generals of the European Commission. As has been demonstrated above, policy advocates with an interest in sport can push their agenda in a wide number of policy subsystems.

This venue exploitation has however not been without challenge. In *UK v. Commission*, the ECJ held that each budget item must have a legal base.[5] As a result, the Commission was forced to abandon its Eurathlon programme. As part of a review into the impact of the ruling on sports programmes in the EU, the Commission asked Deutsche Sportbund (the German Sport Federation) to carry out a study into the way in which sport can be integrated into Community aid programmes. The result once again demonstrated the huge range of activities within which sport plays or could play a part. Both the Coopers and Lybrand and Deutsche Sportbund reports demonstrate how fragmented EU involvement in sport is. However, some effort has been made on the part of the EU to co-ordinate sporting activity.

The activities of most of the Commission's Directorate Generals have an impact, direct or indirect, on the operation of sport. The activities of the Competition Policy Directorate (formerly DG IV) have the greatest impact. The formal responsibility for sport within the Commission lies with the Education and Culture Directorate (formerly DG X: Information, Communication, Culture and Audio-Visual). Within the Directorate, the Sports Unit has been created to organise the sporting activities of the Commission.

The Parliament's influence on sport is two-fold. First, the EP can exert influence through its formal legislative, scrutiny and budgetary powers. Although no legal Treaty competence exists for the EU to act directly in sporting matters, much EU legislation has a major indirect impact on sport. The Parliament has been influential in shaping such legislation as it did, for example, via the tabling of amendments to the Television Without Frontiers Directive. Within the Parliament's committee structure, sporting issues are discussed in the Committee on Culture, Youth, Education, the Media and Sport. The Committee on Legal Affairs and Citizens' Rights also has an input. The Parliament can further influence sporting issues through debates, questions, writing to relevant parties and tabling resolutions. The Parliament's ability to modify and approve the EU's budget grants it some influence over the modest amount spent on sport by the EU. The second mechanism by which the EP can influence sporting issues is via the EP's Sports Intergroup, a cross-committee, cross-party discussion forum for sports-related matters (currently inactive). Established in 1992, the Intergroup has no formal power, although it has become a popular point of access for representatives of not only the EU but also many governmental and non-governmental sports organisations. The Committee of the Regions (COR), a 222 member advisory assembly on regional matters has some input into sporting issues through its Subcommission for Youth and Sport. The COR gives its opinions on sports-related Commission proposals.

Member state activity in sport has increased since *Bosman*. The Amsterdam Declaration and subsequent Presidency Conclusions illustrate this trend. The general legislative activity of the Council of Ministers does affect sport in Europe, even though sport is not the intended target of its action. As the EU has no Treaty competence in sports, the Sports Ministers do not pass legislation but do occasionally (informally) meet. In addition to ministerial meetings, member states also co-operate through meetings of European Sports Directors (national ministry officials).

Finally, ECJ rulings have incrementally established the legal principles regulating the relationship between the EU and European sporting interests. *Walrave*, *Donà*, *Heylens*, *Bosman*, *Deliège* and *Lehtonen* confirm the ECJ's importance.

Advocates operating within policy subsystems or working through the range of institutional venues mentioned above usually find themselves able to exploit institutional rules to their advantage. Put another way, advocates find it difficult to control the agenda, and hence policy evolution by mono-polising institutional rules and procedures. As Marks *et al.* remind us, in each of the four stages of the EU's policy process they examine (policy initi-ation, decision-making, implementation and adjudication), decision making capabilities are shared by a range of actors and not monopolised (Marks *et al.* 1996).

In terms of policy initiation (both legislative and 'think-tank' in nature) the Commission has a privileged position. Article 211 of the EU Treaty grants the Commission the sole right of legislative initiative. As such policy must be drafted by the Commission and during the policy process the Commission has the right to amend or withdraw its proposal. This power grants the Commission considerable influence over the political agenda, although it should not be assumed that the Commission works totally auton-omously in this respect. Other EU institutions exert influence on the Commission. First, the Commission itself should not be considered as a monolithic entity. Embedded within the Commission's architecture are numerous Directorates General, each with its own organisational style and culture and each able to exert influence over policy making in its early stages (Cram 1994). Second, the Commission must be sensitive to the wishes of the member states, particularly as the Commission's network of consultation channels includes representatives of the member states. Article 208 permits the Council to request the Commission to undertake any studies and submit proposals the Council considers desirable for the attainment of the Treaties common objectives. European Council meetings and Presidency Conclusions frequently place pressure on the Commission to submit or revise proposals. Soft law measures attached to Treaties have a similar effect as of course do legally binding Treaty Articles. Third, the Parliament can exert influence on the Commission. Article 192 permits the Parliament to request Commission action in a policy area covered by the Treaty. The Parliament's budgetary and supervisory powers can also be employed to either compel or cajole the Commission to act. In the area of non-compulsory expenditure the Parliament has equal budgetary authority with the Council and Commission.

In addition to the influence of other EU institutions, the Commission's right of initiate is also influenced by pressure group activity. Most academics would agree that interest groups exert influence over the composition of Commission proposals, even if they disagree over how to precisely account for this. Interests are increasingly becoming institutionalised within EU decision making, be that through the establishment of informal networks of actors or formally through new consultative institutions such as the Committee of Regions. Citing Commission figures, Peterson and Bomberg claim that 20 per cent of Commission proposals originate as a response to requests from other EU institutions, member states or interest groups; 35 per cent stem from international obligations; 25–30 per cent from amendments to or codifications of existing law; 10 per cent as a result of Treaty obligations; and 5–10 per cent as a result of spontaneous Commission initiatives (Peterson and Bomberg 1999: 38). A general lack of resources contributes to the size of spontaneous initiatives. A general conclusion to be drawn in terms of policy initiation is that, although the Commission has a strong position, plenty of avenues exist for advocates to push their own particular idea.

Decision-making competences are even more dispersed. The process of agreeing legislation in the EU is a function shared by the Council and the Parliament. Prior to the signing of the Single European Act (SEA), the Parliament could only give a non-binding opinion on Commission proposals prior to the Council disposing the legislation. Following the SEA the Parliament acquired a second reading and greater scope to influence legislative proposals (the co-operation procedure). Since the Maastricht and Amsterdam Treaties, the Parliament is now considered the Council's legislative equal (the co-decision procedure). Furthermore, the use of qualified majority voting (QMV) in the Council further reduces the amount of veto points in the policy process. In budgetary matters, competences are also shared between the Parliament, Commission and Council.

Although the Commission holds considerable powers in relation to the implementation of policy, yet again it does not monopolise this function. The

Commission shares this function with national, sub-national and non-state actors such as interest groups. The same is true of adjudication. The ECJ is supported by the Commission, national courts and individual litigants.

Of course, a focus only on the formal institutional venues open to advocacy coalitions will only give a one-dimensional insight into coalition strategies. An examination of the informal/normative dimension of institutions also reveals many useful insights. As March and Olsen remind us, 'the polity is something different from, or more than, an arena for competition among rival interests' (March and Olsen 1989: 159). However, norms can take many forms and identifying them, let alone explaining the impact on coalition strategies and policy evolution is not always easy. Some of the most important are as follows:

Legal norms   The build up of legal norms is crucial to the construction of a policy environment (governance regime) within which policy evolution takes place. In particular, ECJ jurisprudence or the Competition Policy Directorates quasi-jurisprudence shapes this environment. The relationship between the ECJ's work and that of the Commission is very close. The Commission's use of the Court's *Cassis de Dijon* judgment to promote mutual recognition is one example.[6] The close relationship between the *Bosman* ruling and the Commission's testing of sporting practises against competition law is another. The use of soft law by the member states and the Commission is a further legal norm to have evolved within the EU. Soft law refers to rules of conduct which in principle have no legally binding effect but which in practise may have a significant impact on policy. Soft law frequently offers guidance as to the interpretation and scope of application of EU law and in some circumstances it has acted to progressively 'harden' policy areas on the margins of the EU's legal remit. The use of soft law has characterised much of the development of sports policy. This reflects a lack of a formal Treaty base to take 'harder' measures.

Institutional cultures   The culture of an institution can have a profound affect on policy evolution (Armstrong and Bulmer 1998: Chapters 2 and 3). Institutional culture may be 'open' thus privileging all advocates, 'selectively open' thus privileging some advocates or 'closed' thus denying all advocates access. The culture of smoke filled rooms and fireside chats within the European Council is just one example of this. Different institutions also have varying dispositions. Some Directorates General within the Commission have a particularly *dirigiste* disposition whereas others operate in a more *laissez faire* manner. Armstrong and Bulmer point to the conflicting cultures within the Transport Directorate and the Competition Policy Directorate that led to a divergence of opinion over the granting of state aid to airlines (Armstrong and Bulmer 1998: 60). Similarly, the Competition Policy Directorate's economic approach to sport conflicts somewhat with the

Education and Culture Directorate's more socio-cultural approach. The same is true of the committee system within the Parliament. Sporting discussions taking place within the EP's Committee on Culture, Youth, Education, the Media and Sport take a different course to those discussed within the Committee on Legal Affairs and Citizens' Rights.

Institutional norms   Institutions also develop routinised patterns of behaviour. Despite the widespread provision for qualified majority voting in the Council, consensual decision making is still preferred. In particular, the Council frequently employs the principle of relative stability to decision making. Under such circumstances, the Council ensures that 'losers' in a policy decision are compensated by concessions in another part of the policy or indeed in another policy altogether. Package deals and issue linkage have therefore become a standard practise in Council decision making. Norms such as relative stability can have profound effects on policy. It is becoming usual each year for the Council to be faced with a proposal from the Commission recommending a reduction in fishing effort. If the proposal recommends a 10 per cent reduction in catch size for a certain species, the effect of relative stability is to greatly reduce this reduction or to allocate the 'losers' higher allocations elsewhere. Environmentalists wishing to influence the Commission proposal may take this decision making norm into account when formulating their suggested reduction figure. Partisan mutual adjustment is another important norm. Although decision makers are partisan, they are capable of compromise. The EU has developed sophisticated mechanisms to manage conflict. Issue linkage and package deals are two examples of this. Others include conciliation procedures, co-ordinating mechanisms and policy forums. Peterson and Bomberg identify other institutional norms (Peterson and Bomberg 1999: 53–58). 'Negotiated enforcement' as opposed to imposed enforcement is frequently preferred by the Commission in cases that are politically sensitive. Finally, an increasingly institutionalised norm is the use of the subsidiarity principle. This norm became associated with the greater devolution of policy-making functions to national and sub-national authorities.

Conclusions

The sports policy subsystem was created as a result of *Bosman*. Prior to that sport was discussed in a wide range of policy subsystems, many of them underpinned with Single Market as opposed to socio-cultural values. *Bosman* emerged from one such interaction between sport and a non-sports-related Single Market subsystem. Dissatisfaction with the lack of a more holistic and co-ordinated approach to sport led to the creation of the socio-cultural advocacy coalition. The coalition has been successful in creating a sports policy subsystem in which the previously dispersed discussions on sport have become more co-ordinated. The formation of a separate sub-system is an essential pre-requisite for policy change. However, alone it is insufficient to change the direction of policy. The institutional resources of the rival coalitions determine the extent to which coalition competition results in policy change.

Peterson and Bomberg describe the EU's policy process as containing 'multiple sources of unpredictability' (Peterson and Bomberg 1999: 58). This supports Armstrong and Bulmer's assertion that the EU represents 'a classic case of governance without formal government' (Armstrong and Bulmer 1998: 71). Within the context of EU subsystems this frequently means that advocacy coalitions are able to go shopping in multiple venues in order to affect policy. The Single Market coalition is institutionally strong. The logic of negative integration is firmly enshrined in the Treaty. Furthermore, through *Walrave, Donà, Heylens* and *Bosman* the ECJ has enshrined the economic definition of sport in law. The Single Market actors have therefore already undermined the policy core belief system of the socio-cultural coalition. Unless the socio-cultural coalition is able to respond in order to protect their policy core beliefs, the subsystem will become monopolised. However, as illustrated above, the socio-cultural coalition is also institutionally privileged. Since Maastricht, the logic of positive integration has more firmly established itself within the culture of integration and this has been supported by institutional moves to strengthen socio-cultural actors. In particular, the Parliament has benefited from institutional reform. The most significant development for the socio-cultural coalition has however been the involvement of the member states within the subsystem.

The member states are able to assert themselves within the subsystem through a variety of non-legal, semi-legal and legal manoeuvres. The member states are able to exert political pressure through the adoption of soft law measures. Furthermore, they alone possess the ability to amend the Treaty. Institutions and policies are not immune from reform, even though unanimity is often required to do so. The ECJ and the Commission operate under the threat of sanction. As Craig and De Búrca argue, the ECJ is not immune from political pressures.

> It is certainly aware of the political environment in which it acts and its judgements are at times influenced by relatively non-legal arguments made by the member states before the Court – often when they relate to the potential financial impact of a ruling – or by critical responses from national and from Community sources. (Craig and De Búrca 1998: 81)

The decision by the member states to insert the Barber protocol into the Maastricht Treaty stemmed directly from their concern over the ECJ's ruling in *Barber*.[7] The Protocol has subsequently affected ECJ decision making in this field. The member states possess various options for safeguarding sports structures within the legal framework of the Treaty. A Barber style protocol approach is one method. In addition, the member states could amend the Treaty itself through inserting an Article for sport or by exempting sport from individual passages within the Treaty. These powerful institutional resources are keenly resisted by the Single Market coalition as the wielding of such powers has the potential to undermine their deep and policy core beliefs.

A situation has therefore emerged within the sports policy subsystem which allows the rival coalitions to take measures which could undermine each other's deep and policy core belief systems. Past experience, calculations of future losses and the EU's culture of mutual adjustment between actors contributes to policy-oriented learning within the subsystem. Policy-oriented learning takes place as actors seek to protect their deep and policy core beliefs. It results in the rival advocacy coalitions compromising their secondary beliefs. Channels for such learning and compromise have been established within the EU. In terms of sport, the EU has established forums through which compromise can take place such as the 1999 EU Conference on Sport and the annual meeting of the European Sports Forum. The Education and Culture Directorate has also emerged as an important policy broker.

Throughout this text it is argued that compromise has been essential to the birth of EU sports law and policy. Compromise within the sports policy subsystem has taken place within the secondary aspects of the coalitions belief system. The 'separate territories' approach has emerged from this compromise. Separate territories is a concept developing within national legal jurisdictions for dealing with sports-related cases. As Beloff *et al.* argues, English courts are increasingly favouring public law principles to resolve cases which on the face of it concern private transactions between economic agents (Beloff *et al.* 1999: 3–4). Accordingly, the courts are defining territories of sporting autonomy and judicial intervention. The construction of a similar separate territories approach within the context of the EU allows both advocacy coalitions to safeguard their deep and policy core belief systems. Increasingly therefore the subsystem argument concerns the respective size and definition of the territories. If compromise within the secondary aspects of the belief system proves mutually beneficial, conflict over policy core beliefs will not develop.

The development of the separate territories approach within the sports policy subsystem is significant. As Beloff *et al.* argue, 'the cornerstone of what could be called the founding principles of sports law is the definition of the respective territories of the courts and the bodies which govern sport' (Beloff *et al.* 1999: 4). By constructing separate territories within the context of the EU's legal system, the EU has acknowledged the existence of a body of law dealing specifically with sport (EU sports law). Rather than EU sports law flowing from legislative activity, the birth of sports law is a tactic employed to avoid the use of legislation specifically directed at sport (such as a Treaty Article). A curious situation has therefore arisen in which the EU pursues a *de facto* sports policy, defined not by primary or secondary legislation but by legal doctrines specific to sport.

The next three chapters develop these themes by examining the nature of the debate within the sports policy subsystem. Chapter 4 examines the role of the Court of Justice in establishing important principles governing the relationship between sport and the EU. Chapter 5 examines the movement of sport from the systemic agenda to the institutional agenda as a result of the actions of the Competition Policy Directorate. Chapter 6 examines attempts by the socio-cultural coalition to politicise the sports policy subsystem and re-focus the prevailing regulatory model to one in which the socio-cultural aspects of sport are more widely recognised and protected.

Notes

1   OJ No. C-329, 31/12/90.
2   Directive 85/337/EEC, OJ L 175, 5/7/85.
3   Directive 92/43/EEC, OJ L 206, 22/7/92.
4   Evidence to support this claim stems from (1) the post-*Bosman* expansion in the sports-related caseload of the Competition Policy DG and Court of Justice and (2) anecdotal observations made by the author at sports law conferences where law firms had representation.
5   Case C-106/96, *UK* v. *Commission* ECR I-02729.
6   Case 120/78, *Rewe-Zentral AG* v. *Bundesmonopolverwaltung für Branntwein* (Cassis de Dijon) [1979] ECR 649. Re: a German law laying down minimum alcohol content in certain drinks.
7   Case C-262/88, *Barber* v. *Guardian Royal Exchange Assurance Group* [1990] ECR I-1889. Re: occupational pensions.

4

Sport and the European Court of Justice

The ECJ is an important agenda setter. Court rulings play an important part in defining the content of the EU's systemic agenda and the conditions under which an issue is transferred to the institutional agenda for active policy development. The ECJ's line of reasoning in relation to sport has been developed within the context of a number of important institutional relationships. As such, the ECJ's role in establishing the boundaries of EU sports regulation is not deterministic.

In *Walrave, Donà* and *Heylens*, the ECJ established important principles concerning the relationship between sport and EU law.[1] In the event, the lack of enforcement from the Commission limited the scope of these rulings. In *Bosman*, the principles established in previous case law were extended. As the Commission was more energetic in enforcing *Bosman*, so the ruling took on enormous legal significance for sport.[2] The rulings in *Deliège and Lehtonen*, which placed some limit on the application of EU law to sport, took place in the context of an on-going political discussion within the EU on how to reconcile EU law with sports social significance.[3] Whereas *Walrave, Donà, Heylens* and *Bosman* took place in an environment where the construction of the Single Market was seen as paramount, *Deliège and Lehtonen* reflected greater sensitivity to the socio-cultural dimension of European integration. *Deliège and Lehtonen* therefore represent the ECJ's contribution to the construction of the separate territories.

This chapter examines the ECJ's sports-related jurisprudence in six parts. The first part reviews the role of the ECJ in the process of European integration. The second examines the Treaty provisions relating to the free movement of workers and the right of establishment and the freedom to provide services. The third section analyses the significance of the ECJ rulings in *Walrave, Donà* and *Heylens*. Section four examines the impact of the *Bosman* ruling and section five reviews the case law in *Deliège* and *Lehtonen*. The final section draws some conclusions.

So Europeanisation : i) acting in it own right
or. ii) strategically advancing its
own belief system.

**WHERE POLICY MAKING HAS
BECOME ITS OWN**

The European Court of Justice and European integration

IMPLIC: ATTORE
- lead to no-integration
- lead to no-implementation

Most writers agree that the ECJ's activities have made an important contribution to European integration. The ECJ has successfully extended the scope of EU law through the establishment of the principles of direct effect and supremacy.[4] This has equipped the ECJ (supported by national courts and individual litigants) to develop substantive law in the field of the free movement of goods, labour, services and capital. Whilst the influence of the ECJ on these issues is not questioned, no consensus exists on how and why the ECJ has been able to achieve this. A vibrant debate has ensued enriching both political science and law. Distilling the essentials of this debate, four broad approaches can be identified.

Activism The first approach sees the ECJ as an autonomous political QUOTE actor seeking to strategically advance its own position and European integration in a manner consistent with its belief system. Not all writers agree that this has had a positive impact on integration (see for example Weiler 1981 and Rasmussen 1986). In particular judicial activism contributed not only to a reluctance of the member states to integrate through supranational channels, but also to disruptions and blockages in the EU's political decision-making process. Other writers have been more positive on the effect of ECJ jurisprudence on integration. Burley and Mattli have argued that the ECJ has incrementally constitutionalised the Treaty of Rome, a process that has 'laid the foundations for an integrated European economy and polity' (Burley and Mattli 1993). Adopting a neo-functional analysis, Burley and Mattli argue that law has spilled over from the purely economic sector to new spheres, including new policy areas such as occupational health and safety, social welfare and education. Just as Haas argued economics acted as a mask for political integration, so Burley and Mattli argue law acts as a mask for politics. Furthermore, this mask is protected by a GOOD shield that insulates the ECJ from political interference. This is because policy makers view law as technical and the ECJ couches its judgments in apolitical terms. In addition to analysing economic to political functional spillover, Burley and Mattli examine functional spillover in terms of legal principles. To illustrate this point the relationship between the *Van Gend and Loos* case and the *Costa* v. *Enel* case is examined.[5] Once the principle of direct effect was established by the ECJ, it became necessary and indeed logical to establish the principle of supremacy. Without supremacy, direct effect could not be fully realised, an example of incomplete integration. Burley and Mattli also detect a strong political spillover dimension in the work of the ECJ. In particular, they detect a bottom-up shift in expectations and responses to cases from member governments, national courts and individual litigants. The preliminary reference procedure assists this connection between legal jurisdictions.[6]

Legalism   The second approach rejects the notion of judicial activism. The ECJ operates above politics and simply applies the law in a neutral manner consistent with the role ascribed to it under the Treaty. If the ECJ has advanced integration through its jurisprudence, it has done so in a manner consistent with the pro-integrative logic of primary and secondary legislation.

Intergovernmentalism   The third approach (very broadly referred to here as intergovernmentalism) also rejects the idea of a judicially active and autonomous ECJ. ECJ rulings reflect the interests of the member states and do not run contrary to them. If they did, member states hold the power of sanction over the ECJ through the revision of the Treaty, which could alter the structure and role of the Court (see for instance Garrett and Weingast 1993). Occasionally governments may be prepared to accept short-term losses in order to secure wider long-term gains. This interpretation accounts for instances where ECJ rulings appear to run contrary to member states interests, yet the governments do not retaliate.

Multi-level governance   The final broad interpretation (and one consistent with the approach adopted in this text) seeks to locate the ECJ's contribution to European integration in a wider context. For example, Wincott claims that whilst it is misleading to see the ECJ as an institution that has forced or engineered integration it is similarly misguided to see the ECJ as an agent of the member states (Wincott 1996: 170–184). Wincott claims 'an analysis which attributes a rational and synoptic control of European integration to a single institution or group is likely to be misleading' (Wincott 1996: 170). As such, even though the ECJ has had an impact on European integration, it remains one actor among many. For example, the ECJ is dependent on a number of relationships in order for it to advance integration. *true.*

- *ECJ–member state*   The ECJ's role in the integration process was initially sanctioned by the member states and can be changed through Treaty revision. Furthermore, the member states can exploit a number of venues in order to limit the impact of past and future ECJ rulings. Changes to secondary legislation agreed by the Council of Ministers represent the most formal method, although political pressure can be imparted on the ECJ through soft law measures. Political Declarations released as annexes to Treaties or in the form Presidency Conclusions are often influential. In the case of pension rights, the member states added a protocol (the Barber Protocol) to the Maastricht Treaty preventing the retroactive application of the ruling. It has been noted that following the protocol, the ECJ 'moderated its activism in this area' (Hix 1999: 128).
- *ECJ–European Parliament*   Given the expansion of the European Parliament's legislative capabilities, the ECJ has the potential to be

influenced by legislation agreed jointly between the Council and the Parliament.

- *ECJ–Commission*   The ECJ has formed a close supranational alliance with the Commission. For instance in terms of widening the scope of the free movement of goods principle, the Commission made legislative use of the ECJ's *Cassis* judgement. In relation to gender equality, the ECJ played a crucial role in giving expression to the Commission's calls for the implementation of Article 141 (Wincott 1996). Furthermore, the emergence of a merger control policy demonstrates the interplay between judicial and legislative actions (Bulmer 1994).
- *ECJ–national courts*   Without the support of national courts, the ECJ would have been unable to develop many of the legal principles which today define the EU's legal order. Article 234 creates a bridge between the two legal orders by allowing national courts to seek guidance from the ECJ. This procedure has allowed the ECJ to issue preliminary rulings on the correct interpretation of EU law.
- *ECJ–individual*   The principle of direct effect has enabled individual litigants to defend their rights under EU law before national courts. Individuals, including companies, therefore have a stake in the EU's legal order and in this capacity are supported by lawyers.

Whilst therefore the ECJ plays an important role in developing legal principles and substantive law, its role should be placed in context. The ECJ constrains and is constrained by multiple actors operating within the EU's legal community. The development of new substantive areas of EU policy results from a complex interplay of forces involving many actors. The ECJ's role in sports regulation illustrates these complexities.

Free movement in the European Union

Article 3(c) of the Treaty requires 'the abolition, as between member states, of obstacles to the free movement of goods, persons, services and capital'. According to Article 12, for this to be achieved, 'any discrimination on grounds of nationality shall be prohibited'. Three further Articles elaborate this goal in the specific fields of employment (Article 39), establishment rights (Article 43) and service provision (Article 49).

because it is anti-competitive

The free movement of workers
Article 39 provides for:

1 Freedom of movement for workers shall be secured within the Community.
2 Such freedom of movement shall entail the abolition of any discrimination based on nationality between workers of the member states as regards employment, remuneration and other conditions of work and employment.
3 It shall entail the right, subject to limitations justified on grounds of public policy, public security or public health:

a to accept offers of employment actually made;

b to move freely within the territory of member states for this purpose;

c to stay in a member state for the purpose of employment in accordance with the provisions governing the employment of nationals of that State laid down by law, regulation or administrative action;

d to remain in the territory of a member state after having been employed in that State, subject to conditions which shall be embodied in implementing regulations to be drawn up by the Commission.

4 The provisions of this Article shall not apply to employment in the public service.

The passing of secondary legislation has served to implement Article 39. For instance Directive 68/360 ensures rights of entry and residence. Regulation 1612/68 regulates access to and conditions of employment. Regulation 1251/70 establishes the right to remain in the territory of a member state after employment there. Directive 64/221 establishes the rights of member states in connection with the derogations outlined in Article 39(3).

Article 39 is directly applicable.[7] Furthermore, in *Walrave and Koch* and more recently *Bosman*, the ECJ established that Article 39 is capable of having horizontal as well as vertical direct effect. In *Walrave* the ECJ held that the 'prohibition of such discrimination does not only apply to the action of public authorities but extends likewise to rules of any other nature aimed at regulating in a collective manner gainful employment and the provision of services'.[8] Also in *Walrave* the ECJ held that Article 39 would apply to work situations carried out outside the EU if the legal relationship of employment was entered into within the EU. Similarly, the reverse applies to instances whereby the legal relationship was formed outside the EU but the effect of the measure is felt within it. The prohibition on direct discrimination based on nationality extends to indirect discrimination in circumstances in which nationality neutral measures act as restrictions to free movement.[9]

Article 39 and subsequent secondary legislation establishes the rights of workers. The Treaty itself does not attempt a definition of a worker, although the ECJ has employed the word widely. In *Lawrie-Blum* the ECJ defined a worker as someone who performs services for and under the direction of another in return for remuneration during a certain period of time.[10] In *Walrave* the ECJ held that the work must constitute an economic activity within the meaning of Article 2 of the Treaty.[11] The ECJ regards most forms of non-trivial work as genuine work.

The right of establishment

Article 43 provides for:

Within the framework of the provisions set out below, restrictions on the freedom of establishment of nationals of a member state in the territory of another member state shall be prohibited. Such prohibition shall also apply to restrictions on the setting-up of agencies, branches or subsidiaries by nationals of any member state established in the territory of any member state.

Freedom of establishment shall include the right to take up and pursue activities as self-employed persons and to set up and manage undertakings, in particular companies or firms within the meaning of the second paragraph of Article 48, under the conditions laid down for its own nationals by the law of the country where such establishment is effected, subject to the provisions of the Chapter relating to capital.

The right of establishment refers to the right of individuals and firms to establish a business in a member state other than their own. Article 43 is directly applicable and directly effective.[12]

Freedom to provide services

Article 49 provides for:

Within the framework of the provisions set out below, restrictions on freedom to provide services within the Community shall be prohibited in respect of nationals of member states who are established in a State of the Community other than that of the person for whom the services are intended.

The Council may, acting by a qualified majority on a proposal from the Commission, extend the provisions of the Chapter to nationals of a third country who provide services and who are established within the Community.

The term 'service' is defined in Article 50(1) as being 'normally provided for remuneration, insofar as they are not governed by the provisions relating to freedom of movement for goods, capital and persons'. Such services include industrial and commercial services and the activities of craftsmen and professionals, excluding transport, insurance and banking for which alternative Treaty provisions exist. The right to provide services is afforded to individuals and firms. The right of establishment and the right to provide services is limited by the public policy, public security and public health limitation contained in Directive 64/221.

The *Walrave, Donà* and *Heylens* cases

As the EU is not an omni-competent organisation, it must be established that sport falls within the scope of the above Treaty Articles. The case law of the ECJ has established that Articles 39, 43 and 49 apply to sport. The Commission has also established that Article 81 and 82 dealing with competition law also apply (considered in Chapter 5).

Walrave *v.* Union Cycliste International *1974*

Bruno Walrave and Noppie Koch were two Dutch professional pacemakers in motor-paced cycle races. Participants in these races ride pedal powered cycles. Each participant has a pacemaker on a motorcycle whom he follows. The pacemakers, who wear special clothing, aim to create a moving vacuum for the cyclist (stayer) to ride in. This enables the stayer to achieve speeds in excess of what a 'normal' cyclist could achieve. This can be as much as 100 kilometres per hour. The role of the pacemaker is therefore central to the sport, unlike the role of pacemakers in many other sports such as athletics. The pacemaker enters into a contract with the stayer, a cycling association or a sponsor. Until 1973, the pacemaker did not have to be of the same nationality to that of the stayer.

In November 1970, the Union Cycliste International (UCI, the international association for cycling sport) reviewed its rules on the conduct of motor-paced races for the forthcoming medium distance world cycling championships. From 1973, the pacemaker and the stayer had to be of the same nationality. UCI justified this action on the grounds that World Championships are intended to be competitions between national teams. Believing there to be a paucity of good Dutch stayers, Mr Walrave and Mr Koch acted as pacemakers for non-Dutch stayers, including Belgians and Germans. Faced with a restriction on their livelihood, they regarded this rule change as being discriminatory and a breach of EU law. Having failed to secure the repeal of the rule change, the two pacemakers initiated proceedings against the UCI, the Dutch cycling association and, because the championships were to be held in Spain, also the Spanish cycling association.[13] Walrave and Koch wanted the rule to be repealed and wanted an injunction requiring the UCI to allow the pacemakers to take part in forthcoming events. The case was brought before the Arrondissementsrechtbank (District Court) in Utrecht in 1973 and referred to the ECJ using the reference procedures outlined in Article 234 of the Treaty. In answering the questions posed by the referring court, the ECJ came to the following conclusions.

First, the District Court asked the ECJ to rule on the compatibility of UCI's rule with Articles 12, 39 and 49 of the Treaty and Regulation No. 1612/68 of the Council of 15 October 1968 on the freedom of movement for workers within the Community. The ECJ initially had to establish whether EU law was applicable to sport. Paragraph 4 of the ruling established that, 'having regard to the objectives of the Community, the practice of sport is subject to Community law only in so far as it constitutes an economic activity within the meaning of Article 2 of the Treaty'.

Second, flowing from this general principle, the ECJ held that when the purpose of this 'economic activity' is to gain employment or remunerated service, it comes within the scope of Articles 39 to 42 or 49 to 55 of the Treaty, depending on the individual circumstances of the case.[14] These Articles give effect to the general rule of Article 12 prohibiting discrimination on nationality. No distinction was therefore made between sport as an economic activity and other forms of work or services. Only when the practice of sport is of 'purely sporting interest', did the ECJ make such a distinction. As such national teams can discriminate on the grounds of nationality.[15]

Third, the prohibition of discrimination applies not only to the actions of public authorities but also to rules of any other nature aimed at collectively regulating gainful employment and services.[16] Articles 39 and 49 therefore carry horizontal direct effect.

Fourth, relating to the applicability of EU law to events of world-wide significance, such as the cycling championships in question, the ECJ ruled that the rule on non-discrimination applies to all legal relationships in so far as these relationships, by reason either of the place where they are entered into or the place where they take effect, can be located within the territory of the EU.[17]

In accordance within the division between interpretation and application, the ECJ referred its answers back to the national court leaving it to determine whether EU law applied to the case and whether the pacemaker and the stayer were a team. In the event, Walrave and Koch declined to press for a judgment by the Arrondissementsrechtbank because the UCI had allegedly threatened to withdraw paced cycle racing from the World Championships (Weatherill 1989).

Donà *v.* Mantero 1976[18]

The second occasion on which the ECJ dealt with a sports-related case concerned nationality rules in Italian football. The Italian Football Federation, the Federazione Italiana del Gioco del Calcio (FIGC) controls the game of football in Italy. Under its rules, players are required to hold a federation membership card. Only the FIGC can issue such a card. Article 28(g) of the federation's rules stated that normally only players of Italian nationality, residing in Italy could be issued with the card. An exemption was made for foreign nationals who have never been members of a foreign federation who are resident in Italy and ask to be enrolled as youths, amateurs or for recreational purposes. For all other players the FIGC had total discretion as to whether a card was to be issued.[19] The rules effectively placed a heavy restriction on non-Italian footballers playing professional football in Italy. A challenge to these rules was brought by an agent who had attempted to recruit players from abroad. The agent had been hired by the chairman of an Italian league football club who wanted to explore the possibilities of bringing foreign players to the club. The agent, Gaetano Donà placed an advert in a Belgian sports newspaper. When, however, he claimed the costs of this advert back on expenses, he was refused on the grounds that he had acted too soon and Italian league rules prevented the use of foreign players. Mr Donà sued for the amount of the advert before the Giudice Conciliatore di Rovigo.

The Giudice Coniliatore di Rovigo referred the case to the ECJ. In particular, the national court asked the ECJ to establish if the nationality requirement for playing in professional football matches in Italy was compatible with EU law. The national court asked for clarification, initially on two key questions. First, whether Articles 12, 39 and 49 of the Treaty confer upon all nationals of the member states of the EU the right to provide a service anywhere in the EU and, secondly, whether football players also enjoy the same right where their services are in the nature of a gainful occupation. Depending on the answers to these two questions, a further two were asked. First, the national court asked the ECJ to rule whether this right may also be relied on to prevent the application of contrary rules drawn up by a sporting federation that regulates football on the territory of a member state. Second, the national court asked the ECJ whether the right in question is directly effective. On first sight, these four questions appear disproportionate for the purposes of the case. Some commentators have suggested the case was contrived for the purposes of opening the Italian football league to foreign players (Blanpain and Inston 1996).

Previously in *Walrave* the ECJ had established that sport is subject to EU law when it is practised as an economic activity and has the character of gainful employment or remunerated service. In particular, Articles 39 to 42 or 49 to 55 are applicable in this connection. These provisions give effect to Article 12 of the Treaty, prohibiting discrimination on the grounds of nationality.

Trabucchi, the Advocate General appointed to the case, appeared to suggest in his opinion delivered on 6 July 1976 that restrictions on nationality in football matches may be justified. He argued:

> there is, in my view, nothing to prevent considerations of purely sporting inter-
> est from justifying the imposition of some restriction on the signing of foreign
> players or at least on their participation in official championship matches so as
> to ensure that the winning team will be representative of the state of which it
> is the champion team. A condition of this kind seems all the more reasonable
> when it is borne in mind that the team which wins the national championship
> is often chosen to represent its own state in international competitions.

Trabucchi was therefore of the opinion that even the rules of sporting organisations run as an economic concern may be exempt from the application of non-discriminatory Treaty provisions. Sport may be a business, but it may still also be simultaneously practised as an activity of purely sporting interest. The question is whether these restrictions are appropriate and proportionate to the end pursued. In answer to the referred questions, the ECJ partly confirmed the main thrust of Trabucchi's argument. The ECJ held:

1 Rules or a national practice, even adopted by a sporting organisation, which
   limit the right to take part in football matches as professional or semi-
   professional players solely to the nationals of the State in question, are
   incompatible with Article 12 (ex 7) and, as the case may be, with Articles
   39 to 42 or 49 to 55 (ex 48 to 51 or 59 to 66) of the Treaty, unless such rules
   or practice exclude foreign players from participation in certain matches for
   reasons which are not of an economic nature, which relate to the particular
   nature and context of such matches and are thus of sporting interest only.

2 Article 39 (ex 48) on the one hand and the first paragraph of Article 49 (ex 59) and the third paragraph of Article 50 (ex 60) of the Treaty on the other – the last two provisions at least in so far as they seek to abolish discrimination against a person providing a service by reason of his nationality or the fact that he resides in a member state other than in which the service is to be provided – have direct effect in the legal orders of the member states and confer on individuals rights which national Courts must protect.

Once again, the ECJ referred its answers back to the national court for application.

UNECTEF *v.* Heylens 1987[20]

Although players are the most important feature of the sporting contest, many other individuals are involved in its production. In this connection, sports clubs also employ physiotherapists, coaches, dieticians, psychologists and trainers. Member states impose restrictions on foreign nationals wishing to take up such posts. For example, the individual in question is normally expected to be suitably qualified. In instances whereby qualifications are not awarded by bodies within the member state, member states are under a EU obligation to recognise equivalent qualifications gained in other member states. For some professions the EU has established specific mutual recognition standards. However, in many instances no such standards exist. Member states must therefore take appropriate measures to assess an individual's suitability. This is achieved by comparing the candidate's credentials with those required by national rules. The exercise of this judgement has however been called into question.

The *Heylens* case concerned a French requirement that in order to be a football trainer in France, a person must be the holder of a French football-trainer's diploma or a foreign diploma which has been recognised as equivalent by the French government. George Heylens, a Belgian national, trained the Lille Olympic Sporting Clubs football team, a French club. His application for recognition of a Belgian diploma was rejected by the French Ministry of Sport. In the statement of reasons, the Ministry referred to the negative opinion of a special committee. However, the special committee gave no reasons for their negative opinion. The French football-trainers' trade union (UNECTEF) prosecuted Heylens and the directors of the football club before the Lille Criminal Court because of his continued employment with the club. The question of the compatibility with EU law of the French system for deciding on the equivalence of diplomas law was referred to the ECJ.

The ECJ referred to the fundamental right of workers to move freely within the EU. In this connection, the ECJ reiterated that member states must take all appropriate measures to ensure the fulfilment of the obligations arising from the Treaty. Nevertheless, the ECJ held that in the absence of harmonisation of conditions of access to a particular occupation, the member states are entitled to lay down the knowledge and qualifications needed in order to pursue it and to require the production of a diploma certifying that the holder has the relevant attributes.[21] However, the ECJ held that a decision refusing to recognise the equivalence of a diploma must be reviewable to see whether it is compatible with Article 39 and to allow the person concerned to ascertain the reasons for the decision.

Comment on Walrave, Donà *and* Heylens

Combining the answers provided by the ECJ in *Walrave, Donà* and *Heylens*, it is possible to draw a number of conclusions relevant to the question of the pre-*Bosman* relationship between sport and EU law:

1 The ECJ has clearly established that sport is subject to EU law in so far as it constitutes an economic activity within the meaning of Article 2 of the Treaty. Exemptions from the principle of non-discrimination are permitted but linked with the practise of sport on a non-economic basis. As such, Article 39 does not concern itself with the composition of national teams.

2 Footballers are considered to be workers (employees of clubs) and as such are protected by Article 39. The broad definition of a worker adopted by the ECJ means that not only professional but also semi-professional and amateur players are included if they provide services in return for remuneration. Players who are not remunerated by the club but are financially rewarded indirectly (for instance through sponsorship) are not considered workers. Solo players who are not employed and remunerated by a club are also not considered workers in the context of Article 39 (but see below).

3 Article 39 is not only vertically directly effective, it is also horizontally directly effective. As such, Article 39 covers the activities of private sports associations.

4 Articles 43 and 49 dealing with establishment rights and freedom to provide services also apply to sport. Sportsmen and women who provide services but are not employed by clubs are afforded protection from discrimination by these Articles. As with Article 39, the discriminatory rule in question must be economic in nature and not of purely sporting interest. Two cases in English law illustrate this. In *Wilander* v. *Tobin* the Court of Appeal indicated, without deciding, that the sanction of suspending players who failed drug tests in tennis falls outside the scope of Article 49 as it concerned a rule governing sporting conduct.[22] The players in question argued that the rule prevented them from supplying services within the EU. Similarly in *Edwards* v. *BAF and IAAF*, no breach of Article 49 was found concerning the International Amateur Athletics Federation's doping rules.[23] These rules were also considered to be essentially concerned with sporting conduct and as such fell outside the scope of Article 49. However, as Lord Woolf argued in *Wilander*, EU law still has the

potential to apply to the rules concerning the conduct of sport as well as to rules affecting the economic activity of sport.

5 Sports associations are entitled to lay down the knowledge and qualifications needed to take up employment but they must provide reason why they refuse to recognise a foreign diploma as equivalent. Furthermore, such decisions must be reviewable to establish compatibility with Article 39.

URBSFA and others v. Bosman[24]

Despite the growing body of case law relating to discriminatory practices in sport, the European Commission appeared unwilling to fully enforce the *Walrave* and *Donà* rulings. Consultations between the Commission (Internal Market DG) and UEFA on the continued use of nationality restrictions in European football continued unsuccessfully until the *Bosman* judgement. In 1978, an agreement between Commissioner Davignon and UEFA was concluded by which the federations had to modify their internal rules in order to abolish discrimination on the grounds of nationality. A temporary agreement was reached permitting first and second division clubs to restrict non-nationals to two per match. Despite objections from the Commission and the European Parliament, the restrictions remained in place. In December 1984, the Commission once again requested that discriminatory rules be amended to conform to EU law, this time by 1 July 1985. The response of UEFA and the national football associations was piecemeal. At the conference of the national Football Associations of EU member states held in July 1985, the associations approved a four-point plan proposed by UEFA.

1 Maximum of two non-nationals to be fielded per match.
2 'Sporting' nationality to be granted after five years' uninterrupted activity for a single association.
3 Qualifying period for applications for 'sporting' nationality to commence 1 July 1984.
4 Re-examination of the problem in 1989 to analyse the results obtained.

In September 1985, Commissioner Sutherland signalled his dissatisfaction with the agreement. Not only had UEFA failed to abide by the July deadline, but fundamentally UEFA's plans still contravened EU law. It was Sutherland's view that, 'players have their rights under Community law . . . if a player has the chance to secure his own future during a relatively short career then who are the Commission to stop him? We are trying to ensure that there is no restriction on freedom' (Grayson 1994: 274).

Accordingly, the Commission once again requested that discriminatory practises in sport be abolished. At a further meeting between the Commission and UEFA/national federations in June 1987 the Commission proposed:

1 The participation of three nationals from another member state in all official matches during the 1988–89 and 1989–90 seasons.
2 Continuous progress towards the achievement of total freedom of movement, to be completed by 1992.
3 The creation of an evaluation group to consider the problems surrounding the free movement of professional players and its impact on professional football in general.

The proposals proved unacceptable to UEFA, although in 1991, after
further consultations between the two parties, UEFA adopted the 3+2 rule.
From July 1992, clubs could play not more than three non-nationals in the
team and two 'assimilated' players who have played in the country in question for five years uninterruptedly, including three years in junior teams.
Initially, this rule applied to top division sides and was to be extended in the
1996/1997 season to all other non-amateur league's. Individual associations
could frame rules allowing more foreign players to play. However, the 3+2
rule applied universally in club matches organised by UEFA. The *Bosman*
ruling brought an abrupt end to the 3+2 formula.

The Commission's attitude towards discriminatory practises in sport
throughout this period was somewhat contradictory. The Commission
adopted a generally consistent view that discriminatory practises in sport
should be abolished. However, they failed to ensure compliance with EU law
and instead favoured a negotiated settlement with UEFA in the form of a
gentleman's agreement. How can this be accounted for? First, the
Commission recognised that, although sport could be defined as an economic activity, it still possessed certain qualities necessitating a softer interpretation of the law. Despite previous ECJ cases, European football in the
late 1970s and early 1980s was regarded as a marginal economic activity at
best. Second, the Commission appeared reluctant to use the direct sanction
of competition law against UEFA. The status of the Competition Policy
Directorate in the 1970s and early 1980s was not as established as it is today
(see next chapter). Furthermore, the question of the relationship between
sport and competition law was nascent. However, by 'sanctioning' the 3+2
nationality rule, the Commission was effectively sanctioning discriminatory
practises.

Background

On 10 May 1988, Jean Marc Bosman, a Belgian national, signed a two-year
contract with the Belgian first division football club, SA Royal Club Liégeois
(RC Liège). His contract with the club guaranteed him a gross basic salary,
excluding bonuses of 75,000 Belgian Francs (BFR) a month, up until its expi-
ration on 30 June 1990.[25] Under Article 5 of his contract with the club, it
was agreed that on expiry, either naturally or prematurely, the football club
would retain the player's registration. Any future transfer of the player at the

end of his contract would then be regulated by the rules of the Belgian Football Association.

In April 1990, two months before the end of the Bosman's contract, RC Liège offered the player a new one-year contract at BFR 30,000, the Belgian leagues (URBSFA) minimum wage.[26] Bosman rejected the new terms as it represented a significant pay cut. In accordance with Article 46 of the Associations rules on transfers of professional and non-amateur players on expiry of their contracts, the club placed him on the transfer list as a 'compulsory transfer' at a price of BFR 11,734,000, a price fixed by a calculation made on his last wage and the minimum in the event of him being transferred without the agreement of RC Liège. This means that if the player and the acquiring club agree to the transfer and the transfer fee set by the association's rules is paid, the transfer can go ahead even without the agreement of the vendor (the 'compulsory' transfer).

No club showed an interest in signing Bosman on a 'compulsory' transfer. On 1 June, the 'compulsory' element of the transfer came to an end and the period of 'free' transfer started. In this period a transfer fee can be freely negotiated as long as all three parties, including the vendor agrees. Bosman attempted to set up his own exit from the club by contacting an interested second division French league side, SA d'Économie Mixte Sportive de L'Union Sportive du Littoral de Dunkerque (US Dunkerque) who were prepared to offer the player BFR 90,000 a month. On the 27 July 1990, US Dunkerque and RC Liège agreed on the terms of the player's temporary transfer. The player was to move to US Dunkerque for one season in return for a payment of BFR 1,200,000, payable on receipt of the transfer certificate from URBSFA. US Dunkerque were given an option to purchase the player on a permanent basis at the end of the initial period for a further fee of BFR 4,800,000. The contracts between Bosman and US Dunkerque and US Dunkerque and RC Liège were conditional on the Belgian Association issuing a transfer certificate that was to reach the French Football Federation by 2 August.

Concerned about the solvency of Dunkerque, RC Liège did not seek the necessary international certificate from the Belgian Association. The transfer collapsed and under Article 46(5)(a) of the Belgian Association rules, RC Liège secured his suspension from the Belgian Football Authority on 31 July 1990. In its letter to the Association and to the player, the club explained, 'since no Belgian or foreign club has wished to transfer you and you have refused to sign that contract we find ourselves obliged to suspend you' (cited in Blanpain and Inston 1996: 62).

Unable to play professional football, Bosman applied to the Tribunal de Première in Liège on 8 August 1990. In addition to his main claim, Bosman applied for an interim order guaranteeing him three things. First, he wanted RC Liège and URBSFA to pay him BFR 100,000 a month whilst he found alternative employment. Second, to facilitate his search for alternative employment, Bosman wanted an order restraining RC Liège and URBSFA from claiming or levying any sum when appropriate work was found. Third, he wanted the case to be referred to the ECJ for a preliminary ruling.

On 9 November 1990, the Tribunal de Première ordered RC Liège to pay Bosman BFR 30,000 a month, granted the restraining order and referred the case to the ECJ seeking a preliminary ruling on the compatibility of the transfer system with Articles 6 and 39 of the Treaty. On 28 May 1991, on appeal, the Cour d'Appel in Liège quashed the Tribunal de Première's ruling relating to the preliminary reference to the ECJ. The first two orders relating to a monthly salary and a free transfer were however upheld. In June 1991, in response to this case, the ECJ withdrew Case-340/90 from its register.

Having been granted a free transfer, Bosman joined a French second division club, Saint-Quentin in October 1990. At the end of the season, that contract was terminated. In February 1992, Bosman signed for Saint-Denis de la Réunion, a contract also terminated after a short period. In May 1993, he then signed for a third division Belgian team, Royal Olympic Club de Charleroi. Suspicion grew that Bosman had been blacklisted by most European clubs.

In the main proceedings in August 1990, also brought before the Tribunal de Première, Bosman claimed damages against RC Liège. This related not only to breach of contract but also to the legality of the transfer system. In August 1991, Bosman brought action against UEFA as well attempting to have UEFA's transfer rules declared null and void and in breach of Articles 39, 81 and 82 of the EU Treaty. In April 1992, Bosman amended his claim against RC Liège and UEFA and brought a separate action against URBSFA. In these further applications, Bosman sought further compensation and attempted to reactivate the preliminary reference to the ECJ.

On 11 June 1992, the Tribunal de Première Instance ruled that RC Liège had acted unlawfully in causing Bosman's transfer to US Dunkerque to collapse. For this, Bosman was to be compensated. In addition, the national court made a reference to the ECJ for a preliminary ruling on the interpretation of Articles 39, 81 and 82 of the Treaty in relation to the operation of the transfer system. A further appeal was held before the Cour d'Appel in Liège in October 1993. The findings of the Tribunal de Première Instance were upheld and the Cour d'Appel made its own reference to the ECJ. Acting on a suggestion from Bosman, the national court also requested an examination of the rules relating to restrictions on foreign players. The Cour d'Appel submitted the following questions to the ECJ:

> Are Articles 39, 81 and 82 of the Treaty of Rome of March 1957 to be interpreted as: (1) prohibiting a football club from requiring and receiving payment of a sum of money upon the engagement of one of its players who has come to the end of his contract by a new employing club; and (2) prohibiting the national and international sporting associations or federations from including in their respective regulations provisions restricting access of foreign players from the European Community to the competitions which they organise?

These two questions relate to two UEFA sanctioned practices regarding transfer fees and restrictions on foreign players. First, under the UEFA international transfer rules, a club selling a player is entitled to compensation for training and development from the acquiring club, even if the player was no longer under contract with the vendor. Only the first club is entitled to compensation for training whereas each subsequent club is only entitled to a development fee. If the club's valuation of the player differs, a board of experts established by UEFA fixes the fee having taken into account the gross income of the player in the preceding season multiplied by a factor depending upon the player's age.

The second question related to the widely employed practise in European football of restricting the number of foreign players able to play for a club. After protracted consultations between the European Commission and UEFA, the 3 + 2 rule was adopted (see above). The ECJ handed down its full judgement on 15 December 1995. By doing so, the ECJ supplied the definitive answers to the questions posed by the national court.

Transfer rules

In relation to the application of Article 39 concerning transfer rules, the ECJ did not significantly diverge from the opinion of Advocate General Lenz. The ECJ dismissed the claims of URBSFA, UEFA and some national governments that Article 39 was not applicable. URBSFA had claimed that only the major clubs are economic units and that rules on transfers relate only to the relationship between clubs. UEFA had claimed that EU authorities have always respected the autonomy of sport and to change the transfer system would fundamentally affect the whole organisation of sport.[27] The German government had claimed that football is not an economic activity at all and sport should be seen in the same light as culture. In addition, the German government, referring to freedom of association and subsidiarity, argued that the EU must limit their involvement in this area to what is strictly necessary.[28]

The ECJ repeated the findings of the Advocate General in relation to the definition of sport as an economic activity.[29] Furthermore, the ECJ agreed with Advocate General Lenz in relation to the issue of transfer rules only concerning the relationship between clubs and not the relationship between club and player. If a player's employment opportunities are restricted by this relationship between clubs, then Article 39 is relevant.[30] In relation to UEFA's claim that an adverse ruling would have huge consequences for the organisation of football, the ECJ held that the consequences of a judgement cannot be allowed to interfere with the principle of law, nor its application.[31] On the question of the cultural analogy, the ECJ argued that this cannot be accepted because the original reference from the national court did not relate to the conditions under which EU powers of limited extent may be exercised but on the scope of the freedom of movement of workers guaranteed by Article 39.[32] Regarding the issue of freedom of association, the ECJ held that the rules laid down by sporting associations cannot be seen as necessary to ensure enjoyment of that freedom by those associations, by the clubs or players.[33] Finally, in relation to the claim that the principle of subsidiarity applies, the ECJ held that this principle cannot be used to restrict the exercise of rights conferred on individuals by the Treaty.[34] On the question as to whether the dispute between Bosman and URBSFA was wholly internal, the ECJ ruled that, although case law had established that Article 39 cannot be applied to situations that are wholly internal to member state, the cross border requirement had been in evidence as Bosman was seeking to move abroad.[35]

Accordingly, the ECJ held that Article 39 does apply to the rules laid down by URBSFA, FIFA or UEFA, thus confirming the horizontal direct effectiveness of Article 39. Having established this fact, the ECJ proceeded to assess the extent to which transfer rules form an obstacle to freedom of movement for workers. In this connection the ECJ agreed with Bosman and the Advocate General that these rules did constitute such an obstacle.[36] This point is not affected by the fact that UEFA's 1990 transfer rules state that the business relationship between the two clubs is to exert no influence on the activity of the player, who is free to play for his new club. Despite this reference, the purchasing club must still pay a fee to the vendor. As such the vendor maintains a financial interest in the player, even though they hold no contractual interest in him. This is an obstacle to the freedom of movement of workers. Furthermore, the fact that these rules are equally applied is irrelevant.

The ECJ held that the 'public interest' justification for the maintenance of the transfer system claimed by the defendants should also be dismissed. URBSFA, UEFA and the governments of France and Italy had claimed that transfer rules are justified by the need to maintain a financial and competitive balance between clubs and to support the search for talent and the training of young players.[37] In this connection, the ECJ agreed with the Advocate General that this aim was legitimate but less-restrictive measures could achieve the same aims as the transfer system.[38]

In answer to the first question posed by the national court, the ECJ therefore clearly answered that Article 39 precludes the application of transfer rules which permits payment for an out-of-contract player wishing to move between clubs in different member states.

Nationality restrictions

The ECJ drew the same conclusion in relation to the application of Article 39 to rules restricting the number of foreign players eligible to play for clubs. The ECJ held that Article 39(2) guarantees freedom of movement for workers and the abolition of any discrimination based on nationality. Nationality quotas clearly represent a breach of these provisions even though the rules relate to the fielding of players and not to their employment.[39] It is after all unlikely, although not unheard of, for clubs to employ players they are incapable of fielding. Having established the existence of an obstacle to free movement, the ECJ reviewed the arguments presented by UEFA, URBSFA and some national governments justifying such restrictions on the grounds that they were non-economic sporting rules. The ECJ rejected this justification in accordance with the Opinion of the Advocate General. First, on the question that nationality restrictions maintain the link between club and country, the ECJ held that no rule has been established linking a club to a locality, therefore none should exist linking a club to a country. Second, on the issue relating to nationality restrictions being necessary to ensure a pool of players eligible to play for the national team, the ECJ argued that no rules exist limiting a national team's choice of players to one association. National teams can still pick eligible players who play abroad. Third, the ECJ held that nationality restrictions do not maintain a competitive balance between clubs because the richer teams can still recruit the best national players regardless. Finally, in relation to UEFA's argument that nationality restrictions were sanctioned by the European Commission, the ECJ held that the Commission does not possess the power to authorise practices that are contrary to the Treaty.[40]

To the second question posed by the national court, the ECJ therefore once again held that Article 39 had been breached, this time in relation to the use of nationality restrictions. In relation to the application of Articles 81 and 82 (ex 85 and 86), the ECJ simply remarked, 'since both types of rule to which the national Court's questions refer are contrary to Article 48 (now 39), it is not necessary to rule on the interpretation of Articles 85 and 86 of the Treaty'.[41] On the grounds mentioned above, the ECJ answered the questions posed by the Cour d'Appel, Liège in the following way:

1 Article 48 of the EEC Treaty precludes the application of rules laid down by sporting associations, under which a professional footballer who is a national of one member state may not, on the expiry of his contract with a club, be employed by a club of another member state unless the latter club has paid the former club a transfer, training or development fee.
2 Article 48 of the EEC Treaty precludes the application of rules laid down by sporting associations under which, in matches in competitions which they organise, football clubs may field only a limited number of professional players who are nationals of other member states.
3 The direct effect of Article 48 of the EEC Treaty cannot be relied upon in support of claims relating to a fee in respect of transfer, training or development which has already been paid on, or is still payable under an obligation which arose before the date of this judgement, except by those who have brought proceedings or raised an equivalent claim under the applicable national law before that date.

The imposition of the temporal limitation on the judgement concerning the transfer system avoided the inevitable chaos a retroactive ruling on transfers would have created. Nevertheless, the impact of *Bosman* on sport had immediate effects (see for instance Morris *et al.* 1996, Miller 1996, Gardiner *et al.* 1998, Beloff *et al.* 1999 and Caiger and Gardiner 2000).

First, clearly the international transfer system and nationality rules had to be re-modelled. Nevertheless, the ruling does not directly affect transfers when a player is in contract. The ruling only affects players who are out of contract.

Second, internal transfer rules remain only theoretically untouched by *Bosman* because the ECJ decided to base the ruling on Article 39, not Article 81 relating to restrictive agreements. Article 39 applies only to the international transfer system and not to situations that are wholly internal. As such, national transfer rules continue to apply to cases where a player moves between two clubs in the same association. However, following *Bosman*, the Commission held the opinion that certain aspects of national transfer systems violate Article 81. Although the indirect consequence of the ruling saw most internal transfer rules being reformulated in Europe, the Commission continued their investigation into such rules leading to the total reformulation of transfer rules in 2001 (see next chapter).

Third, the ruling does not affect transfers of non-EU nationals from one EU/EEA state to another. Furthermore, the ruling does not concern transfers from the EU to third countries. However, although non-EU/EEA players cannot rely on the ruling in relation to transfers, players who are nationals of a country that has concluded an association or co-operation agreement with the EU prohibiting discrimination on the grounds of nationality cannot be excluded from playing in a team because of their nationality. This also assumes that the free movement provisions have direct effect. Such countries include Morocco, Tunisia, Algeria, Turkey, Poland, Slovakia, the Czech Republic, Bulgaria and Romania. Norway, Iceland and Liechtenstein are part of the European Economic Area (EEA) and are thus fully covered by the ruling. As such the ruling fully applies to 18 European countries.[42] The application of Article 81 may however alter the situation regarding the transfer of players from third countries.[43]

Fourth, the ruling does not affect the composition of national teams. This is because Article 39 relates only to economic activity and national teams are not deemed as such.[44] Is this view still defensible? In modern international sport many sportsmen and women have entered into appearance contracts with their national associations (Hoskins 1999: 10–11). As Leeds United and Rio Ferdinand discovered, participation in the Football World Cup can have an enormous influence on a player's value.[45]

Fifth, the ruling was not restricted to football. Sport, in so far as it constitutes an economic activity, is subject to EU law. This means that all sports in Europe operating restrictions on EU citizens and similar transfer rules to football, must comply. The main sports to be affected are ice hockey, basketball, handball and rugby. Clearly not all sports are as commercially developed as football.

Comment on Bosman

The ECJ first had to establish the applicability of Treaty rules to sports bodies. In this connection the ECJ did not break new ground by merely confirming the findings in *Walrave* and *Donà* which established that sport is subject to EU law in so far as it constitutes an economic activity. In addition the ECJ confirmed the horizontal direct effectiveness of Article 39. The reach of Article 39 (and for that matter 43 and 49) went beyond the acts of public authorities to cover the actions of private individuals and firms. Article 39 therefore covers any rules aimed at regulating employment in a collective manner. If Article 39 was not horizontally directly effective, private actors could effectively re-construct restrictions previously abolished between states.

The ECJ then needed to establish whether the rules on eligibility criteria and international transfer constituted restrictions. In this connection, the ECJ went beyond a mere confirmation of previous sports-related case law by suggesting that all restrictions to free movement (and not just discriminatory ones) are caught within the scope of Article 39.

Nationality rules   The ECJ found that UEFA's 3 + 2 nationality rules clearly placed foreign nationals at a disadvantage in comparison to home nationals. However, the ECJ held that nationality rules were not simply an example of discrimination, but were an obstacle to free movement as they restricted access to the employment market. This represents 'a significant change of emphasis' and one which potentially has far-reaching consequences for sport (O'Keefe and Osbourne 1996: 119). By taking this stance, the ECJ has established a much stronger link between sport and the EU. If nationality restrictions are not to be simply considered an issue of discrimination but rather an obstacle to free movement, then potentially a much greater range of sporting rules will be caught by the scope of Article 39. Therefore, rather than 'contracting' into the Treaty, sport must now justify why it should 'contract' out of it.

Transfer system   On transfers, the ECJ held that the nature of the transfer rules imposed non-discriminatory restrictions on players, even though such rules govern business relations between clubs. The ECJ decided to view the transfer rules as a restriction despite the fact that the existence of the transfer rule did not make it more difficult for a player to move between clubs in different member states than between clubs in the same state. As such, the ECJ held that the application of Article 39 went beyond a mere prohibition of discrimination, but extended to all restrictions. This extension had first been made in *Ramrath* and in *Kraus*, two cases unconcerned with sport.[46] However, *Bosman* differed from these cases because the restriction was not created in the host state but the home state, i.e. Bosman's own state of Belgium. Bosman's freedom of movement was restricted by the actions of parties within his own country, not the host country. Although previous cases prohibited restrictions being placed on an individual leaving a state (as opposed to entering) in relation to Article 43, this was the first occasion it was extended to Article 39. This broadening took place despite the ruling in *Keck*[47] in which the ECJ held that Article 28 (free movement of goods) does not apply to rules on certain selling arrangements provided that they apply to all relevant traders within the national territory and that they affect in same manner, in law and in fact, the marketing of domestic and imported goods. A case can therefore be made to apply *Keck* to *Bosman* given that transfer rules applied equally to all clubs in all member states and affected foreign and domestic transfers equally. The ECJ chose not to extend *Keck* beyond the free movement of goods, instead relying on the *Alpine Investments* ruling.[48] *Alpine* concerned restrictions within the host state affecting access to the market of another member state. *Keck* concerned the rules of the 'importing' state. The ECJ therefore made a distinction between the two cases equating *Bosman* with *Alpine* and not *Keck* (O'Keefe and Osbourne 1996: 116–118).

Having established that nationality rules and transfer rules constitute restrictions on mobility, the ECJ had to examine the question of justified restrictions and proportionality. At issue here was the sporting exception. Restrictions of a discriminatory nature can only be justified if covered by Article 39(3) relating to grounds of public policy, public security or public health. Non-discriminatory measures can only be justified by 'imperative reasons' such as the need to protect sports social function. However, as indicated above, these justifications do not take sport outside the scope of EU law. This is a significant finding and one which distinguishes *Bosman* from earlier sports-related case law. The ECJ indicated that sport possesses particular features that mark it out from other 'normal' industries. However, the justifications submitted to the ECJ in support of the maintenance of nationality rules and the transfer system were rejected, thus placing further limits on concept of a sporting exception. Such restrictions were not considered proportionate to the aims submitted. Basing their judgement on the opinion of the Advocate General, the ECJ argued that alternative measures such as collective wage agreements and financial redistribution between the clubs were more proportionate measures. Both mechanisms contain features that would arguably be considered illegal in 'normal' industries. Whilst, therefore, the ECJ's ruling represented a damning condemnation of traditional sporting practices, it is incorrect to assume that the Court treated sport in the same manner as any other industry. Arguably, therefore, the birth of EU sports law had its roots in *Bosman*. Nevertheless, *Bosman* had more to do with the Single Market project and the scope of Article 39 than it did sport. The sweeping condemnation of all out-of-contract payments rejected any notion of a reformed transfer system – a possibility raised by the Advocate General.[49]

[handwritten note: ~Became EU law because of ECJ ruling: no going back.]

Article 39 : free moment of workers

Nevertheless, *Bosman* has far-reaching consequences for sport. Sport is clearly subject to EU law and Article 39 is horizontally directly effective. Furthermore, Article 39 extends beyond the prohibition of discriminatory practices to include non-discriminatory practices which restricts free movement. By adopting such an approach the argument is now less concerned with whether sport falls outside the Treaty but under what circumstances are sports rules justifiable under the Treaty. However, the key implication of *Bosman* related to enforcement. The full consequences of *Walrave* and *Donà* did not occur because the Commission did not rigorously enforce the rulings. Following *Bosman* the Commission became more energetic in enforcing the competition policy implications of the ruling. This has had a profound effect on how sport is being regulated in the twenty-first century.

the implication was enforcement
× IMPACT of BOSMAN RULING

The *Deliège* and *Lehtonen* cases

As indicated above, in *Bosman* the ECJ recognised 'the considerable social importance of sporting activities'.[50] However, it went on to explain why nationality restrictions and the operation of the international transfer system could not be justified and as such exempted from the application of Article 39. Nevertheless, as Foster explains, 'in retrospect this paragraph can be seen as the genesis of the Court's attempt to formulate a policy of non-intervention in sport' (Foster 2000a: 47). The ECJ has recently been requested to consider two further sports-related disputes, one concerning judo, the other basketball.

Christelle Deliège *v.* Asbl Ligue Francophone de Judo and Others[51]
In *Deliège*, the ECJ heard a case concerning a Belgian judoka who claimed that her career had been impeded by the refusal of the Belgium judo authority to allow her to participate in the 1992 Olympic Games held in Barcelona and the 1996 Games held in Atlanta. In order to participate in these events potential participants needed the authorisation from the relevant national federation. Although considered a very good judoka, Miss Deliège failed to make the Belgian Olympic team, having failed to achieve the necessary qualification criteria. Failure to gain selection would undoubtedly inhibit her career. Miss Deliège believed that, although judo is considered an amateur pursuit, she was carrying out an economic activity and as such had economic rights guaranteed by Articles 49, 81 and 82 of the EC Treaty. The case was referred to the ECJ by the Tribunal de Première de Namur who asked:

> Whether or not it is contrary to the Treaty of Rome, in particular Articles 49, 81 and 82 of the Treaty, to require professional or semi-professional athletes or persons aspiring to professional or semi-professional activity to be authorised by their federation in order to be able to compete in an international competition which does not involve national teams competing against each other.

As in *Bosman*, the ECJ did not address the question of competition law. On the question of the freedom to provide services, the ECJ confirmed that the activities of athletes (even amateur athletes) are capable of falling within the scope of Article 49. Organising the sporting contest allows the organisers to commercially exploit the secondary features of the contest such as broadcasting and sponsorship rights. Furthermore, Deliège received a grant to train and compete. Despite giving clear guidance in this matter, the ECJ did not form an opinion on whether Miss Deliège's activities were economic in nature. This was for the national court to decide. The ECJ did however acknowledge the 'considerable social importance of sport'[52] and did refer to the Amsterdam Treaty's Declaration on the social significance of sport.[53] In this connection, the ECJ considered the selection rules derived from a need inherent in the organisation of the sport and as such were not to be considered a restriction on the ability to provide services. Allowing anyone to compete in competitions is clearly unworkable. However, the ECJ held that sports organisations must be able to demonstrate that selection rules are based on objective justifiable principles. On 11 April 2000, the ECJ delivered its judgement. It held:

> A rule requiring professional or semi-professional athletes or persons aspiring to take part in a professional or semi-professional activity to have been authorised or selected by their federation in order to be able to participate in a high-level international sports competition, which does not involve national teams competing against each other, does not in itself, as long as it derives from a need inherent in the organisation of such a competition, constitute a restriction on the freedom to provide services prohibited by Article 49 of the EC Treaty.

Lehtonen and Castors Canada Dry Namur-Braine *v.* Fédération Royale des Sociétés de Basketball and Ligue Belge-Belgische Liga[54]

The second case concerned transfer deadlines in Belgian Basketball. Jyri Lehtonen, a Finnish Basketball player was transferred from a Finnish to a Belgian basketball team. However, the Belgian basketball federation refused to register him on the grounds that the transfer had not taken place within the specified 'transfer window'. Un-registered players are prevented from competing in Belgian competitions. In Belgium, players are unable to be transferred outside these transfer seasons. This is a common practise in European sport. To make matters worse for Castors Braine, the Belgian team who had acquired Lehtonen, they had already played him in a winning game only to have the result over-turned due to the breach of transfer rules. Lehtonen and Castors Braine applied to the Court of First Instance in Brussels for an interim order on the over-turned match and the sanctions imposed on Lehtonen. The national court referred the following question to the ECJ:

Are the rules of a sports federation which prohibit a club from playing a player in the competition for the first time if he has been engaged after a specified date contrary to the Treaty of Rome (in particular Articles 12, 39, 81 and 82) in the case of a professional player who is a national of a member state of the European Union, notwithstanding the sporting reasons put forward by the federations to justify those rules, namely the need to prevent distortion of the competitions?

In answering the above question, the ECJ was guided by *Walrave, Donà* and *Bosman* in deciding that the activities of sport are subject to EU law and that employees of sports clubs are to be considered workers. However, as in *Deliège*, the ECJ acknowledged the 'considerable social importance of sport' and made further mention of the Amsterdam Treaty's Declaration on the social significance of sport.[55] On the question of whether the rules on transfer deadlines constituted a restriction on free movement, the ECJ found that the rule in question was such an obstacle even though the restriction related to fielding players and not employing them. The ECJ then had to decide whether such restrictions were justifiable and proportionate. Could the rule be justified as non-economic in nature and as such of sporting interest only? In the Opinion of the Advocate General, the protection of a sporting competition against distortion is in the public interest. As such public interest justifications could be employed to protect transfer deadlines. The ECJ agreed with the submissions of the Basketball Federation that rules on transfer deadlines were sporting rules which were necessary for the organisation of the game. Late transfers could substantially alter the sporting strength of teams in the course of the championship thus calling into question the proper functioning of sporting competition. However, the ECJ argued that such rules must not go beyond what is necessary for achieving the desired aim. The differential treatment of players from inside and outside Europe, which the rules promoted, went beyond what was necessary and as such were prohibited by Article 39.[56] Again, the ECJ did not address the question of competition law. Therefore in answer to the questions referred by the Tribunal de Première Instance, Brussels, on 13 April 2000, the ECJ held:

> Article 39 EC precludes the application of rules laid down in a member state by sporting associations which prohibit a basketball club from fielding players from other member states in matches in the national championship, where they have been transferred after a specified date, if that date is earlier than the date which applies to transfers of players from certain non member countries, unless objective reasons concerning only sport as such or relating to differences between the position of players from a federation in the European zone and that of players from a federation not in that zone justify such different treatment.

Comment on Deliège *and* Lehtonen

Deliège and *Lehtonen* bring a degree of respite for sport without undermining previous sports case law. As Bell and Turner-Kerr remark, 'at a time when it seems that the legality of nearly every sports regulation is being called into question, it is at least welcome for the ECJ to recognise that there are certain areas where sports governing bodies retain the authority and competence to regulate the disciplines for which they are responsible' (Bell and Turner-Kerr 2002: 260). In essence the rules which sports bodies retain competence over concern those which are inherent in the conduct and/or organisation of sporting events.

The significance of *Deliège* lies in the ECJ's view that selection criteria do not necessarily constitute a restriction under Article 49. This places a small limit on the application to sporting contexts of the freedom to provide services provisions. In *Lehtonen*, the significant finding is that, even though transfer windows do constitute a restriction to free movement, they are able to be justified on sporting grounds and as such are capable of being exempt from the application of Article 39.[57] The Opinion of the Advocate General who equated such sporting interest arguments not with sporting autonomy justifications but with the 'public interest' justification is potentially significant. If sports bodies are able to connect sporting interest arguments with public interest justifications, this could act as a vehicle for the protection of the remaining autonomy sports organisations possess. Given that the purpose of Articles 39 and 49 is to protect workers and not the organisation of sport, the public interest finding could prove a significant precedent for sports bodies, particularly given that the Commission are beginning to draw similar findings in connection with their sports-related competition law case load.

The *Bosman* ruling demonstrated that the ECJ was sensitive to the economic context surrounding the recently completed Single Market project. The *Deliège* and *Lehtonen* rulings also need placing in context. First, the rulings took place within the context of an on-going discussion in the EU on how best to reconcile the economic and socio-cultural dimensions of sport within the EU structure.[58] Significantly, in both cases the ECJ made mention of the Amsterdam Treaty's Declaration on Sport, even though it carries no legal force. The reference to the Declaration indicates that the ECJ has been sensitive to this debate. Although the ECJ has consistently refused to answer referred questions concerning competition law, the reference to the Declaration has undoubtedly informed the Commission's approach to sport.

Second, *Bosman* allowed the ECJ to clarify and extend some important issues relating to the scope of Article 39. The legal broadening that took place in *Bosman* was arguably as significant to the free movement of workers as the wide definition of restriction adopted in *Dassonville* was to the free movement of goods.[59] As such, following *Bosman*, *Lehtonen* placed limits on the scope of Article 39 in a manner similar to *Keck's* limitation of Article 28 following *Dassonville*.

Nevertheless, as Foster argues, there are limits to the rulings. In *Lehtonen*, the ECJ made specific mention of the impact transfer deadlines have on play-off games.[60] Does this justification extend to all-play-all leagues? Some sports prevent a player from competing for two separate sides in a knock-out competition but allow this in a league format. As such, 'the general legality of transfer deadlines per se cannot safely be assumed by the judgment' (Foster 2000a: 49). Furthermore, in *Deliège*, it remains unclear exactly what objective standards for selection are. Objective criteria is apparent in sports such as tennis and golf where rankings and handicap determine competition entrance. However, subjective criteria is apparent in other team sports where picking players who 'blend' is more important than picking the best players. *Deliège* also avoided the question of selection for national teams. The ECJ held that it was affiliation to the appropriate national federation that was the basis for selection to international tournaments and not nationality (Foster 2000: 51). In a wider sense, the key limit to the rulings is that very little sport has been taken outside the scope of the Treaty. In fact, by finding that unpaid amateur sports men and women are workers, the rulings have effectively further undermined the concept of sport as a non-economic activity.

Conclusions

The value of an actor-centred institutional analysis is demonstrated when observing the impact of ECJ jurisprudence on the sports policy subsystem. An 'old' institutional analysis would tend to confirm the privileged position the Court enjoys in terms of interpreting and applying the law. A 'new' institutional analysis reveals the extent to which informal practices and complex institutional relationships have affected the development of EU sports law and policy.

The ECJ is clearly an important agenda setter in the EU in that it not only defines the content of the EU's systemic agenda, it also specifies the conditions under which an issue is transferred to the institutional agenda for active policy development. The role of the ECJ in this respect should not however be viewed as deterministic. The relationship between the ECJ and the other EU institutions is crucial for policy definition. Sufficient sports-related case law exists to illustrate this point. ECJ rulings in *Walrave* and *Donà* established sport as an item on the EU's systemic agenda. The rulings established that sport was subject to EU law whenever practiced as an economic activity. The rulings should be seen in the context of the time. The 1970s have been characterised as a period of stagnation for the EU. Economic and political crisis contributed to a slowing of 'ever-closer union'. In the absence of a political impetus, the ECJ ensured the original Treaty of Rome bargain was continued. Hence, *Walrave* and *Donà* served to widen the scope of the Treaty and afford greater protection to workers. The impact of the rulings on sport was however limited. The Commission did little to enforce the central findings in the cases, preferring instead a negotiated settlement with the sports authorities. As such, sport remained in a largely latent regulatory space and the transfer of sport from the EU's systemic to the institutional agenda remained incomplete.

The major impetus for sports eventual passage on to the institutional agenda for active EU consideration came with *Bosman*. *Bosman* destroyed the Commission's negotiated settlement approach. The changed economic status of sport contributed to the ECJ's forceful ruling and the Commission's more energetic use of competition law to enforce *Bosman*. Despite the submissions of various governments in *Bosman*, the ECJ's ruling was also a response to a political impetus. Although a legal and bureaucratic exercise of immense proportions, the newly completed Single Market represented a triumph of political will. The ECJ's extension of the scope of Article 39 was consistent with the broad thrust of the Single European Act/Single European Market project. As such, sports functional link to the Single Market was an unanticipated consequence of the wider Single Market project. Sport now operated within a EU regulatory environment. The legal consequence of *Bosman* was that the EU no longer had to justify why sport was subject to EU law, but rather sport would have to justify why it should be exempt from the Treaty. Even so, the acknowledgement by the ECJ that sport was different to other 'normal' industries may be interpreted as the genesis of EU sports law.

Items on the EU's systemic agenda are often transferred on to the institutional agenda with definitional bias. Sport, for instance, was transferred through a legal/regulatory venue involving a close relationship between the ECJ and the Commission. However, the EU's institutional agenda is very open. As an item for active policy consideration, sport has proved a relatively malleable item. The rulings in *Deliège* and *Lehtonen* again reflect the political context of the day. The ECJ has confirmed that sport is subject to EU law but has given clearer guidelines on sporting justification arguments. In this connection, the ECJ has been sensitive to the post-*Bosman* political debate on how to reconcile EU law with sports social status. *Deliège* and *Lehtonen* represent the ECJ's contribution to the construction of the separate territories approach and, therefore, the development of EU sports law. The member states, the European Parliament and the Education and Culture Directorate General have been active in promoting this message. *Deliège* and *Lehtonen* have also informed the activities of the Directorate General for Competition Policy. Whereas the ECJ has responded to the political debate by being sympathetic to the 'inherent sporting rule' justification when deciding cases, the Commission has recently indicated that exemptions from competition law may be an appropriate way of reconciling EU law with sports social status. It is to this that the next chapter turns.

Notes

1　Case 36/74, *Walrave and Koch* v. *Association Union Cycliste Internationale* [1974] ECR 1405. Case 13/76, *Donà* v. *Mantero* [1976] ECR 1333. Case 222/86, *UNECTEF* v. *Heylens* [1987] ECR 4097.

2   Case C-415/93, *Union Royale Belge Sociétés de Football Association and Others* v. *Bosman* [1995] ECR I-4291.

3   Joined cases C-51/96 and C-191/97, *Deliège* v. *Asbl Ligue Francophone de Judo and others* [2000] ECR I-2549. Case C-176/96, *Jyri Lehtonen and Castors Canada Dry Namur-Braine* v. *Fédération Royale des Sociétés de Basketball and Ligue Belge-Belgische Liga* [2000] ECR I-2681.

4   Case 26/62, *Van Gend en Loos* v. *Nederlandse Administratie der Belastingen* [1963] ECR I. Case 6/64, *Costa* v. *ENEL* [1964] ECR 585.

5   See note 4.

6   Article 234.

7   Case 167/73, *Commission* v. *French Republic* [1974] ECR 359. Re: nationality restrictions in the French maritime sector.

8   *Walrave*, para 17.

9   Case 152/73, *Sotgiu* v. *Deutsche Bundespost* [1974] ECR 153. Re: the discriminatory granting of allowances to workers.

10 Case 66/85, *Lawrie-Blum* v. *Land Baden-Württemberg* [1986] ECR 2121.

11 *Walrave*, para. 4.

12 Case 2/74, *Reyners* v. *Belgian State* [1974] ECR 631. Re: refused admission to the Belgian bar on nationality grounds.

13 The Spanish cycling association was later dismissed from the suit. At the time, Spain was not a member of the EU.

14 *Walrave*, para. 5.

15 *Walrave*, para. 8.

16 *Walrave*, para. 17.

17 *Walrave*, para. 28.

18 Case 13/76, *Donà* v. *Mantero* [1976] ECR 1333.

19 Facts taken from Opinion of Advocate General Trabucchi, Delivered on 6 July 1976.

20 Case 222/86, *UNECTEF* v. *Heylens* [1987] ECR 4097.

21 *Heylens*, paras. 8–10.

22 *Wilander* v. *Tobin* [1997] EuLR 265.

23 *Edwards* v. *British Athletics Federation and International Amateur Athletics Federation* [1997] EuLR 721.

24 Case C-415/93, *Union Royale Belge Sociétés de Football Association and Others* v. *Bosman* [1995] ECR I-4291.

25 With bonuses and other payments, the players' average monthly earnings were in the region of BFR 120,000.

26 As specified in the statutes of ASBL Union Royale Belge des Sociétés de Football Association (URBSFA).

27 *Bosman*, para. 71.

28 *Bosman*, para. 72.

29 *Bosman*, para. 73.

30 *Bosman*, para. 75.

31 *Bosman*, para. 77.

32 *Bosman*, para. 78.

33 *Bosman*, para. 80.

34 *Bosman*, para. 81.

35 *Bosman*, paras. 88–91.

36 *Bosman*, para. 104.
37 *Bosman*, para. 105.
38 *Bosman*, para. 110.
39 *Bosman*, para. 120.
40 *Bosman*, paras. 123–136.
41 *Bosman*, para. 138.
42 In case C-438/00, *Deutscher Händballbund e. v. v. Maros Kolpak* (pending), the Advocate General has formed the opinion that rules of a sports association restricting the participation of Slovak players in Championship and Cup matches of federal and regional leagues are contrary to Article 38 of the EU–Slovakia Agreement.
43 Note the opinion of the Advocate General in Case C-246/98, *Tiborbalog* v. *Royal Charleroi Sporting*, Opinion of 29 March 2001 (case subsequently withdrawn). See next chapter.
44 See Case 13/76, *Donà* v. *Mantero* [1976] ECR 1333.
45 Ferdinand joined Leeds from West Ham in November 2000 for £18 million. Following a series of good performances for England in the 2002 Japan/South Korea World Cup he joined Manchester United for £30 million in July 2002. Now let's never mention it again.
46 Case C-106/91, *Ramrath* v. *Ministre de la Justice* [1992] ECR I-3351; Case C-19/92, *Kraus* v. *Land Baden-Württemberg* [1993] ECR I-1663.
47 Joined cases C-267 and 268/91, *Keck and Mithouard* [1993] ECR I-6097. Re: the prohibited practice under French law of reselling goods at a loss.
48 C-384/93, *Alpine Investments BV* v. *Minister van Financiën* [1995] ECR I-1141. Re: a Dutch ban on unsolicited telephoning of potential customers.
49 Opinion of the Advocate General, para. 239.
50 *Bosman*, para. 106.
51 Joined cases C-51/96 and C-191/97, *Deliège* v. *Asbl Ligue Francophone de Judo and Others* [2000] ECR I-2549.
52 *Deliège*, para. 41.
53 *Deliège*, para. 42.
54 *Lehtonen*.
55 Paras. 32 and 33 *Lehtonen*.
56 Players from a federation outside the European zone were subject to a transfer deadline of 31 March, whereas players inside the European zone were subject to a transfer deadline of February 28.
57 *Lehtonen*, para 51–55.
58 See Chapter 6.
59 Case 8/74, *Procureur du Roi* v. *Dassonville* [1974] ECR 837. Re: the importation into Belgium of a consignment of Scotch whisky purchased from French distributors without a certificate of origin required by Belgian law.
60 *Lehtonen*, para. 55.

5

Sport and EU competition law

[handwritten annotation: Commercial significance over + above social, cultural and educational dimensions.]

In applying EU competition law to sport, the Directorate General for Competition Policy (herein referred to as the Commission) has been caught between three powerful forces. First, the Commission has a constitutional commitment to promote and protect the free market principles on which much of the Treaty of Rome is based. In this capacity it shares a close relationship with the ECJ. The ECJ's rulings in *Walrave*, *Donà* and *Bosman* have played an important role in placing sport on the EU's systemic agenda in a regulatory form. The Commission has a constitutional obligation to follow the ECJ's line of reasoning on sport, given its role in enforcing ECJ rulings. As such, sport has passed on to the EU's institutional agenda through the regulatory venue, the prevailing definition stressing sports commercial significance over and above its social, cultural and educational dimensions.

The second major influence on Commission jurisprudence in the sports sector is administrative. Although primary and secondary legislation has equipped the Commission with the necessary legal powers to execute this commitment, it lacks the necessary administrative means to carry out formal investigations into abuses in all sectors of the economy. In the face of a large *[handwritten: So non-action not always wanted.]* and growing caseload, the Commission has had to adopt creative means in order to turn over cases. In particular, the Commission has resorted to the use of informal procedures to settle cases rather than adopting formal deci- *[handwritten: with this one? yes]* sions. For some time it has been felt by Commission officials that the procedures for applying competition law are in need of reform. It is within this context that in September 2000, the Commission proposed a regulation to devolve its competition powers to national courts and regulatory agencies.[1] The proposed Regulation seeks to establish a system whereby 'both the prohibition rule set out in Article 81(1) and the exemption rule contained in Article 81(3) can be directly applied by not only the Commission but also *[handwritten: Do they now?]* national courts and national competition authorities'.[2] This would in effect end the Commission's monopoly over the application of Article 81(3). Whilst the Commission's proposal acknowledges that the system worked well with six member states, the monopoly has created difficulties for the uniform application of competition powers in an enlarged EU. However, the very reason for needing reform may hinder the viability of the Commission's proposal. For national regulatory bodies to play a more active role in applying competition law requires familiarity with existing practice in case law. Due to the resource problem, the Commission has however settled many cases through negotiation rather than formal channels. In areas such as sport, where the use of soft law is most pronounced, case law precedents are thin.

The third pressure is political. Although the Commission has been fairly successful in shielding itself from close member state control, it does not operate in an environment immune from the wider political context. The EU's institutional agenda is very open and affords actors the opportunity to exploit a multiplicity of venues in order to influence policy. As such, once an item reaches the institutional agenda a range of actors can become involved in the policy debate. In the case of sport, not all have accepted the definition of sport adopted by the ECJ and the Commission. The application of EU competition law has evolved in the context of an on-going debate in the EU as to the real nature of sport. Should sport merely be seen as an economic activity or does sport possess social, cultural and educational values worthy of protection from law? The member states have emerged as a powerful advocate of this more broad-based approach to sport. This has involved the construction of the separate territories approach for sport. The Commission is central to the construction of this approach, although, as is discussed below, the proposal to devolve competition powers (particularly the exemption procedure) to national regulatory authorities may pose some difficulties for the construction of the separate territories.

The Commission's constitutional obligation to safeguarding the fundamentals of the Single Market has therefore had to be balanced by administrative and political pragmatism. The Commission has generally adopted a two-fold strategy. On the one hand it has consistently followed the ECJ's line that sport is subject to EU law whenever practiced as an economic activity. This allows the Commission to claim that the fundamentals of the Single Market have not been compromised. On the other hand, the Commission has been willing to recognise sports social, cultural and educational values when considering the applicability of exemptions. In this connection, the Commission has to make a distinction between rules that are of sporting interest only and rules which have commercial implications. As the Commission has acquired more experience in these matters so it has been more active in formulating a competition law separate territories approach. The Commission hopes that this approach will add more legal certainty to what is a relatively new area of Commission activity.

This chapter explores these issues in six sections. The first section reviews EU competition law, concentrating in particular on restrictive practices and abuses of dominant positions in the Single Market. The second section examines the generic relationship between sport and competition law. Should sports rules fall within the scope of competition law? Sections three, four and five analyse the specific relationships between sport and competition law. The sports market comprises three markets (Egger and Stix-Hackl 2002: 85–87). The exploitation market, in which clubs and federations exploit secondary features of their performances such as broadcasting rights, exclusive distribution networks for ticket sales and merchandising arrangements, is considered in section three. Section four analyses the contest market where the actual product, the sporting contest, is made. Rules concerning the organisation of sport are addressed in this section. Section five examines the supply market – the market in the buying and selling of players. The final section examines the Commission's general approach to sport by reviewing the sports-related case law within the context of the Commission's paper on the development of a framework for the application of competition law to sport, the first formal exploration of the viability of constructing separate territories of sporting autonomy and competition law.

European Union competition policy

Article 3 of the EC Treaty states that the activities of the Community should include the establishment of a system ensuring that competition in the Single Market is not distorted. Following the signing of the Treaty of Rome, the precise nature of this system was set out in Articles 85–94 of the Treaty (now 81–89). The two Articles most relevant to the sports sector in Europe are Articles 81 (ex 85), dealing with restrictive practices by undertakings and Article 82 (ex 86), concerning the abuse of a dominant position by an undertaking.

Despite the Treaty base for competition policy being established by the Treaty of Rome, a fully fledged competition policy did not come into operation until the passing of Regulation 17/62 establishing the procedures for applying the competition provisions contained in the Treaty. Although this body of primary and secondary legislation granted the Commission considerable scope for applying competition law, it was not until the 1980s that it began to fully exercise the full potential of their powers. Doern and Wilks identified three reasons accounting for this. First, the EU entered a new phase of development in the 1980s as domestic neo-liberal ideas found expression at the European level through the exercise of tighter rules of competition. Second, the political leadership of Sutherland and Brittan contributed to the visibility and the maturation of the Directorate General for Competition Policy. Third, through this leadership, the Commission sought innovative ways of expanding the scope of European competition policy, the creation of the Merger Regulation being the highlight of this activity (Doern and Wilks 1996: 232). By the 1990s the Commission had established a strong reputation for itself. However, the problem of a lack of resources persists.

This problem has resulted in a slow turnover of cases and the increased use of administrative procedures rather than formal decisions to decide cases.

Today, competition policy is exercised with both economic and political objectives in mind. In economic terms, the competition provisions are consistent with the free market ethos that underpinned much of the Treaty. Only in selected areas such as agriculture can an overtly protectionist agenda be detected. The belief in the market mechanism was clear, but only by enforcing strict rules of competition can the EU hope to establish many buyers and sellers within the market which would help improve the allocation of resources and in turn benefit consumers. As competition policy has evolved, so these rules have been central to the establishment of a more economically and politically cohesive Single European Market and increasingly a tool for helping European undertakings compete in the global marketplace.

Article 81

Article 81 comprises three paragraphs:

1 The following shall be prohibited as incompatible with the common market: all agreements between undertakings, decisions by associations of undertakings and concerted practices which may affect trade between member states and which have as their object or effect the prevention, restriction or distortion of competition within the common market, and in particular those which:
   a directly or indirectly fix purchase or selling prices or any other trading conditions;
   b limit or control production, markets, technical development, or investment;
   c share markets or sources of supply;
   d apply dissimilar conditions to equivalent transactions with other trading parties, thereby placing them at a competitive disadvantage;
   e make the conclusion of contracts subject to acceptance by the other parties of supplementary obligations which, by their nature or according to commercial usage, have no connection with the subject of such contracts.
2 Any agreements or decisions prohibited pursuant to this Article shall be automatically void.
3 The provisions of paragraph 1 may, however, be declared inapplicable in the case of:
   • any agreement or category of agreements between undertakings;
   • any decision or category of decisions by associations of undertakings;
   • any concerted practice or category of concerted practices,
   which contributes to improving the production or distribution of goods or to promoting technical or economic progress, while allowing consumers a fair share of the resulting benefit, and which does not:
   a impose on the undertakings concerned restrictions which are not indispensable to the attainment of these objectives;
   b afford such undertakings the possibility of eliminating competition in respect of a substantial part of the products in question.

Accordingly, for Article 81 to apply a number of conditions must be met. First, it must be determined by the Commission that an agreement between undertakings, decisions by associations of undertakings and concerted practices has taken place. Although the term agreement is not defined in the Treaty, the Commission has usually adopted a wide interpretation of it. Similarly, the term undertakings is not defined and again the Commission's wide interpretation brings into the definition any entity engaged in economic or commercial activity involving the provision of goods and services. Undertakings whose activity only generates a small profit and even non-profit undertakings are included in this definition. Should such entities co-ordinate their activities they may be described as associations of undertakings. Anti-competitive effects stemming from decisions by associations of undertakings also fall within the scope of Article 81. Such decisions need not be formally constituted. For example codes of conduct have been regarded as decisions. If undertakings co-ordinate activity between themselves in such a way as to fall short of an agreement, then this behaviour may amount to a concerted practice.

The second condition required for Article 81 to apply concerns the nature of the agreement. Article 81 seeks to prevent agreements which have as their object or effect the prevention, restriction or distortion of competition within the Single Market. Article 81 itself lists some agreements which distort competition. The definition of anti-competitive agreements has widened through the jurisprudence of the Commission and the ECJ. For instance in the *Consten* case the ECJ extended the scope of Article 81 beyond horizontal agreements (for instance, agreements between undertakings operating at the same level in the system of distribution) to vertical agreements (for instance, agreements at different levels such as between producers and distributors).[3] Furthermore in *Consten*, the ECJ argued that if it can be determined that the object of the agreement was the prevention, restriction or distortion of competition, the agreement can be condemned without further market analysis of its impact. Therefore such an analysis is only required in circumstances where the agreement in question has the effect (and not the original intention) of being anti-competitive. Agreements which are of minor significance will not be caught by the provisions of Article 81 and will therefore be subject to the *de minimis* limitation. In such circumstances and others where the agreement falls outside the scope of Article 81(1), the Commission will issue a negative clearance. Negative clearances constitute a formal decision.

The third condition relates to the requirement that the agreement must affect trade between member states. Agreements which only affect trade within one member state or agreements the impacts of which lie outside the EU are unlikely to be caught by the scope of Article 81. The ECJ has given guidance concerning the calculation as to whether an agreement affects inter-state trade patterns.[4]

The Commission can become aware of potential illegalities in a number of ways. First, it can launch its own investigation. The Commission's powers of investigation are considerable and are detailed in Regulation 17/62. These include the power to request information, the ability to scrutinise documentation and ask on the spot questions and the right to enter premises. Second, as the Commission currently has a monopoly over the right to issue exemptions, a self-notification system is in operation for undertakings to inform the Commission of agreements and practices. Finally, individual complainants bring potential abuses to the attention of the Commission.

Having become aware of potential competition violations, the Commission must resolve the case. Again, a number of options are available to it. First, due to the political and administrative pressures the Commission works under, many cases are settled through informal channels. Undertakings seeking a negative clearance or exemption from Article 81 will notify the agreement in question to the Commission. Following the notification, a series of informal consultations between the relevant party and the Commission takes place. Aspects of the agreement which the Commission objects to are removed. The Commission then usually issues a 'comfort letter' informing the party that the agreement does not infringe Article 81(1) or that an exemption is suitable. These letters do not hold the legal force of a Commission decision but are a useful way of communicating the Commission's views. Frequently, the undertakings themselves favour this negotiated settlement. The problem with the informal soft law approach is that the legal environment is not clarified. Firms are not guided by the legal certainty formal decision making creates. Particularly in relation to the regulation of new sectors such as sport, the lack of legal principles often creates confusion (see below). The Commission is aware of this and has introduced a more formal comfort letter which it publishes in the *Official Journal*. This gives them a more formal appearance and notifies interested third parties of the 'decision'. This allows third parties to submit observations prior to the Commission formally closing the file. In addition, the Commission has relied heavily on other informal tools to communicate their position. These include press releases, notices and annual reviews. As with comfort letters, these tools hold no legal effect. The cumulative impact of them in establishing *de facto* precedents is however considerable.

The second method of resolving cases involves the Commission taking a formal decision to grant negative clearance. The Commission follows this course of action if it believes that the agreement or practice falls outside the scope of Article 81. The third method involves the Commission finding that an agreement infringes Article 81. In these circumstances it will send a statement of objections to the relevant parties outlining the case against them. Once the parties have responded to the statement of objections a hearing is convened. In effect the Commission acts as prosecutor and judge. A formal decision of a finding of infringement may result from this procedure in which case the Commission can declare the agreement void (Article 81(2)). The Commission also has the power to issue interim orders.

The final method involves applying the exemption criteria outlined in Article 81(3). Agreements which contribute to improving the production or distribution of goods or to promoting technical or economic progress, while allowing consumers a fair share of the resulting benefit, may be exempted from the application of Article 81(1). Under the provisions of Regulation 17/62, the Commission has the power to grant individual and block exemptions. An individual exemption can only be granted if the agreement in question has been notified to the Commission. Formal individual exemptions issued by the Commission can only be granted if the four conditions contained in Article 81(3) are applied. Exemptions are published in the *Official Journal* and are reviewable by the Court of First Instance (CFI) and the ECJ on further appeal. The formal process of issuing individual exemptions is however time consuming. A lack of resources and the requirement to issue speedy decisions has contributed to the wider use of the Commission's informal procedures for communicating their thoughts on a particular agreement. For these reasons, the Commission has also made more use of the block exemption procedure. Block exemptions are more generic in nature and cover particular agreements in a whole sector. In addition to the Commission, the Council has the legal right to issue block exemptions under the authority of Article 87 (State Aid). Examples of block exemptions include Liner shipping agreements and motor vehicle distribution agreements (Goyder 1998: 131).[5] The Commission's proposal to amend the procedures for applying competition law by replacing the current system of self-notification with a devolved competition regime involving national courts and national regulatory authorities will, if accepted, affect the current system for granting individual exemptions (see above).[6]

Article 82
The focus of Article 82 concerns:

> Any abuse by one or more undertakings of a dominant position within the common market or in a substantial part of it shall be prohibited as incompatible with the common market insofar as it may affect trade between member states. Such abuse may, in particular, consist in:
> a directly or indirectly imposing unfair purchase or selling prices or other unfair trading conditions;
> b limiting production, markets or technical development to the prejudice of consumers;
> c applying dissimilar conditions to equivalent transactions with other trading parties, thereby placing them at a competitive disadvantage;
> d making the conclusion of contracts subject to acceptance by the other parties of supplementary obligations which, by their nature or according to commercial usage, have no connection with the subject of such contracts.

To establish whether Article 82 applies to any given context, the Commission must identify the existence of two conditions. First, it must establish whether an undertaking has a dominant position. Second, it then has to decide whether it has abused this dominance. It is the abuse of dominance and not the sheer existence of dominance that is illegal. In this connection, the Commission must demonstrate that the abuse has had an appreciable impact on trade between member states. Unlike Article 81, there is no provision for negative clearance or exemptions under Article 82.

A position of dominance is potentially anti-competitive because within the relevant market, an undertaking may have such power that its behaviour has a negative impact on competitors and consumers. In order for the Commission to establish whether an undertaking has a dominant position it must define the 'market'. This involves determining the relevant product market and the geographical market. The definition of the market is important because if effective competition exists within the market, the effect of an anti-competitive agreement would be limited and even self-defeating for the offending undertaking. The product market refers to 'all those products and/or services which are regarded as interchangeable or substitutable by the consumer, by reason of the product's characteristics, their prices and their intended uses'.[7] The wider the product market is defined the more difficult it is to identify dominance. Substitutability refers to the ability of consumers to obtain similar goods within the relevant market (demand substitutability) and the ability of undertakings to supply similar goods (supply substitutability). The Commission often employs the 'SSNIP' test to determine substitutability (Weatherill 2000: 275). According to this test the Commission must decide whether consumers would switch to other goods in response to an increase in the range of 5–10 per cent in the price of the good in question. Defining the geographical market is important as Article 82 is only breached where dominance occurs within the common market or a substantial part of it. In this instance the wider the market is defined, the easier it is to apply Article 82. Various tests exist for determining dominance within the market. These include identifying the market share of the undertaking and of competitors, examining the financial and technical resources at the undertakings disposal, analysing the ability of undertakings to control production and distribution and examining the actual conduct and performance of an undertaking (Kent 2001: 256).

Having defined the market in order to determine dominance, the Commission must then identify whether an undertaking has abused its dominant position. Abuse essentially refers to conduct which influences the structure of a market in a way which weakens competition. Article 82 provides guidance as to the types of agreement that might be considered abusive. As with Article 81, the abuse must affect trade between member states.

The procedures available to the Commission for the enforcement of Article 81 and 82 are contained in Regulation 17/62. The Commission has wide powers of investigation and has the ability to fine undertakings up to 1 million euros or 10 per cent of the undertaking's global turnover – whichever is greater. Decisions of the Commission are reviewable before the CFI and on further appeal the ECJ. Alternatively, complainants can bypass the public enforcement procedures of the Commission and rely on private enforcement before national courts to challenge alleged anti-competitive practice. As the Commission proposal to amend competition law procedures outlined above illustrates, the Commission is keen to extend the use of private enforcement. However, as is examined below, the proposal to also devolve the exemption procedures outlined in Article 81(3) to national authorities raises important questions concerning the future definition of the separate territories concept for sport.

Sport and competition law

The discussion of the above general principles of competition policy gives rise to more specific questions concerning the applicability of such principles to sport. A number of questions arise in relation to the applicability of Article 81.

First, are sports organisations considered 'undertakings'? Amateur and professional sports organisations and individuals will be considered undertakings if they are engaged in economic or commercial activity involving the provision of goods and services even if this activity generates little profit or indeed their activity is not for profit. On first appearance, sports organisations are primarily concerned with regulating sporting conduct. Rules concerning the operation of the off-side rule in football are clearly of sporting interest only. However, sports organisations have a wider responsibility to ensure the commercial success of their sport. Frequently, international federations gather receipts from national associations and are centrally involved in a range of economic activities including exploiting broadcasting and sponsorship rights. National associations also have a responsibility for marketing broadcasting rights on behalf of participants. Similarly, clubs are to be considered commercial undertakings. Such commercial activity ranges from ticket sales to transfer dealings. In some cases clubs are quoted on the stock exchange in the form of public limited companies. Finally, players are paid for their services. Some football clubs are prepared to pay large sums to secure the services of the better players. This desire to attract the best not only improves sporting performance, it also contributes to the commercial potential of a club. Given that this activity need not generate profit, it is clear that sports organisations should be considered undertakings.

Second, do sports rules constitute 'agreements'? Given the broad definition of agreements employed by the Commission and the ECJ, it is of little doubt that rules relating to, for example, the transfer of players are agreements by undertakings or associations of undertakings. The relevant strength of the international federation must be taken into account when deciding whether an agreement has been reached between undertakings (such as clubs) or by an association of undertakings (such as the international federation). Organisations such as FIFA and UEFA have statutes whose nature clearly indicates regulatory strength. However, not all rules contained in these statutes are commercially based. The difficulty for the Commission lies in distinguishing between rules which are inherent to the sport and rules which have commercial implications. The distinction is not always clear-cut. Furthermore, the Commission need not be convinced by the assertion by sports organisations that the *object* of a particular rule was sporting in nature as they can examine the *effect* of this rule. Rules which initially were designed for sporting reasons may have assumed greater economic importance due to developments in the sector (Pons 1999: 7). Therefore sporting rules having commercial implications can still be caught within the scope of competition law.

Third, do sports rules have the potential to prevent, restrict or distort competition in the EU? Rules which have a minor impact on competition are not subject to EU competition law. Nevertheless, as in any other sector, horizontal and vertical sporting agreements do have the potential to be caught within the scope of competition law. Of course competition in the sports sector is not necessarily the same as in other sectors due to the unique interdependence within the sector. This leads to a supplementary question concerning the overall place of sport within competition law. The business of sport is different to other businesses in one important respect – participants in the sports market rely on each other for their success, they do not seek to eliminate competition. Oligopoly would not serve the interests of the remaining powerful participants who rely on competition to make the game in question interesting and unpredictable. Furthermore, in many sports, such as football, large clubs benefit from the available pool of talent cultivated by smaller clubs. The Commission is therefore faced with returning to the question of what constitutes a sports rule and what is a commercial rule. Case law is beginning to provide some answers to this question (see below).

Fourth, do sports rules affect trade between member states? Much European sport is based on a single structure model. An international federation controls the activities of the national associations who in turn regulate competition within their jurisdiction. It is clear therefore that many sports rules have international implications. This is most clearly demonstrated in relation to rules governing the transfer of players. Again, not all rules have international implications. Stevenage Borough's claim against the Football League failed because the League ruling preventing the club entering the Football League from the non-leagues did not affect trade between member states.[8] Stevenage had argued that membership of the Football League would enable them to compete for a place in European competitions – a remote prospect (Beloff *et al.* 1999: 146).

An area where competition policy may not apply?

Finally, if the activities of sport are covered by Article 81, should sport qualify for an exemption under Article 81(3)? Individual agreements could be exempt or agreements pertaining to the wider sports sector could qualify for a block exemption. This issue is dealt with more fully below and in the concluding section of this text.

Much of the reasoning advanced above supporting the view that the activities of sport's organisations are subject to Article 81 also applies to Article 82. Nevertheless, further questions remain concerning the issue of dominance in sport. In particular, are sports organisations capable of assuming a position of dominance within the relevant market? The answer to this question lies in the definition of the market. Egger and Stix-Hackl argue that, although the relevant product market for sport differs from other sectors, a market (three altogether) still exists (Egger and Stix-Hackl 2002: 86). The first is the exploitation market in which clubs and federations exploit secondary features of their performances such as broadcasting rights, exclusive distribution systems for ticket sales and merchandising arrangements. The second is the contest market where the actual product, the sporting contest, is made. To stage an effective contest, rules regulating competition between participants and rules limiting access to sporting competitions are formed by sports governing bodies. The third market is the supply market where clubs buy and sell players.

A potential for a finding of dominance is enhanced due to a number of factors. First, the European model of sport necessitates international sports federations to assume considerable (even monopolistic) control over the activities of members. The 'market share' of organisations such as UEFA is therefore considerable. Potentially compounding this dominance is the restrictive rules often employed by governing bodies to maintain the single structure model. Clubs could also be regarded as having a dominant position should they co-ordinate their activities. It is less likely an individual club would be found to have a position of dominance although the definition of the relevant market may show otherwise. Second, if it is to be accepted that the sports market consists of three markets, undertakings operating within them are more likely to assume a position of dominance than if the market was defined in a wider sense. This links into the third reason – the potential for a finding of dominance is enhanced by the limited scope for demand- and supply-side substitutability in the sector. These issues are further developed in the review of case law below.

The definition of the geographical market flows from that of the product market. It is difficult to argue against the whole EU being considered the relevant geographical market for agreements concerning the sale of broadcasting rights, rules on international transfer and even ticketing arrangements for major international sporting events such as the football World Cup. Of course the finding of dominance is not in itself illegal. As such, the Commission must establish whether an abuse of this dominance has taken place. The development of Commission jurisprudence in this field is beginning to identify examples of abuse in the sports sector (see below).

The case law of the ECJ and Commission confirms sport's relationship with EU law. The *Walrave* and *Donà* cases established that sport is subject to EU law whenever practiced as an economic activity. Nevertheless in the immediate aftermath of these rulings, the Commission did little to enforce the central findings. As a result, throughout the 1970s and 1980s, the Commission took little interest in the operation of sport. At that time the Commission was not best placed to apply the competition implications of these rulings due to its own status and indeed the status of sport. A number of factors changed this.

First, it was not until the maturation of the Directorate General for Competition Policy in the 1980s that the link between sport and competition law became more likely. Second, this maturation coincided with an accelerated push to complete the Single Market. The powerful logic of negative integration served to enmesh new economic sectors within the Single Market. Third, sport began to *practice* as a truly economic activity in the late 1980s/early 1990s. This coincided with an influx of money into sport, especially football, partly as a consequence of technological advances in broadcasting. Fourth, the ruling in *Bosman* served as an important watershed in the thinking of Commission officials and served to confirm sport's status as an economic activity subject to EU law. Whilst the ECJ chose to apply Article 39 to the case, the Commission exploited the competition dimension of the case in order to fully enforce the ECJ's central findings.

Following *Bosman*, rules devised by European sports bodies in order to maintain a competitive balance between participants were increasingly attracting the regulatory interest of the Commission. Given the broad definition of anti-competitive behaviour adopted by the Commission and ECJ, it is clear to see the ease by which sporting rules, many of which were devised in an amateur age, may infringe competition law whenever sport is practised as an economic activity within the meaning of Article 2 of the Treaty. Sporting self-regulation has thus become increasingly challenged from above and below. From below, individual complainants frustrated by the lack of redress within sporting circles used the Commission and the ECJ as a new legal venue. From above, the EU institutions, keen to extend legal rights to all EU citizens, including sports men and women, accommodated such complaints. The Commission has investigated cases relating to the operation of sport in each of the three product markets identified above.

The exploitation market: the marketing of sport

The broadcasting of sport
Sport, and in particular football, has become of critical importance to broadcasters. In Britain, sports broadcasting has been the cornerstone of BSkyB's

[handwritten margin note at top: distortion of the market ultimately undermines consumer freedom of choice. Is this the underlying become for?]

success and the reason for the failure of ITV Digital. Whilst BSkyB prospered following the conclusion of successive contracts to broadcast English Premiership games, ITV digital went into administration and returned its broadcasting licence following the signing in 2000 of the £315 million contract to broadcast lower league games in England, a contract left unfulfilled and ultimately re-negotiated by BSkyB.[9] Just as sport is of critical importance to broadcasters, so the exploitation of broadcasting rights is a major source of revenue for sports clubs, national associations and international federations. Agreements concluded between sports organisations and broadcasters must, in general, comply with Article 81. As such, the Commission has become centrally involved in questions relating to how these rights are exploited.

The precise relationship between sports broadcasting and competition law will depend on the definition of the market. Although the geographical broadcasting market is normally considered national due to linguistic and cultural factors, the universal appeal of sport indicates that a wider geographical market exists. The product market is more complex. Beloff *et al.* identify three issues relevant to the definition of this market (Beloff *et al.* 1999: 150). First, the market needs dividing into pay-TV and free-to-air broadcasters. In this sense sport is more substitutable on free-to-air televi- *[margin: YES]* sion than it is on pay-TV due to the direct relationship between viewing sport and the money paid to watch it.

Second an analysis needs making of the market relevant to the sport in question. Do separate markets exist for separate sports? It is traditionally argued that football should be considered a market separate from other sports. The contrasting fortunes of BSkyB and ITV Digital point to arguments on both sides. Whereas BSkyB's experiment with pay-per-view broad- *[margin: use?]* casting of Premiership matches has proved satisfactory, ITV Digital's attempt to do the same with lower league football was disastrous. The substitutability of football therefore varies. Only top-flight football and perhaps major boxing encounters can truly be considered a separate market from *[margin: or not substitutional options.]* other sports. Such questions are becoming more significant in the new world of multi-channel specialist television.

Third, do separate markets exist in the broadcasting of live sport and recorded sport? The picture once again varies. In the Netherlands, the competition authority has argued that a separate market did exist for broadcasting highlights of sports events. One of the reasons for the failure of Dutch pay-TV channel Sport in 1997, which broadcast live football, was the availability of highlights on free-to-air television (Van Den Brink 2000a: 361–362). The non-substitutability of football in this instance was therefore questionable. However, as Beloff *et al.* explain in the case of Britain, 'BSkyB's success in using live football coverage to sell pay-TV subscriptions indicates that comprehensive highlights programmes such as Match of the Day do not constrain their pricing ability for live football' (Beloff *et al.* 1999: 152).

Although any aspect of a broadcasting contract may fall within the scope of EU competition law, four particular themes have emerged in terms of the sports broadcasting cases to have come before the Commission. The first concerns the practice of collective selling of rights. The second relates to the sale of exclusive rights, a practice often linked to collective selling. The third theme is concerned with the nature in which rights are acquired and the fourth is how events are transmitted.

Collective selling

An established commercial practice in the European sports sector is the central marketing and joint sale of broadcasting rights on behalf of the participants. Participation in the league is often conditional on the acceptance of this practice. Accordingly there is little doubt that collective selling is to be considered an 'agreement' in the context of competition law. [Collective selling is considered vital by sports organisations as it allows them to maximise revenues, thus enhancing their re-distributive capabilities.]

National law will determine who owns the broadcasting rights in the first instance and national regulatory agencies have become involved in central marketing issues. For instance, in Germany, the Federal High Court (Bundesgerichtshof) concluded that the central marketing of European Cup football matches by the national football association was a cartel for which no exemption could be justified.[10] This ruling has since been overturned by legislation with effect from 1 January 1999 due to the addition of section 31, dealing with sport, to the German Competition Act legislation. In Britain, the Restrictive Practices Court held that the £743 million 'bundled' contract between BSkyB and the BBC to show Premier League football was not in violation of the 1976 Restrictive Trade Practices Act.[11]

If inter-state trade in broadcasting services is affected, the Commission becomes the relevant regulatory agency. A number of competition concerns may stem from collective selling. First, does the prevention of clubs from entering into individual agreements with broadcasters amount to a restriction of competition and fall within the scope of Article 81(1)? If the central marketing of broadcasting rights is necessary to ensure the survival of the smaller participants in the league (the so-called solidarity argument) should an exemption under Article 81(3) be granted? Second, does collective selling affect competition between broadcasters by reducing the number of available rights on offer? Clearly if clubs could market their own rights more broadcasters could enter the market for them. This may have implications for the creation of a single European market in broadcasting. Finally, does collective selling constitute an abuse of a dominant position by the vendor? In this connection, leagues themselves can be considered undertakings. Given that sports clubs cannot realistically operate outside a league structure and a condition for league membership is the acceptance of broadcasting rules, it follows that a position of dominance on the part of the league can be deduced. Article 82 may therefore also be relevant.

Collective selling in sport has only recently been addressed by the Commission. In the Deutscher Fubßball-Bund (DFB) case the German National Football Association has requested a negative clearance or an exemption from the application of Article 81 in respect of the collective sale of the television and radio broadcasting rights for professional football matches in Germany.[12] The DFB organises football competitions in Germany and collectively sells the broadcasting rights to the games on behalf of the participants. The DFB redistributes the revenues gained from these broadcasting contracts back to the participants. The contracts in question concerned the rights to show first and second division Bundesliga games primarily on a free-to-air basis but with some provision for a limited number of games to be shown on a pay-TV basis. The DFB claims authority to enter into such contracts as chief organiser of the events. Furthermore, the DFB claim that central marketing performs an important solidarity function in German football in that money is redistributed fairly between participants. The pro-competitive effects of central marketing therefore outweighs the anti-competitive effects. At time of writing, the Commission has yet to form an opinion on this matter.

In the UEFA Champions League case, UEFA applied for a negative clearance or an exemption from Article 81 in respect of the central marketing of commercial rights to the UEFA Champions League.[13] 'Commercial rights' refer to the television rights, sponsorship rights, supplier rights, licensing rights and intellectual property rights. UEFA organises the Champions League, a prestigious tournament involving teams finishing in the highest places of domestic leagues. UEFA centrally markets the broadcasting rights to these games on behalf of the participants and allocates most of the revenues to these teams (hence the financial importance for clubs to qualify for the Champions League).[14] Smaller amounts are redistributed to grass roots football. The rights were sold as a bundle on an exclusive basis for up to four years to one broadcaster in each member state. Although the broadcaster is normally a free-to-air operator, they could sub-license some games to pay-TV operators. UEFA justified central marketing by claiming that without it there would be a diminution of the UEFA Champions League brand. This would have the effect of making the competition less visible and attractive and therefore have a consequential impact on sponsors, clubs, broadcasters and spectators. Furthermore, central marketing serves a solidarity function and hence enhances competition rather than restricts it.

In July 2001, the Commission opened proceedings against UEFA concerning the collective marketing of the television rights for the Champions League.[15] In particular, the Commission objected to UEFA's practice of selling the rights exclusively to a single broadcaster in each state. It is the Commission's contention that this practice restricts competition in the market for such rights, as only larger operators are able to afford the rights. This may have a consequential impact on broadcasters and viewers.

Less-established broadcasters are unable to penetrate the market. This may have the effect of slowing down the use of new technologies such as internet and mobile phone use. Furthermore, the Commission believes that viewers are denied wide access to televised matches. Due to the nature of the exclusive contracts, some live games remained unexploited therefore denying fans the ability to view live games. Other broadcasters (such as regional broadcasters or broadcasters embracing new technology) willing to broadcast these games were denied the opportunity by the exclusive contract. In the statement of objections the Commission made it clear that, although the final decision will be informed by the Nice Declaration on Sport, if less-restrictive means are available to secure UEFA's objectives, a negative clearance or an exemption will not be granted.

In light of the Commission's objections, UEFA re-worked their selling policy leading to a more favourable response from the Commission.[16] In the revised plans from 2003/2004, UEFA retains the right to sell live television rights and highlights for a period of no more than three years. However, delayed television rights and new media rights will be co-exploited by UEFA and the clubs. In essence, the media rights are exploitable in 14 packages. For instance package 1 (the 'gold' package for broadcasting live games) sells the rights, including highlights, for the first and third pick of games on match day. Package 2 (the silver package) does the same for the second and fourth pick of games. These packages are to be sold by UEFA to free-to-air and/or pay-TV. In other packages involving less-attractive games, delayed transmission, archives and radio and internet broadcasting, the clubs are given greater freedom to exploit the rights. The Commission has agreed that UEFA's amendments will allow for new market opportunities for a wider number of operators, both broadcasters and clubs, and viewers will benefit by being able to view a larger number of games. The Commission has given its preliminary approval of the modified arrangements and has invited interested third parties to submit observations. This informal decision will be published in the *Official Journal* in the form of a notice. Should no further objections arise from the market-testing procedure, the Commission has committed itself to taking a formal decision in the form of an exemption under Article 81(3).

The significance of the Commission's approach lies in their (conditional) willingness to acknowledge the specificity of sport. In a Competition Policy Newsletter, the Commission stated,

> the special characteristics of the sport in question have to be taken into account. These could include, for example, the need to ensure solidarity between weaker and stronger participants or the training of young players, which could only be achieved through redistribution of revenue from the sale of broadcasting rights. Such aims would have to be a genuine and material part of the objectives and ones which could not be achievable under less restrictive arrangements. (Commission of the European Communities 1998: 26)

As such, the Commission has indicated that in some circumstances collective selling does have a place in sport. This view was confirmed in the Formula One investigation (see below) in which the Commission indicated that collective selling was appropriate due to the specific characteristics of motor sport and in particular Formula One.[17]

Exclusivity
Exclusivity is closely connected to collective selling. By denying a competitor access to broadcast a particular sporting event, the purchaser of the exclusive rights can maximise viewing figures thus helping the operator to either honour public service commitments or maximise advertising and/or subscription revenues. New subscription-based TV operators have increased competition in the broadcasting market and have undoubtedly served to increase the price of such rights through their subscription-based ability to bid high. Although this may have increased revenues for sporting organisations, free-to-air access to sporting events is limited. The Television Without Frontiers Directive is partly concerned with this issue of public access to sporting events.[18] However, there are also competition policy considerations to be taken into account. Exclusivity may have market foreclosure implications by denying broadcasters the opportunity to develop commercially through the acquisition of rights. Given the importance of sport to new broadcasters, exclusivity may result in the stifling of attempts to establish a single European market in broadcasting.

Nevertheless, in previous case law concerning the granting of copyright licences the Commission and the ECJ have indicated that they are not opposed to exclusivity *per se*.[19] However, the Commission will investigate such arrangements if they unduly restrict competition in the broadcasting sector. This is consistent with the Commission's desire to realise a free market in broadcasting requiring the reduction of barriers to market entry. The sale of exclusive broadcasting rights, sold on long-term contracts, may be viewed as one such barrier to market entry. The Commission believes that exclusive deals may be exempt from competition rules when they are granted for a brief time and are limited in their scope and effect. The market power of the buyer and seller must be taken into consideration as must the potential for market foreclosure. Long contracts may be acceptable if the purchaser is a new market entrant requiring a substantial contract to become established. Occasionally, new entrants invest heavily in new technology necessitating longer contracts in order to counterbalance the risk of market entry. An exemption under Article 81(3) may be granted in such circumstances. An exemption may be granted if exclusive rights are reasonably sublicensed, thus allowing wider access to the rights to other market players. However, 'sublicensing is not by itself either a satisfactory or a convenient way of solving the competition problems of sports broadcasting' (Commission of the European Communities 1998: 27). The cost of the sub-licensing and the nature of the material offered (edited/unedited for example) are considerations. The licensees must genuinely benefit from the arrangement.

The Commission is gathering more experience in these matters. The first example concerns the agreement between British Satellite Broadcasting (BSB), now British Sky Broadcasting (BSkyB) following a merger in 1990, and the English Football Association to show live English football matches between 1988 and 1993 to a subscription audience.[20] The Commission exempted the agreement, even though the contract was for five years, because the Commission felt that as a new operator, embracing new technology, BSB needed a long-term contact to establish its operations. However, as (now former) Commissioner Van Miert announced in 1997, 'looking back . . . the five year period approved by the Commission was probably too long because the broadcasting technique in question became established more rapidly than had been expected' (Van Miert 1997).

Van Miert's more hard-line stance on long exclusive contracts was demonstrated in KNVB case.[21] On this occasion the Commission did not sanction what it regarded to be an anti-competitive agreement between the Dutch Football Association and Sport 7, a Dutch television channel. Under the terms of the agreement the KNVB granted Sport 7 exclusive rights to Dutch football over a seven-year period. The agreement was notified to the Commission in May 1996. The Commission objected on two counts. First, seven years was deemed to be excessively long for an exclusive contract that denied competitors broadcasting access. This could act as a potential barrier to entry for new operators in the market. Second, the Commission objected to a renewal clause in the contract that would have unfairly privileged Sport 7 in the tendering procedure at the end of the term.

Collective purchasing
The widely used system of collective selling and the high costs associated with the acquisition of exclusive rights has contributed to the practice of broadcasters grouping together to collectively purchase sports rights. Sports rights are often out of the financial reach of individual broadcasters. Collective purchasing agreements allow broadcasters to not only spread the cost of rights but also to share the risk for broadcasting events.

Collective purchasing is a tool employed by the European Broadcasting Union (EBU). In order to improve the collective bidding power of the public service broadcasters, the EBU was established in 1950. Since the trend towards the deregulation of the broadcasting market and the rise of new commercial operators in the 1980s, the work of the EBU has become more important to public service operators attempting to keep pace with the rising cost of broadcasting rights. Historically, membership of the EBU has only been open to broadcasters with a public service obligation. Commercial operators cannot join and the EBU has no commercial aim, although a few commercial operators have achieved membership due to 'various anomalies and historical accidents' (Collins 1994: 121). Based in Geneva and Brussels the EBU operates the Eurovision network of programme exchanges and acts as a collective purchasing agent for its members. This form of collaboration is clearly aimed at securing a competitive advantage for EBU members at the expense of commercial operators. However, with the evolution of a EU broadcasting and audio-visual policy, the activities of the EBU have become increasingly called into question (Humphreys 1996).

In both the *Screensport* v. *EBU Members* case and the *EBU-Eurovision System* case, the Commission identified a restriction of competition stemming from the EBU's collective purchasing arrangements. In the *Screensport* case the Commission refused to grant an exemption because the nature in which the EBU provided exclusive sports rights to Eurosport effectively foreclosed the market to Screensport, Eurosports main competitor.[22] In the *EBU-Eurovision System* case concerning the EBU's Eurovision programme sharing arrangements, the Commission believed that once acquired, the EBU were unfairly denying non-EBU members access to sporting rights. In order to qualify for an exemption under Article 81(3) of the Treaty the Commission imposed strict sub-licensing conditions.[23] The Commission decision was however annulled by the CFI following an appeal by a commercial broadcaster.[24] The CFI considered that the Commission had not adequately considered the anti-competitive consequences of the EBU's membership rules when granting an exemption. The EBU subsequently amended their membership rules and the Commission formally approved the EBU-Eurovision system in May 2000.[25] The exemption is granted until 31 December 2005.

In a further case concerning collective purchasing, the Commission raised objections to an agreement between Telefónica and Sogecable to exploit rights to broadcast football in Spain. The Commission was concerned that such collaboration could foreclose the market to cable and digital competitors of Telefónica and Sogecable. Following the issuing of a statement of objections to Telefónica and Sogecable in April 2000, improvements to the arrangements were made by the two parties.[26]

Broadcasting restrictions

UEFA not only has responsibility for marketing broadcasting rights, it also controls the cross-border transmission of football matches through the provisions of Article 14 of its Statute.[27] The reason for this is that UEFA fears that attendances at 'live' matches and indeed participation at all levels, would be adversely affected by broadcasting matches played at the same time. Since being introduced in 1988, UEFA's broadcasting regulations have however been challenged by various broadcasters. The Commission's investigations into them have centred on their compatibility with Article 81 of the Treaty. The cross-border trade in the broadcasting of football matches between member states could be restricted by their application. In addition, the regulations prevent national football federations from freely marketing their transmission rights in the Single Market. As a result of Commission scrutiny and after consultations between UEFA and the Commission, the broadcasting regulations have been amended, first in 1993 and most recently July 2000 following the 1998 issuing of a statement of objections by the Commission outlining the breach of Article 81. In April 2001, the Commission decided that UEFA's new rules on the broadcasting of football matches as amended in July 2000 fall outside the scope of EU competition rules as no appreciable restriction of competition could be identified and neither was inter-state trade appreciably affected by these arrangements. The rules allow national football associations to block the broadcasting on television of football during two and a half hours either on Saturday or Sunday to protect stadium attendance and amateur participation in the sport. The Commission closed the case with a formal decision in April 2001.[28]

Ticketing arrangements
Ticketing arrangements for major sporting events arguably falls between the exploitation market and the contest market. On the one hand ticketing is a method of marketing the game whereas on the other it is an essential component of organising the competition. As ticketing arrangements for major sporting events are linked to exclusive distribution networks, it is dealt here within the context of the exploitation market. It has become an established commercial practice for the organising committees of sporting events to enter into agreements with ticket distributors, guaranteeing for the distributor, often for a high price, the exclusive right to distribute the tickets within each of the member states. Rather than being one single market for ticket sales in the EU, nationally tied exclusive agreements create fifteen different markets (based on EU15). Very often, only residents of the country in which the exclusive ticket distributor is based can purchase tickets. In effect, therefore, each country is given a ticket quota which the exclusive distributor then sells to the public. The alleged benefit of this system is two-fold. First, it guarantees a fair and equitable distribution of tickets to fans of all countries, large and small, who want to purchase tickets. Second, it ensures spectator separation along national lines. This is considered an important safety feature.

The ticket distribution system for the 1990 World Cup finals held in Italy was investigated by the Commission, the first example of Commission involvement in ticketing arrangements for sporting events.[29] In November 1989, the Commission received a complaint from travel agent Pauwels Travel against the FIFA Local Organising Committee Italia '90, 90 Tour Italia SpA and NV CIT Belgique. In this case, the organising committee of the World Cup entered into agreements with a range of tour operators guaranteeing them the exclusive right to sell tickets within the country they were based. Pauwels Travel wanted to put together and sell a package deal for Belgian fans wishing to travel and stay in Italy and also to gain entrance to the stadiums. However, Pauwels was not the exclusive tour operator authorised to sell package deals in Belgium. When Pauwels attempted to purchase tickets by other sources, the authorised agent in Belgium initiated legal action against them before the Belgian courts. The Commission objected to this arrangement arguing that it contravened Article 81(1). The use of exclusive agents effectively foreclosed the market to other travel agents. No fine was imposed on the organisers as the offence was the first of its kind to be investigated by the Commission and the Commission noted that ensuring spectator separation and hence safety was a legitimate aim. As such, the decision did not establish a free market for tickets. It simply prohibited exclusive arrangements from being disproportionately restrictive.

The most high-profile Commission investigation into ticketing arrangements for a major sports tournament came with France '98 World Cup case. After being chosen as host for the 1998 World Cup Finals in July 1992, the French World Cup organising committee, the Comité Français d'Organisation (CFO), began consultations in 1994 on the mechanism by which the 2,666,500 available tickets were to be distributed (Weatherill 2000a). Most of the tickets were distributed amongst national football federations, official tour operators and sponsors, although 749,700 were distributed by the CFO to the public. These tickets were only available to those with a French address.

The CFO gained approval from the Commission for its distribution system in June 1997. The Commission claim that at this time they were unaware of the nationality requirement even though the CFO had informed the Commission of the details outside the scope of the official notification and the France '98 web-site had been opened since May 1997. Furthermore, in June, prior to the clearance, the Commission received a complaint regarding the discriminatory arrangements (Weatherill 2000a: 278). Nevertheless, the consequence of withholding a percentage of the tickets exclusively for the French market soon became clear as football federations, fans and even some governments complained that the distribution system had discriminated against non-French fans resulting in insufficient tickets being available to foreign fans. The Commission's response was to issue a warning letter to the CFO on 20 February 1998 requesting an adaptation of its sales policy. By that time only a small number of tickets remained. The basis of the request was that the ticket distribution system adopted by the CFO had breached Article 82 of the Treaty dealing with abuse of a dominant position. In a news release on 23 March the CFO made clear it was prepared only to distribute 50,000 of the 160,000 remaining tickets to the foreign federations with the other 110,000 being sold directly by the CFO to citizens of the 15 EU states plus Norway, Iceland and Liechtenstein.[30] These tickets went on sale in April.

Articulating the concerns of many European football fans, 32 Members of the European Parliament (MEP's) and 41 Belgian football fans brought a case against the CFO before the Tribunal de Grande Instance in Paris (Corbett 1998).[31] The basis for the complaint was that the distribution of World Cup tickets not only breached Article 82 of the Treaty but also breached Articles 12 (ex 6) and 49 (ex 59). Article 12 prohibits any measure within the scope of the Treaty that discriminates on the grounds of nationality. Article 49 prohibits restrictions on freedom to provide services within the EU. The case was considered as inadmissible by the French court and as such failed.

On 20 July the Commission issued a formal legal decision against the CFO.[32] The Commission concluded that the CFO's discriminatory ticketing practises amounted to an abuse of a dominant position and as such were contrary to Article 82 of the EC Treaty (and Article 54 of the European Economic Area Agreement). Given the popularity of football and the large demand for tickets, the CFO had a dominant position with respect to distributing tickets. Not only were consumers unlikely to substitute the World Cup 'product' for another event, but the Commission found the relevant geographic market was the entire EU/EEA. Given such a dominant position the organisers should have ensured that they did not abuse this by instituting a discriminatory distribution system. The discrimination against non-French residents was reinforced by the CFO advising such people that tickets could only be obtained from national football federations and tour operators. As the ticketing arrangements were similar to those adopted in previous World Cups, the Commission chose to fine the CFO a symbolic sum of just 1,000 euros. In addition, the Commission acknowledged that the CFO did not have case law guidelines to guide them in their decision to establish such a system. Also, the Commission noted that the CFO had been co-operative and had made more tickets available to non-French customers. In the formal decision, the Commission concluded that future breaches of EU competition law in relation to ticketing arrangements would be dealt with more seriously.

Merchandising
EU case law on merchandising issues in sport is limited even though this activity is becoming an essential component of any sports organisations business strategy. Clubs, players and even competitions are considered marketable commodities. The growth in the market for replica club kits illustrates the merchandising potential of some sports. Generally, national laws concerning trademarks, passing-off and copyright apply to disputes arising from merchandising issues. Occasionally such laws have a EU dimension. For instance in *Arsenal Football Club plc* v. *Matthew Reed*, the ECJ has been requested by the High Court of Justice of England and Wales to decide whether or not non-trademark use can constitute infringement of the registered trademark rights.[33] The Advocate General in the case concluded that

Article 5(1)(a) of the First Council Directive 89/104/EEC of 21 December 1988 relating to trademarks allows the proprietor of a trademark to prevent it being used for commercial purposes by a third party, even if it is perceived as a badge of support, loyalty or affiliation to its proprietor.[34] In a further (pending) case the ECJ is examining whether advertising restrictions at sports venues stemming from French law (the Loi Evin) are contrary to the principle of freedom of services.[35]

The question of the application of competition law to merchandising agreements in sport is equally nascent. As yet, the Commission has only raised specific objections to agreements in the field of product distribution and sponsorship. The Commission has established that the distribution of sporting goods falls within the scope of Article 81. Commission case law in this field concerns restrictions designed to protect exclusive distribution networks. In 1992 a fine was imposed on Dunlop Slazenger International and All Weather Sports for blocking exports of tennis balls to other EU countries in order to protect its sole distributors in those states.[36] Similarly, in 1994, Tretorn was fined for a breach of Article 81(1) relating to an export ban Tretorn had placed on their exclusive distributors of tennis balls.[37] Both cases illustrate the Commission's desire to ensure fair competition between the manufacturers of sports goods and the protection of consumer choice.

Sponsorship arrangements have also been investigated by the Commission. Sponsors are prepared to pay the organisers of sports events significant sums to use the term 'official' (such as 'official ball') in competitions. One example of a Commission investigation into this practice is the Danish Tennis Federation (DTF) case.[38] The DTF entered into agreements with three tennis ball manufacturers which resulted in their make of ball being labelled 'official'. A parallel importer complained to the Commission about market foreclosure. Furthermore, the Commission thought that the term official was misleading for consumers who may assume that the term represents a badge of quality rather than an indication of sponsorship. This was considered inappropriate for items such as tennis balls. Following negotiations between the DTF and the Commission amendments were made to the sponsorship arrangements for tennis competitions in Denmark. Under the new arrangement a more open tendering process is held every two years to decide sponsorship. The term 'official' has also been replaced by 'sponsor'. The case was closed by negative clearance.[39]

Given the commercial importance of marketing in sport, the competition case law is expected to expand. In protecting the rights of market competitors and consumers, the Commission will once again need to distinguish between commercial rules and sporting rules. Rules placing restrictions on sports equipment may for instance be justified. Technological advances in the manufacture of sports equipment can result in the games in question becoming too easy, boring or even dangerous. Technical restrictions on equipment is essential for all sports. Such rules cannot, however, act as a mask for the maintenance of anti-competitive rules.

The contest market: organising the game

Traditionally, sports organisations have operated a system of self-regulation. They have, by and large, remained free to determine the structural and organisational issues surrounding their existence. After all, for sport to be entertaining it needs to be highly organised and restrictions need to be placed on who competes in the sports sector. However, the commercialisation of sport has contributed to the erosion of this autonomy and has served to increase the penetration of EU competition law into sport. Furthermore, as has been established above, the definition of an economic undertaking adopted by the EU institutions is wide. Sports organisations at all levels are commercially active. Restrictions placed on their sporting freedom also affect their commercial freedom. Competition law may therefore have relevance for organisational issues in sport, although once again it must carefully distinguish between justifiable sporting restrictions and unjustifiable commercial restrictions.

Maintaining the single structure model of sport

The first category of competition law interventions concerns the maintenance of the traditional single structure model of sport. Most sport in Europe is organised on this basis. One international federation (in the case of European football, UEFA) controls the activities of its constituent members (single structure national associations such as the English Football Association). UEFA is one regional federation affiliated to the world's governing body FIFA. The federations expect affiliates to participate only in competitions organised by the federations. Single structure arrangements are however by no means universal in sport. Boxing, for example, is organised by a range of bodies. For the EU, the main areas of interest are two-fold. First, the Commission must decide whether restrictive practices employed by federations to maintain the single structure organisation of sport are to be tolerated. Second, if alternative or 'breakaway' structures are established, how best to regulate competition between them. The Commission has been asked to investigate the conduct of competing sporting federations. One of the first cases was a jurisdictional dispute concerning an indoor football league in Belgium. In 1994, the Commission rejected the complaint in question on the grounds that intra-Community trade was not seriously affected (Coopers and Lybrand 1995: 78).

In a similar, but much more high profile case in 1998, Media Partners International Limited, an Italian marketing firm, complained to the Commission about rules adopted by UEFA designed to prevent the establishment of a breakaway league. Media Partners notified the Commission of their intention to establish a new European Football League, independent of UEFA.[40] The new 'super-league' was to consist of 18 founder clubs who would be given three years exclusive participation – a break from the traditional merit-based open model of promotion and relegation practiced in Europe. Other clubs would have to qualify. Those clubs with the largest potential to attract television viewers were invited to become founder members. To entice club participation, Media Partners offered a very large financial inducement totalling £1.2 billion to the participants (Van den Brink 2000a: 365). UEFA rules designed to prevent the establishment of alternative competitions by placing heavy sanctions on participants amounted, it was claimed, to an abuse of a dominant position (Ratliff 1998: 5).[41] The Commission must decide whether it is acceptable to require clubs to leave their national leagues if they participate in an alternative pan-European breakaway league. A precedent exists which may guide Commission action in this area. In the *Danish Co-operatives* case, an agricultural co-operative was permitted to prohibit their members from participating in alternative agricultural co-operatives as the restriction benefited competition.[42] Sport could therefore claim that ancillary restrictions such as UEFA's rule is imperative to the effective operation of the competition in question (Van Den Brink 2000b: 421).

Even if competition law could be relied on to break open UEFA's organisational monopoly, the Media Partners proposal or any future similar proposal would still require Commission approval. It is questionable that any proposal seeking to challenge the single structure model of sport in Europe would pass Commission scrutiny unless the proposal maintains a competitive balance between all participants, large and small. This would require the new organisers to demonstrate a commitment to solidarity within the sport. Should the single structure model be broken, it is unclear to see why, other than to satisfy the Commission, the new league based on commercial imperatives would wish to promote solidarity outside the league it organises. Further questions remain concerning the establishment of a breakaway league. First, should entrance to a new league be based on founder members being granted exclusive participation for three years as Media Partners proposed, Article 81(1) could potentially be relied on as this would foreclose the market to new entrants. Second, are clubs who enter into an agreement to form a new league colluding in the market place, contrary to the provisions of Article 81(1)? Such parallel conduct can amount to a concerted practice and can arguably also be considered an abuse of a dominant position given that the new league would be composed of Europe's top clubs.

In the event, UEFA proposed a counter-measure resulting in the Football Champions League being revamped to accommodate the views of the majority of Europe's top clubs. As the top clubs accepted UEFA's proposal, the Media Partners proposal collapsed.

Multiple club ownership

The second category of competition law interventions concerns the related issue of multiple club ownership. It is becoming common for media companies to seek to own a share in some of Europe's football clubs. In Italy for instance media companies own a share or control AC Milan, Fiorentina, Lazio, Parma and Roma. In Britain, media companies own a stake in Manchester United, Leeds United, Sunderland, Chelsea, Manchester City (all BSkyB), Newcastle United, Aston Villa and Middlesborough (NTL) and Liverpool (Granada). A similar picture is emerging across Europe, although in Britain the Competition Commission recommended the prohibition of the proposed total merger between Manchester United and BSkyB. Concerned at the possible impact on the integrity of its European competitions, UEFA passed a new rule on club ownership in May 1998. In the new rule notified to the Commission for a negative clearance or exemption, UEFA proposed that: (1) no club should have a financial or management interest in another club which participates in the same UEFA competition, (2) no person should be involved in the management of more than one club participating in the same UEFA competition and (3) no person or company may control more than one club participating in the same UEFA competition. UEFA was particularly concerned about contrived results and strategic player transfers although the *Financial Times* also noted that UEFA was worried that multiple club ownership could lead to a challenge to their monopoly over European football (*Financial Times* 1999b). Two football clubs owned by the English National Investment Company (ENIC) appealed to the Court of Arbitration for Sports (CAS) for the rule to be overturned. The clubs in question, AEK Athens and Slavia Prague had qualified for the UEFA Cup Winners Cup along with Vicenza, an Italian club also owned by ENIC. By the terms of the new UEFA rule, only one team could participate in the competition. In August 1999 CAS found in UEFA's favour.[43]

   ENIC subsequently lodged a compliant with the Commission in February 2000 arguing that the rule restricted competition. The Commission's own examination of UEFA's multiple owner rule was concluded in July 2002 with the formal rejection of ENIC's complaint.[44] The Commission found that UEFA's rule is a decision taken by an association of undertakings and as such is theoretically caught within the scope of Article 81. However, the Commission agreed with UEFA that the rule was a sporting rule and was essential in order to maintain the integrity of competition. Although the object of the rule was not to restrict competition, arguably that was its effect. Nevertheless, the Commission concluded that the rule was proportionate in that it did not go beyond what was necessary to secure UEFA's chief objective concerning the integrity of its competitions and it was applied in a non-discriminatory manner.

Club relocation

The issue of club relocation is the third category to have appeared on the Commission's competition policy agenda. The tension between the commercial and socio-cultural dimensions of football has been highlighted by the *Wimbledon, Clydebank* and *Mouscron* cases. Both Wimbledon and Clydebank were reported to have considered asking the Commission to test rules preventing cross-border relocation against EU competition law (Duff 1998: 54). The *Mouscron* case concerned Belgian football club Excelsior Mouscron's request to stage the home leg of a UEFA Cup tie against French side F.C Metz in a nearby Stadium just across the border in Lille, France. UEFA imposed restrictions on Mouscrons ground limiting the normal capacity of 10,000 to just 4,500 and Mouscron argued that, due to the nature of the fixture, they required a larger stadium. UEFA blocked the move arguing that the home-and-away structure of its competitions needed protecting. UEFA maintained that the tie must go ahead in the stadium of the home host (*Financial Times* 1999a). This rule led two public bodies representing Lille and Mouscron to formally complain to the Commission. The Commission rejected the complaint made against UEFA by arguing that, 'the UEFA Cup rule to the effect that each club must play its home match at its own ground is a sports rule that does not fall within the scope of the Treaty's competition rules'.[45] As such the case contains no EU interest.

Formula One

The most high-profile investigation conducted by the Commission concerns the organisation of Formula One motor racing. Not only did the Commission investigate the regulatory role of the sports governing body, it also examined issues relating to the commercial exploitation of broadcasting rights. For the sake of completeness both are considered in this section even though the broadcasting provisions should be read within the context of the discussion on the exploitation market.

In September 1997, AETV, a German television company complained to the Commission arguing that the Fédération Internationale de L'Automobile (FIA) had abused a dominant market position by controlling the broadcasting of motor sport.[46] This complaint was followed in November 1997 by a second complaint, this time by the BPR organisation (known later as GTR). BPR claimed that it was forced out of business by the FIA's regulatory dominance in motor sport. BPR withdrew its complaint following a financial settlement. On the basis of these complaints, the Commission launched an investigation into the activities of the FIA. The Commission drew a preliminary conclusion that Articles 81 and 82 of the EC Treaty were being infringed.

In June 1999 the Commission opened formal proceedings into the commercial practises employed by Formula One and other international motor racing series. In particular, the Commission argued that the FIA has abused its dominant position and has restricted competition. The Commission also communicated this opinion to Formula One Administration Ltd (FOA) and International Sportsworld Communicators (ISC). The FIA organises international motor racing, FOA sells the Formula One television rights and ISC markets broadcasting rights to a number of major international motor sport events.

The Commission identified four competition issues relating to the operation of Formula One.[47] First, the Commission believed that the FIA uses its power to block series which compete with its own events. As the FIA has sole regulatory control over motor racing in Europe, it controls the licensing of participants. The Commission believes that the FIA has used this regulatory dominance to restrict FIA licensees from participating in non-FIA competitions. Track owners, vehicle manufactures, organisers and drivers can be stripped of their license if they participate in non-FIA events.

Second, the Commission claimed that the FIA has used this power to force a competing series out of the market. To support this claim the Commission has argued that a competing promoter, the GTR Organisation, was eliminated from the motor racing market because of the FIA's regulatory dominance. The GTR's series was then replaced with a FIA championship. The Commission believes this amounts to an abuse of a dominant position.

Third, the Commission holds the opinion that the FIA uses its power to acquire all the television rights to international motor sports events. In 1995, the FIA introduced a rule stating that it owned the television rights to all motor sport it authorised. These rights were then transferred to ISC, a company owned by Bernie Ecclestone, also an FIA Vice-President. This means that ISC gains the television rights to all competitions authorised by the FIA. Although these rules were modified in 1998 the Commission still views this as an abuse of a dominant position. Formula One rights are dealt with under a separate agreement (the Concorde Agreement). However, the Commission believes that the effect is the same in that the FIA's dominant position effectively forces rights to be transferred to it. The rights are then transferred to FOA, another company controlled by Bernie Ecclestone. If the FIA acquired the rights abusively, then neither ISC or FOA can be said to have acquired the rights validly.

Fourth, the Commission also believes that FOA and the FIA protect the Formula One Championship from competition by tying up everything that is needed to stage a rival championship. In particular the Commission has identified three examples of attempts to foreclose the market to competition. First, the promoter's contracts prevent circuits used for Formula One races from being used for races that could compete with Formula One. Second, the 'Concorde Agreement' prevents Formula One teams from racing in any other series comparable to Formula One for a very long period of time. Third, the agreements with broadcasters place a massive financial penalty on them, ranging from between 33 per cent and 50 per cent of the price paid, if they televise anything deemed by FOA to be a competitive threat to Formula One.

Despite maintaining objections to the Commission's analysis, the FIA and FOA amended their internal rules in January 2001 leading to the publication of a notice in June 2001 indicating that the Commission took a positive view of the proposed changes.[48] The essentials of the changes agreed by FIA and FOA include:

1 FIA has amended its regulations to strengthen the rights of motor sport organisers, circuit owners and participants, and to make it clear that FIA will act impartially as between all forms of motor sport for which it is the regulator.
2 FIA will no longer have a commercial interest in the success of Formula One and the new rules will remove any obstacle to other motor sports series competing with Formula One.
3 FIA will retain its rights over its championships and the use of the 'FIA' name and Trade Marks but has removed from its rules any claim over the broadcasting rights to events that it authorises and has agreed to waive any claim to broadcasting rights under the relevant clauses in the Formula One agreement (the 'Concorde Agreement').
4 FIA has made it clear that its decisions will always be reasoned, and that those decisions may be challenged before national courts.
5 The FOA group of companies has sold its interest in all forms of motor sport including Rallying and will therefore only have an interest in Formula One (Mr Ecclestone will no longer handle FIA's promotional affairs and will also reduce his role in FIA in other ways).
6 FOA has agreed to limit the duration of its free-to-air broadcasting contracts (to five years in the case of host broadcasters and three years in other cases) and has removed provisions which penalised broadcasters who wanted to broadcast other forms of open wheeler racing.[49]

These Commission enforced changes have had the effect of stripping the FIA of many of its commercial functions thus making the organisation essentially a sports regulatory body. By insisting on a separation between commercial rules and the rules of the game, the Commission has in effect sent a clear message to the sports world on how it practically intends to apply competition law to sporting situations. Given that no further objections were raised by third parties following publication of the notice, the Commission closed the case in October 2001.[50] Privately, the FIA are 'delighted' with the settlement.[51]

State aid

The issuing of state aid to sports clubs is an often overlooked aspect of EU competition law, although one highlighted by the European Parliament as early as 1994.[52] State aid has the potential to affect competition between sporting participants and as such has relevance to the contest market. The Commission has formed an opinion concerning the granting of aid from the French government to professional sports clubs in France.[53] The French government proposed granting a subsidy of up to 2.3 million euro per year to professional sports clubs with state-approved youth training centres. The Commission concluded that the aid was of an educational nature and not state aid. Article 87 of the Treaty prohibits aid granted by member states which distorts competition in trade between member states

The supply market: the transfer system

The supply market refers to the buying and selling of players. Transfer fees have traditionally been a common feature of European sport. For many years, football has operated a system whereby money is exchanged between clubs in order to secure the services of a player. The alleged benefit of transfer fees is that they compensate clubs for the training and development of players. Not only do transfer systems regulate the conduct between clubs, thus denying clubs from freely employing the services of workers they choose, they also impose restrictions on the ability of players to seek alternative employment at another club.

The *Bosman* ruling established that out of contract international transfer payments and nationality quotas were incompatible with Article 39. EU law therefore goes some way to protect the right of free movement for players in the EU. The rights of clubs to freely employ labour was not however guaranteed and some restrictions on players remained after *Bosman.* Although the ECJ did not answer the question concerning the compatibility of the international transfer system and nationality restrictions with EU competition law, the Commission held the view in the aftermath of *Bosman* that 'this is not a reason for not taking into account the application of the competition rules' (Commission of the European Communities 1996: 3). Amendments to the international transfer system made by FIFA/UEFA in light of the ruling in *Bosman* would therefore have to satisfy the Commission.

There can be little doubt that the functioning of international transfer rules is subject to scrutiny by the Commission. International football federations (such as FIFA and UEFA), national associations and clubs are considered undertakings as they are engaged in economic or commercial activity involving the provision of goods and services (see above). In the case of FIFA, UEFA and the national football associations, the label association of undertakings or grouping of associations of undertakings may be more appropriate (Egger and Stix-Hackl 2002: 85). The precise definition of such organisations matters little to the application of Article 81 as all are undertakings. The definition is only of importance when considering issues of liability. Furthermore the transfer system should be considered an agreement between undertakings or a decision of an association of undertakings in the case of FIFA's regulations. As is shown below, the regulations on transfer are contained within FIFA's constitution (statute). In addition, FIFA rules, whether binding on national associations or merely recommendations, are still caught by the scope of Article 81.

Therefore, the transfer system clearly stems from an agreement of or between undertakings. As the rules on transfer stem from FIFA they are the relevant body to be investigated by the Commission. The Commission must then decide if the object or effect of such rules is the prevention, restriction or distortion of competition. Two issues are of relevance in this connection. First, transfer fees have the potential to restrict the clubs source of supply (i.e. players). This strengthens the market position of the large clubs at the expense of the smaller clubs who are unable to develop by attracting new and better players. This limits not only their sporting performance but also their commercial potential. Second, players are also disadvantaged by the transfer system. The requirement to pay a fee for a player has the effect of restricting that players wages and limiting his ability to find employment. Clearly, when assessing these effects, the Commission must examine the pro-competitive effects of transfer fees. These are discussed below and a wider discussion on this matter is provided in the previous chapter.

The Commission must also identify whether transfer rules affect inter-state trade. In all three relevant markets discussed above, football is a highly international game. As such, it is difficult to justify that transfer systems do not have a cross-border impact. Accordingly, the operation of the transfer system is caught by the provisions of Article 81. The difficulty in applying Article 82 relates to the definition of the product market. It is the clubs and not the international federation who compete for the services of players and as such the relevant market is for players.

It is within the context of the above discussion that the Commission has conducted an investigation into transfer rules. In January 1996 the Commission notified FIFA and UEFA that is was launching an infringement procedure based on Article 81(1) against the continued use of their international transfer system and the 3+2 restrictions on foreign players, a clear breach of the *Bosman* ruling. In this letter of notification the Commission informed FIFA and UEFA that following the ruling in *Bosman*, the international transfer system, as notified by FIFA/UEFA to the Commission on 28 July 1995, could not be exempt under Article 81(3) and Article 53(1) of the EEA Agreement. The Commission notified FIFA and UEFA that they must fully comply with *Bosman* within six weeks.

After failing to gain an exemption under Article 81(3), FIFA and UEFA informed the Commission that both the international transfer system and nationality restrictions would be abolished. In 1997 FIFA's new Regulations for the Status and Transfer of Players were adopted. Players would be able to move to another club in a different EU/EEA state at the end of their contract without a transfer fee being payable. Furthermore, in UEFA competitions, clubs were no longer restricted to fielding foreign players within the terms of the 3 + 2 player rule.

Despite the abolition of the international transfer system and nationality restrictions by FIFA/UEFA, the Commission maintained an objection to certain aspects of the remaining transfer system. In June 1996, the Commission notified FIFA/UEFA that in their view Article 81(1) EC and Article 53(1) EEA had been breached by the requirement for payment of fees for international transfers within the EEA of players from third countries at the end of their contracts and the FIFA instruction to national associations in the EU/EEA to establish national transfer systems. On the issue of national transfer systems, the Commission drew the following conclusion:

> The effect of national transfers is normally limited to one member state. However, one cannot exclude the possibility that continuing with national transfer systems may limit the freedom of clubs to hire the players that they want, or that their choice may be distorted by the maintenance of national transfers. One can, therefore conclude that in principle national transfer systems are also incompatible with Article 81 of the Treaty. (Commission of the European Communities 1996: 5)

FIFA and UEFA responded to the Commission's statement of objections by informing them that they did not intend to alter aspects of the transfer system not covered by the ruling in *Bosman*. The Commission informed FIFA/UEFA that given their reluctance to respond satisfactorily to the objections, formal infringement proceedings would be initiated. Little progress was made on the resolution of this issue although high-level talks did take place during the 1997 Amsterdam Summit on the social significance of sport. Although the subsequent Amsterdam Treaty only mentioned sport in a non-legally binding Declaration, the involvement of the member states in sporting issues demonstrated that a school of thought within the EU had emerged which stressed the need to take the specific characteristics of sport into account in the application of EU law in sports-related cases. Despite this breakthrough for the sports world, the fact remained that sport was not granted an exemption by the new Treaty, the Commission still had obligations to act as the guardian of the legal framework of the EU and, furthermore, FIFA/UEFA had yet to satisfactorily address the Commission's objections.

Measures eventually proposed by FIFA/UEFA to alter the international transfer system failed to satisfy the Commission's objections. One measure proposed by UEFA's Executive Committee was the establishment of a standard player–club contract covering initially three years as a trainee and then three years as a professional under contract. UEFA recommended that national associations introduce this type of contract from July 1997. In the initial part of the contract, a transfer fee would still be payable at the end of the term. FIFA/UEFA notified the Commission of this proposal but the Commission took the preliminary view that the maintenance of the transfer system at the end of the initial part of the contract would render the standard contract as being incompatible with Article 39 of the Treaty. In a second proposal, FIFA Circular No. 616, paragraph 2 (adopted 4 June 1997) proposed the introduction of a system whereby the issue of an international transfer certificate could be refused if non-amateur players terminate their contract of employment before its date of expiry. Paragraph 1 of the Circular postponed until 1 April 1999 the abolition of the international transfer system within the EEA to non-EU players reaching the end of their contract. Both measures led to formal complaints being tabled to the Commission by three football clubs and players' organisations in Belgium.

Spurred by such complaints and frustrated by the attitude of FIFA/UEFA, on 15 December 1998, the Commission launched a formal investigation into the operation of the international transfer system. In the letter of objections sent to FIFA/UEFA, the Commission objected to certain provisions within the international transfer system which had the effect of:

1 prohibiting players from transferring to another club following their unilateral termination of contract, even if the player has complied with national law governing the penalties for breach of contract;

2 allowing a club to receive payment for a player leaving a club if the contract has been terminated by mutual consent;

3 encouraging high transfer fees which bear no relation to the training costs incurred by the club selling the player, a practice condemned by the Court in *Bosman* and one which limits the ability of small clubs to hire top players;

4 allowing for a transfer fee to be demanded for the transfer of players (both in and out of contract) from a non-EU country to a member state of the EU and vice versa.

The Commission indicated that the above points infringed Article 81(1) and no exemption could be justified. Point 4 also breached Article 81, although transfers from member state countries to non-EU states will only be caught by the scope of Article 81(1) if the club concerned plays regularly in competitions involving the participation of clubs from member countries. In essence therefore, the Commission held the view in the formal statement of objections that these provisions restrict the ability of clubs to recruit the players they want whilst also limiting the freedom of movement of players.

Once again the game's governing bodies were slow to respond the Commission's statement of objections. The Commission's response to FIFA/UEFA's inactivity came in the summer of 2000. Unless FIFA/UEFA submitted formal proposals to amend the international transfer system by 31 October 2000, the Commission would take unilateral action in the form of a formal decision to secure the changes necessary.

Faced with the possibility of an end-of-year prohibition decision, FIFA and UEFA established a joint transfer task force chaired by Per Ravn Omdal, UEFA vice-president and member of the FIFA executive committee. Throughout September 2000, the task force examined potential amendments to the international transfer system in light of the Commission's objections. In this connection, they received support not only from many of Europe's top clubs, but also from the German Chancellor and British Prime Minister who in a joint statement expressed their support for the current transfer system.[54]

The FIFA/UEFA Negotiation Document
Despite their hostility, the joint FIFA/UEFA transfer task force produced a set a proposals that were duly submitted to the Commission by the imposed October deadline. The proposals were outlined in the form of a 'Negotiation Document'.[55] In the introduction, FIFA/UEFA continued to question the validity of the Commission's complaints, although they did acknowledge that certain aspects of the transfer system needed revising. The document explained that a revised transfer system would need to ensure: (1) that contract stability was maintained, (2) that clubs were rewarded for the investment in the training of young players and (3) that the new system must ensure the redistribution of income which would help maintain a balance between the clubs. Using these principles as a starting point, the Negotiating Document outlined the following proposed changes to the international transfer system.

Prohibition of the international transfer of minors   FIFA/UEFA justified this move in order to avoid the economic exploitation of minors, although this restriction would not apply to instances involving the relocation of the player's family to another state.

Training compensation for young players   Concerned at the deleterious effect the abolition of transfer fees would have on the grass roots of football, FIFA/UEFA proposed the maintenance of fees for the transfer of players up to the age of 23, even if the player had come to the end of their contract with the club. FIFA/ UEFA also noted that training compensation would be financed through 'solidarity mechanisms' such as a levy on transfer fees and a solidarity fund financed by income generated from the central marketing of television rights.

Respect for contracts   FIFA/UEFA considered contract stability as an essential part of professional football not only in terms of team building and fan association with a club but also in terms of employment security for players. As a consequence, the Negotiation Document proposed that contracts lasting up to three years should be respected by both club and player. A maximum contract of five years was proposed.

Transfer periods   For the purposes of maintaining contract stability and protecting the integrity of sporting competition, FIFA/UEFA proposed the introduction of two unified transfer periods with players restricted to one move per season.

An arbitration system   The Negotiation Document proposed the establishment of a new voluntary arbitration system for the resolution of breach of contract disputes. Compensation payments would be agreed by the arbitration board in accordance with national labour laws. However, in order to respect the 'specificity of sport', sporting sanctions could be imposed on players breaching contract or for reasons of other 'unethical behaviour'. If the buying and selling clubs and the player agreed to a transfer fee, the use of the arbitration board would not be required and hence sporting sanctions not imposed. Although the Negotiation Document stressed that the arbitration system was designed for the international transfer system, it could act as a model for national transfer regimes.

Transitional arrangements   The Negotiation Document stressed that a minimum necessity for the world of football is that alterations made to the transfer system protect existing contractual arrangements between clubs and players.

Following the submission of the revised transfer plans, negotiations between FIFA/UEFA and the Commission on the acceptability of the proposals were influenced by three key developments. The first was the rejection of the Negotiation Document by FIFPro, the international football player's union. The second was a tactical dispute between FIFA and UEFA and the third was the discussion of sport at the December 2000 Nice European Council.

FIFPro's objections
Despite being originally involved in the preparation of the FIFA/UEFA Negotiation Document, FIFPro, the international football player's union, failed to support the position taken by FIFA/UEFA within it.[36] FIFPro's objections to the Negotiation Document, outlined in an alternative submission to the Commission, were essential two-fold (FIFPro 2001).

The first issue related to *the rights of players* to seek alternative employment at another club without undue restriction (FIFPro 2001: 6 and 13). In this connection, FIFPro share the concerns of the Commission in relation to the inability of players to unilaterally break a contract of employment with a club and move freely to another once compensation for breach of contract has been paid in accordance with national labour law. In the alternative submission, FIFPro questioned the alleged benefits of this system of player restraint. FIFA/UEFA claim that the restraint is needed in order to ensure contract stability (point 3 of the Negotiation Document). FIFPro argued that in the period between 1996/1997 and 1999/2000 both player mobility and transfer spending have greatly increased.[57] This is because the maintenance of transfer fees gives clubs an incentive to sell contracted players. As such 'stability of contract, therefore, cannot be seriously seen as a positive symptom of the transfer system' (FIFPro 2001). Consequently, the abolition of transfer fees would eliminate this distortion and grant footballers equal rights of freedom of movement enjoyed by other economically active European citizens.

The second main objection forwarded by FIFPro concerned the related issue of the *transfer system and the law* (FIFPro 2001: 6). Although FIFPro agreed with FIFA/UEFA that a balance between clubs needed maintaining and clubs should be encouraged to recruit and train juniors, they argued that less-restrictive means than the transfer system can achieve these objectives. Whereas the FIFA/UEFA Negotiation Document stressed the economic importance of the transfer system for small clubs, the FIFPro report claimed that the distribution of income within football was in decline, primarily as a result of the income generated by the sale of broadcasting rights. Similarly, FIFA/UEFA claimed that the maintenance of the transfer system was required in order to encourage clubs to recruit and train juniors. The FIFPro report found no evidence to support this link, instead pointing out that due to transfer fee inflation, most top clubs have invested heavily in youth academies in order to develop their own juniors. FIFPro pointed out that FIFA/UEFA recognise the growing polarisation between rich and poor in European football yet are misguided to believe that the maintenance of the transfer system is required to prevent the gap growing further. FIFPro therefore questioned the validity of maintaining a system which is anti-competitive and restricts the freedom of movement of players, particularly given that it does not fulfil the objective of redistribution and training incentive stated by FIFA/UEFA.

In essence, FIFPro did not support the FIFA/UEFA Negotiation Document because they identified a hidden agenda implicit within it. This agenda sought not only to protect the transfer system, a system used by the game's governing bodies to 'restrain players' earnings and bargaining power', but also to enhance it and impose on players restraints more onerous than previously existed (FIFPro 2001: 6). In the case of young players (under 23) the FIFA/UEFA proposals could lead to a situation in which a player, having come to the end of his contract, could not leave a club without a transfer fee being paid. This, FIFPro argued, is a return to the pre-*Bosman* days of player restraint and as such a retrograde move. In the case of older players, the imposition of sporting sanctions for breach of contract also represents a restraint, particularly if the player has complied with national labour laws governing breach of contract. Furthermore, the FIFPro report claimed that the formula for calculating compensation fees imposes a fixed fee that bears no relation between the amount of costs actually used in the training of a player and the fee to be paid. 'History shows that such fees operate as a significant and sometimes definitive restraint that cannot only seriously undermine player earnings but also put players out of the game' (FIFPro 2001: 15). This formula would not even afford players the protection of a negotiated transfer fee. FIFPro also rejected the notion of a 'multiplier' within the transfer system which would have the result of inflating fees depending on criteria not related to the 'actual cost' of training.[58] One of these multiplier criteria is the quality of the clubs youth section. Given the financial commitment of top clubs to youth academies, the revised transfer system proposed by FIFA/UEFA would result in resources flowing *to* these clubs and not *from* them. This defeats the redistribution argument for the maintenance of the transfer system as the dominant position of the top clubs is reinforced.

In short, the FIFPro report condemned proposals contained within the Negotiation Document on the revised transfer system and arrangements governing player contracts. In place of the revised transfer system, the FIFPro report recommended the establishment of re-distributional solidarity funds, a solution mooted by the Advocate General in *Bosman*. FIFPro suggested that the solidarity 'pool' would be composed of items such as a proportion of gate receipts, television revenues and merchandising. The legitimate objectives expressed by FIFA/UEFA of ensuring a balance between clubs and the encouragement of youth training would be better achieved through these funds than the restrictive transfer system. The FIFPro report expressed disappointment that both the national leagues and UEFA have failed to fully maximise the potential of such revenue sharing, instead relying on the questionable transfer system to do it for them. On the issue of player contracts, the FIFPro report proposed the use of collective bargaining. FIFPro General secretary, Theo Van Seggelen, threatened to 'go to court in every country' if the FIFA/UEFA proposals were accepted, a threat UEFA described as 'totally unacceptable'.[59]

The FIFA–UEFA split

The December 1999 Helsinki report on sport presented the Commission's position on the relationship between sport and the EU. In it, the Commission stressed that it would take the 'specific characteristics' of sport into account in the application of EU law if these characteristics could be adequately defined by the sports world themselves. The report placed a heavy emphasis on a partnership between the EU and a unified sports world. The dispute between FIFA/UEFA on the one hand and FIFPro on the other did little to communicate to the Commission the existence of a sports world with common concerns. In January 2001 the united front presented by FIFA and UEFA in the Negotiation Document also began to crumble.

The Commission's initial response to the Negotiation Document was cautious. In particular, in ongoing discussions with FIFA/UEFA, the Commission expressed concerns relating to the provisions on: the prohibition of the international transfer of minors, the maintenance of transfer fees for players under the age of 23 and the continued inability of players to end contracts prematurely.

FIFA's response to these concerns was to unilaterally issue a second set of proposals to the Commission in January 2001. FIFA explained: 'with a view to making progress in the negotiations with the European Commission on the reform of the international transfer system, FIFA has elaborated a document, which contains new proposals'.[60] The new FIFA document entitled 'Proposals to Amend FIFA's International Transfer Regulations' contained provisions which would have permitted players to serve three months notice on a club prior to the termination of contract.

UEFA issued a response to the new FIFA document in a media release on the 17 January 2001.[61] In essence, UEFA felt that the new FIFA proposals on transfers undermined their efforts to resolve the dispute with the Commission. Furthermore, UEFA criticised FIFA for the way the new proposals were unilaterally submitted to the Commission. The mid-January news headlines were dominated by reports of a possible formal split between FIFA and UEFA unless the dispute between the two parties could be resolved. For UEFA this split could only be avoided if FIFA declared their new transfer proposals void. Given that FIFA, UEFA and FIFPro now all held competing visions for the future, a solution with the Commission seemed remote. The Helsinki partnership approach had failed to be utilised by the key football authorities. Clearly concerned at UEFA's implied threat, FIFA formally withdrew their transfer proposals on 19 January 2001. The October 2000 Negotiation Document reverted to the default document with which FIFA/UEFA would conduct further negotiations with the Commission.

The Nice Summit

In December 2000, the Heads of State and Government met in Nice to finalise the work of the intergovernmental conference. In essence the leaders of the 15 EU countries met to sign a new Treaty designed to strengthen the internal structure of the EU prior to the enlargement of the Union to include applicant Central and Eastern European countries and Malta and Cyprus. In the run up to that meeting intense lobbying took place by the sports world for a protective protocol on sport to be attached to the new Treaty. Despite support for a protocol on sport from some of Europe's major football-playing nations, no additional mention was made of sport in the Treaty beyond the Declaration annexed to the Amsterdam Treaty. As with the Amsterdam debate, the Commission opposed a legally binding mention of sport in the Treaty for fear of setting a precedent of allowing certain profes-sions exemptions from the Treaty.

Despite this further setback for the game's governing bodies, the member states did release an unusually long Declaration on Sport in the form of a Presidency Conclusion. The provisions relating to the transfer dispute read, 'the European Council is keenly supportive of dialogue on the transfer system between the sports movement, in particular the football authorities, organisations representing professional sportsmen and -women, the Community and the member states, with due regard for the specific require-ments of sport, subject to compliance with Community law'.

The final transfer settlement

Despite the split that emerged between FIFA, UEFA and FIFPro, the Nice Declaration offered football's governing bodies an ideal opportunity to secure a favourable settlement with the Commission. In March 2001 an agreement was reached between the Commission and FIFA/UEFA on the re-structuring of the international transfer system for professional footballers. The agreement represented a compromise between the interests of the two parties and was widely interpreted as a favourable settlement for football's governing bodies. In July 2001 FIFA's Executive Committee adopted a new set of transfer rules in line with the principles agreed with the Commission in March. The new rules came into effect in September 2001 and were based on the following principles:

1 *The protection of minors:* the international transfer of players under the age of 18 is permitted subject to agreed conditions; the football author-ities will establish and enforce a code of conduct to guarantee that train-ing and sporting and academic education be provided.

2 *Training compensation for young players:* in the case of players aged under 23, a system of training compensation should be in place to encourage and reward the training effort of clubs, in particular small clubs.

3 *Maintenance of contractual stability:* contracts to be protected for a period of three years up to 28; two years thereafter. Sporting sanctions can be applied to players unilaterally terminating their contract within this protected time. Financial compensation can be paid if a contract is breached unilaterally whether by the player or the club.

4 *Solidarity mechanisms:* the creation of solidarity mechanisms (based on a proportion of compensation fees) is designed to redistribute a significant proportion of income to clubs involved in the training and education of a player, including amateur clubs.

5 *Transfer windows:* one transfer period per season, and a further limited mid-season window, with a limit of one transfer per player per season.

6 *Dispute resolution:* a dispute resolution and arbitration body is established which does not prejudice the ability of players to seek other forms of legal redress.[62]

FIFPro's threat to *'go to court in every country'* began in Brussels in May 2001. FIFPro sought to question the authority of the Commission to sanction a revised transfer system which FIFPro regarded as deviating from EU law. However prior to the hearing FIFPro applied for an adjournment. At the FIFA Congress at Buenos Aires in July 2001, FIFA announced how it intended to implement the new transfer system. FIFPro sought an adjournment in order to allow time to consider the details of FIFA's new system and include any new provisions in the proceedings. In particular, FIFPro expressed concerns relating to the implementation of the transfer provisions concerning sporting sanctions, the stability period and compensation payments for young players. Wishing the court case to be based on the 5 March agreement with the Commission, FIFA objected to the application for adjournment. In July the court granted the adjournment. In August, before the hearing was re-convened, FIFA and FIFPro reached an agreement on FIFPro's participation in the implementation of the new transfer regime. As part of the agreement, FIFPro agreed to halt their litigation in exchange for FIFPro representatives being able to sit on FIFA's Dispute Resolution Chamber along with representatives of the clubs. FIFPro will also nominate representatives for the new Arbitration Tribunal for Football, to which decisions of the Dispute Resolution Chamber can be appealed. Furthermore FIFA and FIFPro have clarified technical issues relating to the new transfer system and have agreed a system of review and consultation concerning the new system. The new transfer regulations accordingly came into force in September 2001.

The Commission now considers its scrutiny of the transfer system complete. The agreement between the Commission and FIFA consisted of an exchange of letters between the two parties in March 2001. In the Commission letter to FIFA, Commissioner Monti stated, 'your undertaking contains sufficient elements for me to be able to confirm that I no longer have the intention to propose that the Commission adopts a negative decision in the procedure that is open against FIFA as regards the international transfer rules'.[63] In June 2002 the Commission released a press release in which it announced the formal closure of its investigations into FIFA's regulations on international football transfers.[64] Following the entry into force of the new transfer procedure three complaints were withdrawn. Two remaining complaints relating to the transfer system were then rejected by the Commission thus allowing for the closure of the investigation. The two complainants were challenging the prohibition on players unilaterally terminating a contract. As complainants may have recourse to arbitration, national courts and the ECJ (in the later case to challenge the Commission's decision to reject the complaints), the Commission now considers its involvement over. FIFPro described this claim as 'premature'.[65] Due to the informal nature of the settlement, the Commission does still have the right to re-open its investigation should it be dissatisfied with the implementation of the new transfer rules. Furthermore, it is clear that transfer rules are not considered by the Commission to be of purely sporting interest only. Future changes to the rules will continue to require Commission approval. The approach adopted by the Commission does not therefore settle the issue definitively. A challenge to the transfer rules before a national court and potentially the ECJ must therefore remain a future possibility.

In case C-264/98 *Tiborbalog* v. *Royal Charleroi Sporting Club*, the ECJ was expected to hear a case concerning objections to the international transfer system which mirror those of the Commission. Following the remodelling of FIFA/UEFA's international transfer system in March 2001, Tibor Balog (a non-EU player) and ASBL Royal Charleroi Sporting Club (RCSC) reached a settlement meaning that a preliminary reference to the ECJ was no longer required on the question of the movement of out-of-contract non-EU players. Interestingly, before the case was withdrawn the Advocate General (Stix-Hackl) published a negative opinion in which she argued that such restrictions were incompatible with Article 81.[66]

The regulation of players' agents

Of increasing importance to the supply and demand of players is the role of their agents. Following a number of complaints and two petitions from the European Parliament, in October 1999 the Commission launched an investigation into FIFA's rules governing players' agents.[67] FIFA requires players and clubs to use licensed agents who themselves must provide a non-returnable bank guarantee of 200,000 Swiss Francs. The Commission considers these rules as potentially anti-competitive as they may have the effect of denying individuals access to the profession. It is questionable whether the competitive-enhancing features of these rules outweigh their anti-competitive features. As such a less-restrictive approach to regulating player's agents may be proposed by FIFA in the future.

Comment: a competition policy framework for sport

The ruling in *Bosman* had profound consequences for sport. Not only did sport have to adjust to the terms of the ruling, it found itself operating in a new regulatory environment in which competition policy was central. Given the newly acquired commercial status of sport in Europe, the Commission found itself compelled to examine more closely the relationship between sport and competition law. In general, the Commission has consistently held that agreements between undertakings in the sports sector do fall within the scope of competition law. Nevertheless, as the above review of case law illustrates, the Commission is seeking to adopt a more soft-touch approach to dealing with the internal rules of sport. A number of factors explain this.

First, in a short space of time cases before the Commission mounted rapidly. The Commission has had to deal with up to 60 sports-related cases at any one time. This expansion of the Commission's sports-related caseload has placed a strain on the Commission's already over-stretched resources. In other sectors, this strain has resulted in a slow turnover of cases and the increased use of administrative procedures rather than formal decisions to decide cases. In two major cases concerning the operation of Formula One motor racing and the international transfer system for footballers, the Commission has followed an informal negotiated settlement approach rather than taking formal decisions.

Second, the increased involvement by the member states (and other actors in the EU) has compelled the Commission to review their procedures for applying competition policy to sport. The member states responded to post-*Bosman* criticism of the EU's approach to sport through the Amsterdam Declaration. Although the Declaration disappointed those who wished to see a legal competence for sport established within the Treaty, the Declaration has proved extremely significant. In particular, it launched the so-called *new approach* to sport – an approach which in terms of the application of EU law to the sports sector stressed the need to balance commercial calculations with a consideration for sports social, cultural and educational qualities. The Commission's 1999 'framework' paper (see below) was in effect an institutional response to the Declaration.

Finally, as the Commission has gained more experience in sports-related issues, so they are more able to formulate clearer guidelines on the application of competition law to the sports sector. Although the causistic approach by the Commission has appeared haphazard at times, an understanding of the sports sector can only develop with time and through consultations with interested parties.

Faced with the above developments, the Commission has sought ways to establish a new regulatory environment for sport, integrating sporting self-regulation within a EU competition policy framework. However, this separate territories approach has been constructed through a mixture of hard (formal) and soft (informal) law. As is explored below, this raises some important questions about the future viability of the current separate territories approach. The Commission's approach does nevertheless reject the notion of a general block exemption for sport. The Commission is still committed to the development and consolidation of the internal market and is keen to avoid setting a precedent for allowing certain professions exemptions from the Treaty. After all, sport cannot be considered to be the only sector with 'special' characteristics.

The then Competition Policy Commissioner Van Miert signalled his intention to establish such a competition framework for sport in November

1997 at a meeting of the European Sport Forum held in Luxembourg. At this meeting Van Miert stated that 'positive action' must be taken in respect of sport. 'By positive action I mean providing the sporting world with guidelines on what kind of restrictions would be acceptable, given the special features of the sector concerned' (Van Miert 1997). In March 1998, the Competition Policy Director General Alexander Schaub made clear that these guidelines would not include a general exemption for sport from EU competition law. He argued that such an exemption is 'unnecessary, undesirable and unjustified' (Schaub 1998). Furthermore, Schaub made clear that the Commission still felt a strong sense of commitment to the realisation and protection of the fundamental freedoms. In this connection he remarked, 'it would not be fair to consumers and it would not reflect the economic importance of sport if we were merely to sit back and refrain from applying the competition rules. Where we receive legitimate complaints, we must take the necessary action' (Schaub 1998).

In February 1999, the Commission released a paper on the application of competition rules to sport.[68] The paper was the first formal exploration of the separate territories concept. The paper outlined the following principles to be considered when applying EU competition rules to sport:

1 safeguarding the general interest in relation to the protection of private interests;
2 restricting Commission action solely to cases which are of Community interest; ✓ IMPORTANT
3 applying the so-called de minimis rule, according to which agreements of minor importance do not significantly affect trade between member states; ✓
4 applying the four authorisation criteria laid down in Article 81(3) of the EC Treaty, but also refusing an exemption to any agreements which infringe other provisions of the EC Treaty and in particular freedom of movement for sportsmen;
5 defining reference markets pursuant to the applicable general rules adapted to the features specific to each sport.

To provide some guidelines for assessing potential breaches of EU competition policy, the Commission has developed four categories concerning:

1 Rules to which, in principle, Article 81(1) of the EC Treaty does not apply, given that such rules are inherent to sport and/or necessary for its organisation.
2 Rules which are, in principle, prohibited if they have a significant effect on trade between member states.
3 Rules which are restrictive of competition but which in principle qualify for an exemption, in particular rules which do not affect a sportsman's freedom of movement inside the EU and whose aim is to maintain the balance between clubs in a proportioned way by preserving both a certain

equality of opportunities and the uncertainty of results and by encouraging recruitment and training of young players.

4 Rules which are abusive of a dominant position under Article 82 of the EC Treaty. It is not the power to regulate a given sporting activity as such, which might constitute an abuse but rather the way in which a given sporting organisation exercises such power. A sporting organisation would infringe Article 82 of the EC Treaty if it used its regulatory power to exclude from the market, without an objective reason, any competing organiser or indeed any market player who, even meeting justified quality or safety standards, failed not to obtain from said sporting organisation a certificate of quality or of product safety.

The paper makes clear that as guidelines the principles contained in the paper do not prejudice the Commission's existing sports-related investigations. The paper represents something of a shift in thinking by the Commission and has had practical effects in connection with the application of competition law to sport (see above and below). Nevertheless, the limits of the competition law separate territories approach are apparent. Essentially, the Commission's line of reasoning on sport rests on the assumption that the commercial and regulatory functions of sport can be separated. Where sport is practiced as an economic activity, the Commission has indicated that restrictive practices will be challenged unless they can be justified on sporting grounds. In other words, if sports organisations can demonstrate that the pro-competitive features of their rules outweigh the anti-competitive features, the Commission should in principle have no objection.

The Commission will need to distinguish between purely sporting situations which would be considered to be outside the remit of EU competition law and wholly commercial situations, which are not. As the Commission's paper acknowledges, sport in Europe comprises two levels of activity,

> on the one hand the sporting activity strictly speaking, which fulfils a social, integrating and cultural role that must be preserved and to which in theory the competition rules of the EC Treaty do not apply. On the other hand a series of economic activities generated by the sporting activity, to which the competition rules of the EC Treaty apply, albeit taking into account the specific requirements of this sector.[69]

The difficulty clearly lies in situations in which it is difficult to separate these two levels of activity. Furthermore, the difficulty in deciding which rules are inherent to the operation of sport and which are commercially based is apparent. As such any framework for applying competition policy to sport must be very broad in order to accommodate the huge diversity in the sports world. A case-by-case approach to sport is therefore likely to persist, calling into question the usefulness of the framework. Nevertheless, as case law develops so a clearer picture is emerging of the types of agreements that are being considered anti-competitive. In this connection the

Commission is following a dual strategy. On the one hand it has consistently confirmed that sport is subject to competition law. On the other, it has then considered more closely ways in which the specificity of sport can be taken into consideration in the application of law. As such the Commission has not only been able to fulfil its constitutional role as guardian of the legal framework, it has also responded positively to political pressure for increased sensitivity. A review of the case law confirms this approach.

The exploitation market   The Commission's approach to broadcasting has mainly centred on establishing competition within the broadcasting sector. The Commission has recognised that sports rights often form an essential part of any new broadcasting service being offered to consumers. Such rules are therefore essentially commercial in nature. Accordingly, in all of the broadcasting markets discussed above (collective selling, exclusivity, collective purchasing and transmission), the Commission has established that broadcasting rules fall within the scope of Article 81. The Commission's line of reasoning must therefore be seen in the context of their commitment to establish a single market in broadcasting services in which a range of operators, including those embracing new technology, play a full part. This is consistent with the Commission's line in other sectors. However, in each of these broadcasting markets, the Commission has demonstrated a willingness to make more use of exemptions than it has in other sectors. The Commission has therefore explicitly acknowledged the specificity of sport. In the case of Formula One for instance, the Commission acknowledged that the collective sale of broadcasting rights was appropriate for the sport. On ticketing arrangements, even though the Commission adopted a negative decision in the France 1998 case, the size of the fine (a mere 1,000 euros) indicated that the Commission had to once again balance commercial considerations with the specific nature of sport. Finally, in the cases to come before it concerning merchandising agreements, the Commission has consistently sought to limit the anti-competitive impact of exclusive distribution and sponsorship agreements. In this connection, the Commission has taken the view that such rules could not be justified on sporting grounds.

The contest market   On first appearance, the issue of how sports bodies organise themselves would appear to fall outside the scope of EU competition law. This has not happened. The Commission has scrutinised a growing number of cases concerning the organisation of sport in Europe. Unlike with broadcasting rights where competition law was employed to free up the broadcasting market thus allowing for the entrance of new participants, competition law is applied to organisational issues as a way of maintaining a competitive balance between clubs. In both instances, the Commission argues that consumers benefit from such interventions. Hence the Commission has been sympathetic to rules which seek to maintain the single structure model of sport and rules restricting multiple club ownership and club relocation. Furthermore, in the Formula One case the Commission made a concerted effort to separate the FIA's regulatory and commercial functions.

The supply market   In terms of player mobility, the Commission's line has essentially concerned the rights of players as workers and the rights of clubs as commercial undertakings. In terms of post-*Bosman* transfer rules, the Commission initially adopted a hard line. It made it clear that it was not prepared to accept alternatives to the transfer system that compromised EU law. However, the impact of the Amsterdam and Nice Declaration's on sport have altered this view. The March 2001 settlement on transfers reflects a more sympathetic approach to sport. The Commission has accepted the argument that restrictions on player mobility and restrictions on the ability of clubs to employ players without obstruction can be justified in terms of maintaining a competitive balance between participants. Again, therefore, the Commission has acknowledged the specificity of sport within the context of EU competition law.

In applying competition law to sport, the Commission has had to operate within the context of three institutional pressures. First, the Commission is committed (both ideologically and constitutionally) to the promotion and protection of free and fair competition in the Single Market. It is an institution deeply committed to the principles of negative integration. Second, the Commission faces administrative difficulties. The Competition Policy Directorate suffers from a lack of resources and consequently struggles to ensure the widespread application of competition law to all sectors of the economy. It is for this reason that the Commission is committed to reforming the procedures for applying competition law. Third, the Commission must square its commitment to free market principles with the political pressure being applied to it to recognise the specific characteristics of sport when applying competition law to the sports sector.

As a consequence of these pressures, the Commission's approach to sport has been shaped by the use of soft law – another institutional norm within the Commission. Soft law settlement of cases takes the form of the issuing of comfort letters, the publication of notices or even the publication of press releases. The Commission has used these informal channels to resolve cases involving Formula One motor racing, the operation of the international transfer system for footballers, UEFA's central selling of broadcasting rights (which may in time harden with a formal decision) and the issue of club relocation. The Commission has also made use of policy papers to communicate their thoughts on the application of competition rules to sport. The use of soft law allows the Commission to respond to political pressure for a softer touch application of competition law to sport whilst not undermining their commitment to the free market. Soft law also allows for the speedier and less costly turnover of cases. Furthermore sports bodies themselves favour the informal negotiated settlement approach. With the relationship between sport and competition law being a relatively new development, the use of soft law can also be defended on the grounds of flexibility and sensitivity to sport whilst the Commission build up experience of the sector.

Nevertheless, the use of soft law poses some important questions for sports relationship with the EU. In areas where the Commission has resorted to formal decision making such as in the case of UEFA's broadcasting regulations, ticketing arrangements and merchandising agreements, sport can rely on hard law principles to guide them. However, by using soft law, the Commission has in effect constructed legally fragile separate territories for some crucial arrangements in sport. As the Commission's role is central to the success of the separate territories approach, the continued use of soft law is potentially problematic. As the expanded territory of sporting autonomy is not fully underpinned by hard case law, sport cannot readily rely on the long-term soundness of the separate territories. Furthermore, should the Commission's proposals to amend the competition law procedure be adopted, a new set of actors will play an important part in the development of separate territories.

Under the Commission's proposals, in addition to the Commission, national courts and regulatory authorities will also be able to apply the exemption criteria outlined in Article 81(3). The devolution of the powers to apply Article 81 will allow the Commission to concentrate on the most serious abuses of competition law. Sport is unlikely to be considered such an important sector. As such, the national courts and competition bodies will play a more prominent role in the regulation of sport. However, the Commission's proposals assume that these bodies will be able to play a more active part in applying competition law as they are familiar with the competition law procedures and case law. In the case of sport, the Commission's use of soft law has however resulted in a dearth of hard law measures which could guide the national authorities. With the involvement of more, essentially Single Market regulatory actors operating within the sports policy subsystem, the number of available venues for litigants to exploit will also increase. Single Market regulatory 'venue shopping' therefore has the potential to undermine the legally fragile principles of the separate territories approach. As Kinsella and Daly argue, to compound the lack of 'hard' case law guidance, the impending enlargement of the EU will further erode the uniform application of competition law principles to sport' (Kinsella and Daly 2001: 13). As the exemption criteria (both formal and informal) forms an essential tool in implementing the separate territories approach, the future remains uncertain.

The soft law sporting principles contained with the separate territories approach are therefore legally fragile. First, they can become undermined either by a change of approach by the Commission or through the impact of the Commission proposal. In such circumstances, sports bodies are likely to abandon their preference for soft law. They could, with some justification, claim that their legitimate expectations have been eroded by changes in the application of competition law. The Commission is to some extent bound by its informal decision making. Second, the socio-cultural coalition could exploit further institutional venues and themselves go 'venue shopping' in order to secure a more legally robust regulatory environment. Further sub-system activity in the form of coalition venue shopping will therefore undoubtedly change the current separate territories landscape.

The future definition of the separate territories therefore remains uncertain. Pressures such as the expected downturn in television revenues for sport may also impact upon the separate territories. Concerned at the financial health of many of Europe's football clubs, UEFA intends to introduce a club licensing system in the 2004/2005 season. Under the terms of the system, all clubs taking part in UEFA competitions must adhere to 'good governance' criteria. Given that high player salaries are at the root of football's financial problems, the system may act as a vehicle to administer the capping of salaries. The leading clubs in Europe have already agreed in principle to salary capping as a mechanism to control spiralling wage bills. As the details of the salary cap have yet to be published, the Commission has not formed an opinion on its compatibility with competition law. Salary caps are by definition restrictive. Depending on the form they take they restrict the amount clubs can spend on wages thus restricting the supply and demand for players. Capping is therefore likely to be caught within the scope of the EU's competition rules. However, if the financial recession in sport threatens to undermine the game itself, capping may be considered inherent to sport and essential to maintain a competitive balance between the clubs. The Commission's eventual treatment of salary capping will say much about the future definition of the separate territories. As far back as 1997, the Commission has however indicated its support for capping. As then Commissioner Van Miert remarked, 'another avenue which might be worth exploring is that of the salary cap whereby the total expenditure of each club on players' salaries would be limited so as to prevent all the good players joining the rich clubs, possibly with a levy on any clubs disregarding this limit' (Van Miert 1997).

Notes

1 COM (2000) 582 Final, 'Proposal for a Council Regulation on the Implementation of the Rules on Competition Laid Down in Articles 81 and 82 of the Treaty and Amending Regulations' (EEC) No. 1017/68, (EEC) No. 2988/74, (EEC) No. 4056/86 and (EEC) No. 3975/87. ('Regulation Implementing Articles 81 and 82 of the Treaty'), 27/09/00.

2   Ibid., Section 2a.
3   Cases 56 and 58/64, *Consten and Grundig* v. *Commission* [1966] ECR 299. Re: the use of exclusive distribution agreements, the granting of exclusive trademark usage and export bans in the electronics sector.
4   Case 56/65, *Société Technoque Minière* v. *Maschinenbau Ulm* [1966] ECR 235.
5   Regulation No. 870, 1995 and 1475, 1995.
6   COM (2000) 582 Final.
7   Commission Notice on the Definition of relevant market for the purposes of Community competition law, 1997, OJ C 372.
8   *Stevenage Borough FC Ltd* v. *Football League Ltd* [1997] 9 Admin LR 109, Times 1 August, 1996.
9   See Chapter 1.
10 Order of 2 September, 1994, B 6-747000-A105/92, WuW/EBkartA 2682.
11 Judgement of the Restrictive Practices Court (in England and Wales), 28 July 1999 in the matter of the Restrictive Trade Practices Act 1976 and in the matter of an agreement between the Football Association Premier League Limited and the Football Association Limited and their respective member clubs and in the matter of an agreement relating to the supply of services consisting in the broadcasting on television of such matches. The Act has since been replaced by the 1998 Competition Act.
12 Case No IV/37.214 – DFB (1999), OJ C 6.
13 Case No IV/37.398 – UEFA (1999), OJ C 99.
14 Of the total amount, 68.5 per cent is paid to the 24 clubs taking part in the UEFA Champions League (group matches).
15 DN: IP/01/1043. 20/07/01, 'Commission Opens Proceedings against UEFA's Selling of TV Rights to UEFA Champions League'.
16 DN: IP/02/806. 03/06/02, 'Commission Welcomes UEFA's New Policy for Selling the Media Rights to the Champions League'.
17 DN: IP/01/1523, 30/10/01, 'Commission Closes Its Investigation into Formula One and Other Four-Wheel Motor Sports'.
18 Council Directive 89/552/EEC as amended by Directive 97/36/EC.
19 Case 262/81, *Coditel* v. *Ciné Vog Films SA* [1982] ECR 3381 and the Decision of the Commission in Film Purchases by German Television Stations case, OJ L 248.
20 Case No. IV/33.245 – BBC, BSB and Football Association (1993), OJ C 94.
21 Case No. IV/36.033 – KNVB/Sport (1996), OJ C 228.
22 Commission Decision 91/130/EEC, OJ L 63.
23 Case No. IV/32.150, Commission Decision 93/403/EEC, OJ L 179.
24 Joined Cases T-528/93, T-542/93, T-543/93 and T-546/93, *Métropole Télévision SA* v. *Commission* [1996] ECR II-649.
25 Case No. IV/32.150, Commission Decision 2000/400/EC, OJ L 151, 24/06/00.
26 See Commission Press Releases DN: IP/00/372, 12/04/00, 'Commission Ready to Lift Immunity from Fines to Telefónica Media and Sogecable in Spanish Football Rights Case' and DN: IP/00/1352, 23/11/00, 'Commission Withdraws Threat of Fines against to Telefónica Media and Sogecable, but Pursues Examination of Their Joint Football Rights'.
27 Renamed Article 44 by UEFA in 1997. Article 47 of UEFA's Statute 2000 Edition.

28 Case No. 37.576. UEFA's Broadcasting Regulations, Commission Decision 2001/478/EC OJ L 171, 19/04/01. See also Commission Press Release DN: IP/01/583, 20/04/01, 'Commission Clears UEFA's New Broadcasting Regulations'.

29 Cases IV/33.384 and IV/33.378 – Distribution of package tours during the 1990 World Cup, Decision 92/521/EEC (1992) OJ L 326.

30 Comité Français d'Organisation (1998), News Release, Paris 23/3/98.

31 Richard Corbett MEP Press Release, 21/5/98, 'Euro MP's Take World Cup Organisers to Court'.

32 Case No. IV/36.888 – 1998 Football World Cup, Commission Decision 2000/12/EC (2000), OJ L 5, 08/01/00.

33 Case C-206/01, *Arsenal Football Club plc v. Matthew Reed*.

34 Opinion of Advocate General Ruiz-Jarabo Colomer, Case C-206/01, *Arsenal Football Club plc v. Matthew Reed*, 13/06/02.

35 Case C-318/00, *Bacardi-Martini et Cellier des Dauphins*.

36 Commission Decision of 18/03/92, OJ L131.

37 Commission Decision of 21/12/94, OJ L378.

38 See Commission Notice OJ C 138, 09/05/96.

39 DN: IP/98/355, 15/04/98, 'The Commission Conditionally Approves Sponsorship between the Danish Tennis Federation and Its Tennis Ball Suppliers'.

40 Case No. IV/37.400 – Project Gandalf, OJ C 70, 13/03/99.

41 However, questions have been asked concerning the compatibility of the Media Partners Super-league proposal with EU competition law. See van den Brink, J.P. (2000a), EC Competition Law and the Regulation of Football: Part 1, *European Competition Law Review*, Issue 8.

42 See Case C-250/92, *Gøttrup-Klim Grovvareforeninger and Others* (1994) E.C.R. I-5641.

43 CAS 98/200 *AEK Athens and Slavia Prague v. UEFA*, 20/08/99, Lausanne, Switzerland.

44 Case COMP/37 806: ENIC/UEFA. See DN: IP/02/942, 27/06/02, 'Commission Closes Investigation into UEFA Rule on Multiple Ownership of Football Clubs'.

45 DN: IP/99/965, 09/12/99, 'Limits to Application of Treaty Competition Rules to Sport: Commission Gives Clear Signal'.

46 DN: IP/99/434, 30/6/99, 'Commission Opens Formal Proceedings into Formula One and Other International Motor Racing Series'.

47 Ibid.

48 See Notice published pursuant to Article 19(3) of Council Regulation No. 17 concerning cases COMP/35.163 – Notification of FIA Regulations, COMP/36.638 – Notification by FIA/FOA of Agreements relating to the FIA Formula One World Championship, COMP/36.776 – GTR/FIA and others (2001/C169/03), 13/06/01.

49 DN:IP/01/120, 26/01/01, 'Commission Welcomes Progress towards Resolving the Long-running FIA/Formula One Case'.

50 DN: IP/01/1523, 30/10/01.

51 Conversation with FIA member, November 2002.

52 PE DOC A3-0326/94, 27/04/94, 'Report on the European Community and Sport'.

53 DN: IP/01/599, 'Commission Does not Object to Subsidies for French Professional Sports Clubs', 25/04/01.

54 German Government Press Release No.425/00. 09/10/00.

55 Joint FIFA/UEFA Negotiation Document (International Transfer of Players). Available at www.uefa.com, 10/01.

56 FIFPro is the Federation Internationale Des Associations De Footballeurs Professionnels.

57 Using Italy as an example, FIFPro's paper claims that player mobility rose from 15 per cent to 42 per cent in the period in question.

58 Such as a player's ability and potential and the number of players trained by a club.

59 BBC Online, 17/02/01.

60 FIFA Media Release 10/01/01, 'Principles for the Amendment of FIFA's Rules Regarding International Transfers', accessed at www.FIFA.com

61 UEFA Media Release, 17/01/01.

62 DN: IP/02/824, 'Commission Closes Investigations into FIFA Regulations on International Football Transfers', 05/06/02.

63 Letter from Mario Monti to Joseph S. Blatter, 05/03/01 D/000258.

64 DN: IP/02/824.

65 FIFPro press release 13/06/02, 'FIFPro Reacts to Statements of Commission and FIFA'.

66 Case C-246/98, Opinion of 29 March 2001.

67 DN: IP/99/782 21/10/99, 'Commission Launches Formal Proceedings on FIFA Rules Governing Players' Agents'.

68 DN: IP/99/133, 'Commission Debates Application of Its Competition Rules to Sport', 24/02/99.

69 Ibid.

6

Reconciling sport and law

The EU has been characterised as a regulatory state (Majone 1996). Embedded within the EU's constitutional and normative structure is a predisposition for the promulgation and enforcement of rules. In other words, the forces of negative as opposed to positive integration have historically driven the integration process (Pinder 1968, 1993). Knowledge about regulation and not budgets or votes has been the key resource EU officials have striven for. Yet knowledge has a 'dark side' – technocracy (Radaelli 1999b: 758) – and this essentially technocratic 'path' to integration has attracted criticism (see for instance Featherstone 1994). Although defended on the grounds of policy-making efficiency, technocratic integration raises important questions of transparency, accountability, legitimacy and democracy. As a consequence, in recent years evidence suggests that policy subsystems formerly dominated by technocratic and legal norms are becoming increasingly politicised (Radaelli 1999a, b). Radaelli for example has identified the single currency, tax policy and media ownership policy as three areas penetrated by political arguments (Radaelli 1999a).

As illustrated in Chapters 4 and 5, sport emerged on to the EU's systemic agenda through the ECJ rulings in *Walrave, Donà* and *Bosman*. It was then transferred to the institutional agenda through the quasi-legal venue of the Competition Policy Directorate. As such, the sports policy subsystem was initially dominated by legal Single Market regulatory norms as opposed to the essentially political socio-cultural arguments advanced by Adonnino (see Chapter 1 and below). The Adonnino sporting agenda stressed the social, educational and integrationist qualities of sport. For the EU to gain the more widespread support of its citizens, supporters of Adonnino stress the need for the EU's policy remit to reflect more socio-cultural concerns as opposed to narrow economic issues. The danger with the EU's market-based definition of sport adopted by the ECJ and Commission is that it threatens to undermine this agenda. This has contributed to the re-assertion of socio-cultural ideas within the context of EU involvement in sport. As Rochefort and Cobb remind us, '*the uninterested* [or in this case interested] become engaged in response to the way participants portray their struggle' (Rochefort and Cobb 1994: 5).

In order to achieve the full or partial re-definition of sport, the socio-cultural coalition needs to politicise the regulatory environment within which sport operates. The successful politicisation of the sports policy sub-system is an essential pre-requisite for policy change. Without it, the sub-system will continue to be dominated by legal norms and the economic definition of sport will prevail. However, to achieve politicisation the socio-cultural coalition require two conditions to be met.

First, they need to form a cohesive advocacy coalition in order to act as a counterweight to the dominant coalition. Evidence presented in Chapter 3 suggests that the socio-cultural coalition is a coalition of convenience and as such is not such a cohesive force. Within the coalition exist actors with differing visions of the future. For instance, members of the European Parliament's Culture Committee and Legal Affairs Committee are opposed to moves to re-impose sporting restrictions prohibited by *Bosman* whereas other actors such as sports bodies are keen to challenge the ruling. In addition, the Parliament wants to root sport within the Treaty as a way of underpinning EU action in the social and cultural aspects of sport, whereas the desire of sports organisations for sport to have Treaty status is a tactic to limit EU involvement in sport and thus safeguard the autonomy of sport.

The second requirement for the re-definition of sport is the ability to operate successfully in numerous institutional venues. As indicated in Chapter 3, this condition is broadly met. The Commission has the right of legislative and policy initiative, the Parliament has enhanced budgetary and legislative powers and the member states possess the ability to amend the Treaty and to agree politically persuasive soft law. The socio-cultural advocacy coalition therefore possesses considerable institutional resources in order to effect policy re-definition. The effective use of these resources is however problematic. Changes to primary legislation requires the unanimous support of the member states and changes to secondary legislation and budgetary lines requires considerable support within and between the EU institutions. Nevertheless, the lack of cohesion within the socio-cultural coalition and the absence of a Treaty base for sport represent significant obstacles to the fulfilment of the socio-cultural agenda.

This chapter examines the approach adopted by the socio-cultural coalition in six sections. The first examines the birth and development of socio-cultural ideas between 1984 and 1995. The second section analyses the impact of *Bosman* on the nature, organisation and approach of the socio-cultural coalition. Section three examines the first major breakthrough for the socio-cultural coalition – the annexing of a Declaration on Sport to the Treaty of Amsterdam in 1997. The fourth section analyses the impact of the Declaration and examines the birth of the 'new approach' to sports policy established throughout 1998 and 1999. The fifth section examines the 2000 Nice Declaration on Sport. Section six provides the concluding comment.

The birth of socio-cultural ideas 1984–1995

The birth of a socio-cultural sporting agenda can be traced to the 1984 Fontainebleau Summit. With economic and political integration stagnating and the legitimacy of the EU in the mind of the public faltering, the member states needed to 're-launch' European integration. In response, two committees were established to examine the possible avenues for this re-launch. The Dooge Committee reported on political reform and, although the measures were not directly acted upon, the Dooge proposals acted as the basis for discussion on Treaty reform at the 1985 intergovernmental conference. The Single European Act eventually emerged from these discussions.

The second committee (the Adonnino Committee) reported on measures that could strengthen the image of the EU in the minds of its citizens, thus addressing the legitimacy crisis. The creation of the Adonnino Committee marked the formal launch of an institutional commitment to the concept of a people's Europe and the first acknowledgement of the potential political uses of sport. The Adonnino Committee's report suggested a series of short- and long-term proposals that would contribute to the establishment of a people's Europe.[1] The Committee identified eight categories of proposals, one of which concerned youth, education, exchanges and sport. The Committee's recommendations relating to sport are consistent with the general theme of the report. Interventionism and symbolism are evident throughout the Committee's recommendations. The main problem encountered by the Committee in relation to the 'use' of sport for the purposes of advancing the aim of a people's Europe, concerns the organisation of sport itself. The report recognised the autonomy of sporting organisations and was careful not to appear to challenge that autonomy. As a result, the Committee's sporting recommendations merely sought to encourage the sports sector to adopt measures, rather than requesting the European Council or Commission to act. The report's sports-related recommendations read:

> Since ancient times sport has been an important forum for communication among people's. It is an important part of the lives of a large number of people within the Community. That is why it is all the more regrettable that the enjoyment of international competitive sport has been drastically marred recently by hooliganism. The Committee has therefore considered both of the these important aspects below.
>
> 5.9.1. The administration of sport is predominantly the responsibility of sports associations independent of government. The Committee proposes that the sports associations be invited to encourage action where it is consistent with their responsibilities, along these lines:

i   for certain sectors of sport, organisation of European Community events such as cycle and running races through European countries;

ii creation of Community teams for some sports to compete against joint teams from geographical groupings with which the Community has special links;

iii inviting sporting teams to wear the Community emblem in addition to their national colours at major sporting events of regional or worldwide interest;

iv exchanges of sportsmen, athletes and trainers between the different Community countries, to be encouraged by programmes at the level of the Community and the member states;

v   support for sporting activities especially for particular categories of persons, such as the handicapped. Student sport activities should be organised in conjunction with the twinning of schools and towns.[2]

The acceptance of the Adonnino Committee's recommendations marked more of a commitment to the concept of a people's Europe than it did to the development of a sports policy. Nevertheless, the spirit of Adonnino lived on within the EU, with the Parliament emerging as the new natural home for such a movement.

The Parliament's sporting agenda has a strong socio-cultural tradition. The Parliament has acknowledged that, above all, sport is a social pursuit. It not only carries health, educational, cultural and social implications, it can also be used for political purposes. In this connection, sport can aid the implementation of policy goals in other fields and can act as a vehicle through which the EU can connect itself to its citizens through the establishment of a people's Europe. For the Parliament, the expression of these goals is therefore generally considered a priority. Nevertheless, difficulties remain for the Parliament in their desire to advance the Adonnino agenda.

The most obvious barrier is the lack of a Treaty base for sport. This creates practical legislative and budgetary difficulties for the Parliament in terms of developing and funding sports-related initiatives. Elements within the Parliament's Committee on Culture, Youth, Education, the Media and Sport have been active in advancing the case for a Treaty Article on sport which would provide a legal base for legislation and guarantee a budgetary line.

The second major difficulty concerns the prevailing definition of sport adopted by the EU. *Walrave, Donà* and *Bosman* established sports economic link to the Treaty. As such, sport became a Single Market issue rather than a social issue. As the Parliament's Committee on Constitutional Affairs concluded,

> although, it is a good idea that the Union should intervene to tackle a number of very specific problems in the sphere of sport, such as the fight against doping, it is absurd that such measures should be based on the Union's responsibility for the internal market, which results, for example, in ill advised case law such as the Bosman judgement.[3]

The difficulty in attempting to achieve the wider goal of constructing a European federation based solely on economic integration without a commitment to socio-cultural (political) integration is widely acknowledged by many MEPs.

Third, along with the other EU institutions, the Parliament has also had to confront the issue of how to disentangle sports economic function from its social function. Whilst the Parliament primarily sees sport as a social pursuit, it has acknowledged that sport carries out an economic function. The Parliament has had to balance the desire to protect sporting structures from the scope of EU law with the need to protect the rights of workers and consumers within the EU. For example in 1989 the Van Raay report condemned the use of nationality restrictions and the international transfer system.[4]

The Larive report on the European Community and sport[5]
The 1994 Larive report was the result of a number of sports-related reports stemming from the Parliament. These reports included 'Sport and the Community', 'Women in Sport', 'Vandalism and Violence in Sport' and 'Sport in the European Community and a People's Europe'.[6] The Committee on Culture, Youth, Education and Media was responsible for the report with Mrs J. Larive MEP as rapporteur. The catalyst for the report was a motion for a resolution proposed by Mrs Ewing MEP on the protection of popular sporting traditions in Europe. This motion for a resolution sought ways to protect traditional sports from the deleterious consequences of the break up of local communities. Ewing called for the implementation of a framework of law to assure the legal recognition of these traditional games in Europe and the establishment of a body to study, safeguard and promote Europe's sporting traditions.[7]

The report included within its terms of reference a number of motions for resolutions that had been referred to it. The first motion for a resolution, written by Mrs Banotti MEP on the 'Need to Reappraise the EC's Sports Policy' called on the Commission to rethink its approach to sport in the wake of the approved Adonnino report, 1985. In particular, Banotti called into question funding priorities and asked for greater emphasis to be placed on a 'Sport For All' policy that could contribute to the creation of a true 'people's Europe'.[8] The second motion for a resolution was provided by Mr Gutiérrez Díaz MEP in October 1991 on safety in professional boxing.[9] The third motion suggested that a common logo should be worn by athletes from the 12 Community member states taking part in the Barcelona Olympic Games.[10] Written by Mrs Muscardini MEP, the motion recognised the symbolic significance of sport and sought to use this to promote European integration. The common logo would, according to Muscardini, symbolise the athletes membership of the EU as an ideal and unified homeland and as an appeal for democracy for all the people's of Europe. The fourth motion for a resolution related to the outlaw of symbols that incite violence in sport.[11] The authors of the text called on the Commission to assess the situation relating to anti-social practises in sport such as the actions of abusive and racist supporters and the use of totalitarian symbols in sport and take the necessary steps to promote effective legislation that will restore the full harmony and value of sport. The motion sought measures to protect those values in sport that encourages coexistence, understanding and tolerance among peoples, races and cultures. The final motion for a resolution concerning safety of sports installations was written by Mrs Muscardini MEP following the death of a number of fans due to the collapse of a temporary stand in Bastia, France.[12]

The Larive report clearly links the active or passive participation in sport with the social and cultural identity of people. Additionally, this participation has generated significant amounts of economic activity. Accordingly, the report argued that sport should receive political attention in the EU, first in relation to underpinning the process of European integration and secondly in connection to the operation of the Single Market.

The first area covered by the report concerned the relationship between EU legislation and the internal rules of sports organisations. The report challenged the mismatch between the rhetoric of the fundamental freedoms and the practise of sports organisations. Many of the issues raised in the report relating to restrictive practices in sport were dealt with in *Bosman*. Four subdivisions of legislative activity were identified. First, in relation to free movement of persons and services legislation, the report sought to ensure sport for all EU citizens regardless of nationality (a challenge to the use of nationality quotas in sport), the freedom to join and leave sports clubs (a challenge to the rules on transfer of players), the mutual recognition of coaches' diplomas and the freedom to conclude cross-border insurance contracts. Second, concerning free movement of goods legislation, the report commented that the internal market had clarified the position with regard to the cross-border movement of sports goods through VAT Directives, standardisation of technical specifications and issues relating to the composition of sports food. Third, the report commented on how EU rules on competition greatly affect the operation of sport in Europe. Fourth, the application of other general legislative provisions were examined including legislation on animals in sport and the protection of minors. Despite a concern for sportspersons to be afforded the same level of protection under EU law as any other EU citizen, the report was clear that the liberalisation of sporting rules should be accompanied by more socio-cultural measures.

The second main area dealt with by the Larive report concerned the role of the EU in encouraging active participation in sport. The report highlights the job-creation potential of sport, suggesting over 60 million people in the EU (12) belong to sports clubs with tens of million more taking part in sport in a recreational, non-organised way. However, the report suggested that this participation is highly uneven. In this connection, the report urged the EU to encourage a wider participation in sport to include the underprivileged, the disabled and women. Furthermore, participation in sport was identified as a useful tool for counteracting crime, health problems and worker absenteeism. School sport was therefore encouraged, as was the participation of the wider working and non-working population.

Third, the report addressed the issue of combating hooliganism in sport. In addition to raising the profile of fair play campaigns in sport in order to combat 'on-the-field' problems, the report suggested that 'off-the-field' problems such as hooliganism can be dealt with via legislation. In particular, stadium structure and layout specifications can help minimise disorder. Support was given to national measures designed to minimise hooliganism, although it was stressed that nationality should not be used as a reason for refusing or impeding access to sporting events.

The final area dealt with by the report concerned the use of sport in fostering a European identity. The report criticised the EU approach of sponsoring large-scale sporting events with high media interest, questioning the appropriateness of the use of financial resources. Implicitly, the report suggested that this amounts to marketing the EU, whereas the EU should be involved in smaller, more specific projects that are of more relevance to EU citizens. In this respect, the report welcomed the Commission's policy shift on sport which proposed a change in this direction. The report argued that funding priority should be given to small-scale, cross-border projects as this heightens people's awareness of other cultures. In addition, support for national and regional traditional sports should be encouraged as means of protecting traditional sports. The report suggested that one mechanism for advancing the aim of fostering a European identity through sport is to integrate sport into the operation of other Community projects such as the European Regional Development Fund, the European Social Fund, town twinning schemes, the Interreg programme and the Youth for Europe initiative. The report also stressed the importance of European support for sports facilities, European training programmes and sports research/ management initiatives. To help co-ordination in these areas, the report also suggested that sport should be included as an area of formal competence in the Treaty.

The *Bosman* setback 1995–1997

The 1995 *Bosman* ruling represented a set back for many socio-cultural actors despite the Larive report's desire to see the lifting of restrictions placed on the movement of sportsmen and women. *Bosman* confirmed the predominance of the EU's market-based definition of sport at the expense of the social definition. In short, the *Bosman* approach was inconsistent with the Adonnino agenda.

The Pack report on the Role of the European Union in the Field of Sport[13]
In June 1996, the Parliament's Committee on Culture, Youth, Education and
the Media, appointed Doris Pack as rapporteur to a report on the role of the
EU in the field of sport. Additionally, it was decided to include in the report
a motion for a resolution on setting up a European youth sport fund. As with
the Larive report, the report reviewed the significance of the sports sector to
Europe's society and economy. In terms of participation in sport, the report
claimed that over 100 million European citizens participate in sporting activity and that tens of thousands of sports associations organise these activities.
As such, sport 'constitutes a basic cultural and social phenomena'.[14] Sport is
therefore crucial to European society given that access to it promotes 'personal development and a well balanced personality'.[15] In this connection the
report therefore draws similarities between the sports sector in Europe and
the cultural world. Furthermore, the report argues that the love of sport
extends beyond participation to those who are not actively involved. As
such, the report recognises the importance of ensuring citizens gain access to
sporting events and information on them. The emphasis on social interaction is supplemented with a focus on sport as a method of countering the
deleterious effects of smoking, alcohol and drug abuse and a preventative
weapon against potential health problems such as cancer and cardio-
vascular problems. Sport therefore has a role to play in the field of physical
and mental health and social interaction.

The report also emphasised the economic significance of the sports sector
in Europe. According to the report sport generates an estimated 1.5 per cent
of the EU's gross domestic product (GDP) and plays a significant role as a
source of employment. Even though the report welcomed the ECJ's lifting of
restrictions on the mobility of sports men and women in *Bosman*, it claimed
that,

> although the European Union has taken an interest in professional sport as an
> activity, it has, to date, only taken account in a very marginal fashion of the
> cultural, educational and social dimension of sport, and whereas such neglect
> stems basically from the fact that there is no explicit reference to sport in the
> Treaty.[16]

Accordingly, activity in the sports sector has been economically motivated
and not specifically directed at sport. The report therefore called on the intergovernmental conference (at the time still sitting) to include a reference to
sport in Article 128 (Culture) of the revised Treaty (the Amsterdam Treaty)
or to establish a separate Article for sport. The report does, however, express
the opinion that sport should not be exempt from EU law and places a degree
of pressure on sports organisations to ensure that the solidarity of sport is
maintained. In this connection, the report suggests financial redistribution
between sports organisations as an effective mechanism to achieve this solidarity.

This general lack of interest in the socio-cultural dimensions of sport is illustrated by the size of the Community budget for sport. The ECU 3 million 'Sport in Europe' programme (Article B3-305 in the 1997 Community budget) was created by the Parliament and (at the time) financed programmes such as the Eurathlon programme and sports initiatives for the disabled. Only through the activities of the Committee on Culture, Youth, Education and Media and the Committee on Budgets in the Parliament was this expenditure included in the budget. The report criticises the Commission for continually failing to include this programme in its preliminary draft budget. The Commission included Article B3-305 in the chapter entitled 'Information and Communication' within the preliminary draft budget. The report argues that this is 'symbolic of the subsidiary, workaday role ascribed to it by the Commission, which sees it simply as a means of communication'.[17] Furthermore, the report argues that this attitude demonstrates that sport is not considered by the EU on its own merits, but rather as a means of implementing other policies. The report sees a clear division between the rhetoric of a people's Europe and the practise of how sport is dealt with by the EU.

The report recommended that the Commission should establish a task force to examine more closely the relationship between the EU and the European sports sector. A Green Paper should then be produced with a view to elaborate the themes stemming from this task force. The report expressed the view that all dimensions of sport, not just those relating to it as an economic activity, should be taken into consideration. The report also commented that pending the implementation of that action plan, sports initiatives could be promoted through other channels such as the EU's regional and social policies, those concerning education, training and youth exchanges, equal opportunities policy, anti-racist policies and research policies. To ensure some action in these directions, the report also called for the convening of a Council of Ministers for Sport and, to ensure visibility, called for a European Year of Sport.

The Motion for a Resolution relating to the establishment of a European youth sport fund called on the Commission to enter a specific appropriation in the forthcoming budget for youth sport and also to oversee the establishment of a youth sport fund, a solidarity fund paid into by sporting organisations. Additionally, the Resolution called on the Commission to co-operate with member states and European sports bodies to draw up an action programme for youth sport.

In essence the Pack report reflects the more socio-cultural tendencies within the Parliament. The report stresses the multi-dimensional nature of sport, rather than the narrowly economic interpretation applied by the ECJ and the Competition Policy Directorate. In effect, the report seeks the establishment of a European sports policy. First, the report wants sport to be granted a Treaty base. Second, the report wants a more co-ordinated approach to sport to be adopted by the Commission through the adoption of a Green Paper. Third, the report seeks more creative ways of feeding sports initiatives into other programmes. Fourth, the report calls for more funding for sports initiatives and, finally, the report seeks the establishment of a Council of Ministers for Sport. The Parliament is therefore attempting to act as a counterweight in the European policy process to the more market-based motivations of the Commission. Furthermore, the Parliament has signalled, through its budgetary powers and the report that it intends to creatively promote the socio-cultural elements of sport through other policy means. A clear example of this was demonstrated by the inclusion in the revised Television Without Frontiers (TWF) Directive of Article 3a dealing with the broadcasting of sporting events on free-to-air television. This conforms to the general approach of the Parliament, which has traditionally sought to expand the EU's agenda through the creative exploitation of institutional powers.

The Television Without Frontiers Directive
It has already been established by the ECJ that television broadcasts are to be defined as tradable services within the meaning of Articles 49 and 50 of the Treaty.[18] The primary mechanism through which the EU has sought to establish the legal conditions necessary to establish a common market for these broadcasting services in Europe has been through the TWF project. Based on Articles 47 (2) and 55 of the Treaty, the project's provisions on sporting broadcasts represent something of a contradiction. In theory, member states cannot restrict the transmission of services emanating from another member state, yet the amended TWF Directive permits the establishment of such restrictions in sports broadcasting through the creation of national lists to protect major events. Article 3a of the Directive permits member states to draw up lists of protected sporting events that will have to be made available to the public on free-to-air television. Such a restriction on broadcasting services has been defended on the grounds of public interest but must be of non-discriminatory nature and must be proportionate to their objectives. The ECJ has confirmed the validity of public interest arguments in the broadcasting sector.[19]

The TWF Directive resulted from a series of measures adopted by the EU institutions in the field of broadcasting and audio-visual policy (Collins 1994, Humphreys 1996). EU involvement in broadcasting and audio-visual policy had its roots in the early 1980s. The 1982 Hahn report expressed the view that television and the mass media in general could aid the process of European integration through its ability to shape public opinion. Hahn, a German Christian Democrat MEP, argued that political integration in Europe would be difficult to achieve whilst the media remained nationally controlled. The report emphasised how new technology would radically transform the nature of broadcasting in Europe, calling into question traditional nation state forms of broadcasting. The Parliament adopted the Hahn report through a resolution (the Hahn Resolution). As a result of this resolution, the Commission produced an interim report titled, '*Realities and Tendencies in European Television: Perspectives and Options*'. A year after the publication of DG X's interim report, the Commission produced a 1984 Green Paper on the '*Establishment of the Common Market for Broadcasting, Especially by Satellite and Cable*', better known as Television Without Frontiers.[20] Significantly, responsibility for preparing the Green Paper lay, this time, with the more liberal DG III and references to the cultural dimension of broadcasting were kept to a minimum. In light of the Commission's overtly economic justifications, the TWF proposal represented a significant break with the Hahn report and '*Realities and Tendencies*'.

In order to realise a common market in broadcasting, the Commission's Green Paper proposed harmonisation in three areas: advertising, copyright and public order, personal rights and the right of reply. The TWF Directive was agreed in Council by a qualified majority in October 1989 and came into operation two years later. However, many supporters of the Hahn report and 'Realities and Tendencies' were disappointed with the new TWF Directive as it was not a true reflection of the spirit of Hahn. Similar arguments were advanced a number of years later concerning the compatibility of *Bosman* with the Adonnino sporting agenda.

Built into the Directive was provision for review after five years (Article 26). The Commission presented their proposals for review on 31 May 1995. This review gave the Parliament an opportunity to not only re-kindle some of the spirit of Hahn, but also to seek to balance the economic definition of sport adopted in *Bosman* with a socio-cultural sporting measure. The Parliament's ability to do this was enhanced by the new co-decision procedure for agreeing legislation.[21] In accordance with this procedure the Parliament completed its first reading of the proposal on 14 February 1996 by approving the Commission's proposal subject to amendments. The Council adopted a common position on 8 July 1996 and the Parliament held its second reading on 12 November 1996. A final text was agreed between the Parliament and Council in April 1997 after discussions in the conciliation committee. Member states had until December 1998 to transpose the new Directive into national law.

The new Directive made some minor definitional amendments to the original Directive in order to make it more workable. However, the most significant change came in the form of a Parliament amendment designed to guarantee public viewing access to major sporting events on television. Amendment number 20 was agreed by the Parliament during its second reading of the revised Directive.[22] To give effect to the Parliament's amendment, Article 3a was included in the new Directive. The purpose of Article 3a (full text below) was explained in recital 18 of the new Directive.

Recital 18: 'Whereas it is essential that member states should be able to take measures to protect the right to information and to ensure wide access by the public to television coverage of national or non-national events of major importance for society, such as the Olympic games, the football World Cup and European football Championship; whereas to this end member states retain the right to take measures compatible with Community law aimed at regulating the exercise by broadcasters under their jurisdiction of exclusive broadcasting rights to such events'.

Article 3a

1 Each member state may take measures in accordance with Community law to ensure that broadcasters under its jurisdiction do not broadcast on an exclusive basis events which are regarded by that member state as being of major importance for society in such a way as to deprive a substantial proportion of the public in that member state of the possibility of following such events via live coverage or deferred coverage on free television. If it does so, the member state concerned shall draw up a list of designated events, national or non-national, which it considers to be of major importance for society. It shall do so in a clear and transparent manner in due and effective time. In so doing the member state concerned shall also determine whether these events should be available via whole or partial live coverage, or where necessary or appropriate for objective reasons in the public interest, whole or partial deferred coverage.

2 Member states shall immediately notify to the Commission any measures taken or to be taken pursuant to paragraph 1. Within a period of three months from the notification, the Commission shall verify that such measures are compatible with Community law and communicate them to the other member states. It shall seek the opinion of the Committee established pursuant to Article 23a. It shall forthwith publish the measures taken in the Official Journal of the European Communities and at least once a year the consolidated list of the measures taken by member states.

3 Member states shall ensure, by appropriate means, within the framework of their legislation that broadcasters under their jurisdiction do not exercise the exclusive rights purchased by those broadcasters following the date of publication of this Directive in such a way that a substantial proportion of the public in another member state is deprived of the possibility of following events which are designated by that other member state in accordance with the preceding paragraphs via whole or partial live coverage or, where necessary or appropriate for objective reasons in the public interest, whole or partial deferred coverage on free television as determined by that other member state in accordance with paragraph 1.[23]

Article 3a of the Directive therefore permits member states to draw up lists of protected sporting events that will have to be made available to the public on free-to-air television. These lists are then notified to the Commission who must seek the opinion of the so-called 'Contact Committee' composed of representatives of all member states and assess the compatibility of the national measures with EU law. Measures approved by the Commission are published in the *Official Journal of the European Communities.*

In Britain, the Broadcasting Act of 1996, as amended by the Television Broadcasting Regulations 2000, implements the Directive. Part 4 of the Act governs the listing of 'Sporting and Other Events of National Interest'. Section 97 allows the Secretary of State to establish a list of sporting (or other) events of national interest. Sections 98–101 ensure public viewing accessibility to these listed events. Currently in Britain the following events are listed: (Group A): The Olympic Games, the FIFA World Cup Finals Tournament, the FA Cup Final, the Scottish FA Cup Final (in Scotland), the Grand National, the Derby, the Wimbledon Tennis Finals, the European Football Championship Finals Tournament, the Rugby League Challenge Cup Final, the Rugby World Cup Final. (Group B): Cricket Test matches played in England, non-finals play in the Wimbledon Tournament, all other matches in the Rugby World Cup Finals Tournament, Six Nations Rugby tournament matches involving home countries, the Commonwealth Games, the World Athletics Championship, the Cricket World Cup – the Final, Semi-finals and matches involving home nations', the Ryder Cup, the Open Golf Championship.

The justifications in support of Article 3a tend to reflect socio-cultural tendencies inherent within the Parliament. Furthermore, they represent an exception to the general principle of free movement of services in trans-frontier broadcasting enshrined in the TWF Directive. The first justification relates to the concern that the drift towards pay-TV television denies the sporting public the opportunity to watch sport on television. As such major sporting events that are of particular significance to society should be protected (the 'public interest'/'national heritage' argument).

Second, as the original TWF Directive recognised, national media sovereignty no longer fully exists. As such purely national measures designed to ensure unencrypted access would be prone to circumvention by operators external to national jurisdiction. If it is the wish of national authorities to ensure public access to televised major events, then the EU offers an appropriate level of protection given technology driven developments in trans-frontier broadcasting.

Third, given the high level of competition between broadcasters and the small size of potential lists, income to sporting clubs will not be excessively restricted by regulation.

Fourth, as commercial television operators have identified, sport is an important component to schedules due to its popularity. If public service broadcasters are denied major sporting events it may threaten their overall survival in the market place. If this happens, a source of competition will be denied. This argument may however over emphasise the importance of sport to public service broadcasters.

Fifth, by protecting the broadcasting of major sporting events, the EU can demonstrate a degree of visibility and relevance to Europe's public in a manner compatible with historical attempts to create a 'people's Europe'. This approach would be consistent with the general theme of the Hahn report relating to information, media and European integration and indeed the Adonnino Committee's central thrust. It reflects a socio-cultural inspired attempt to redress the market-based approach adopted in the first TWF Directive and the ruling in *Bosman*.

Nevertheless, the Directive goes against a trend in European sport favouring a free market in broadcasting. The arguments are essentially economic. Although free-to-air broadcasting increases viewing numbers, it denies the sporting organisations the ability to realise the full value of their rights. The (as then) Sports Council of Great Britain changed its policy on sports broadcasting to embrace the free market. Until February 1996 the Sports Council supported the listing of designated sporting events. Since this date they have favoured a free market in sports rights thus allowing them to maximise income from their sale. The English football Premier League shares these concerns pointing to the unsatisfactory state of terrestrial broadcasting of sport in the 1980s which limited competition for rights and restricted sports broadcasting income. Revenue generated from television money has enabled English football to invest in new and improved stadiums, better facilities for fans and players and grass roots investment into youth football. As such, it is the view of many European sporting organisations that they are in the best position to make distributional decisions concerning investment in sport and so should be left free to negotiate appropriate broadcasting contracts with a range of operators. The case against regulation of sporting broadcasts is naturally shared by the cable and satellite operators who often require exclusive sporting broadcasts to attract new subscribers.

The Amsterdam breakthrough 1997

The Parliament's response to the ruling in *Bosman* proved influential in highlighting and articulating the concerns of the socio-cultural advocacy coalition. In particular, the Parliament emerged as an important forum through which demands for the incorporation of sport into the Treaty emerged. Although the Parliament's activity pressurised the member states into taking action, the Parliament's socio-cultural agenda tapped into a thread of concern already evident within some national capitals. Not only had the member states agreed to the Adonnino proposals, but following unsuccessful governmental submissions to the ECJ in *Bosman*, a growing number of member states including the Italian, Belgian, French and German governments gave their support to sport's Treaty incorporation. As such, the Parliament's role must be placed in context. Alone, the Parliament lacked the legislative powers to pursue a more holistic approach to sport. Therefore without member state support, the Parliament would have been unable to force the issue of sport on to the European Council's agenda.

Although the TWF Directive was a success for the Parliament, the ECJ's ruling in *Bosman* and the approach adopted by the Commission in applying competition law demonstrated to the socio-cultural coalition the insensitivity with which the EU dealt with sporting issues. The perception was that the EU was not only failing to recognise the social importance of sport, but it was also curtailing sporting 'autonomy'. A Treaty Article was therefore required in order to address these two concerns. As a result, in the run to the Amsterdam Summit, intense lobbying took place for the adoption of an Article for sport in the newly revised Treaty. In particular, the maximalist members of the socio-cultural coalition hoped to ensure greater protection for sports rules from the application of EU law whilst also granting sport a legal base to exploit funding opportunities.

Calls for an Article for sport came to a head at the 6th European Sports Forum where representatives of the National Olympic Committees of the 15 member states and 30 international and European sports federations supported sport's inclusion into the Treaty. Support was also forthcoming from the Parliament, yet crucially not the Commission who wanted to avoid the setting of a precedent for allowing certain professions exemptions from the Treaty and also for fear of sparking inter-DG conflict over the approach to sports policy (*European Voice* 1996). A draft for an Article on sport in the Treaty was agreed by representatives of ENGSO and the EOC's. Its contents give an insight into the objectives of the drafters.

1 The European Community contributes to the development of sport in its member states, taking strict account of the diversity of its public and private structures as well as of the competence of its member states and of the autonomy of sporting organisations with regard to the organisation of sport and its rules. The Community's activities (proceedings) take into account the integrationist qualities of sport within the framework of Europe, its citizens and social dimension.

2 The Community's activities (proceedings) encourage co-operation between organisations responsible for sport in the member states, and fulfil their activities in the following domains:

   • promotion of exchanges between European citizens through the integrationist qualities of sport. These exchanges should contribute to a better knowledge and acceptance of the social and cultural differences between member states.
   • encouragement of participation in sport, as a means of promoting the health of European citizens.
   • support of sporting activities for social ends, aiming to combat unemployment and discrimination, racism and violence, by promoting equal opportunities between men and women.
   • help for sporting initiatives in the realm of education, as much at the level of management training and sports technicians as in the creation of exchange programmes for professions linked to sport. European sporting co-operation founded on sporting institutions and mutual information

on training systems and sporting organisations will be particularly encouraged.

- support for projects aimed at the states of Central and Eastern Europe and projects aimed at co-operation for development.

3 The Community and its member states encourages co-operation with countries outside the Community and with international organisations responsible for sporting matters, particular the Council of Europe.
4 The Community takes into account aspects related to sport in policies conducted on the basis of other clauses of the present Treaty.
5 In order to contribute to the realisation of the objectives set out in the present article, the Council:

- acting according to the procedures of articles 189b (co-decision) and after consultation with the Committee of the Regions, adopts measures of encouragement to the exclusion of all harmonisation of legal and administrative clauses of the member states. The Council decides by unanimity according to article 189b.
- adopts by unanimity the recommendations, as proposed by the Commission.

This ENGSO/EOC memorandum was sent to all representatives on the Reflection Group (the group responsible for managing the Amsterdam IGC process and consisting of representatives of national administrations, the Parliament and Commission). Such an Article would ensure that EU action in the field of sport would reflect the social dimension of sport whilst securing the right for sport to be taken into consideration in the framing of other EU policies. Furthermore, by ensuring that the co-decision procedure applied, the widest possible consultation would have been guaranteed. The independent Treaty Article approach was just one approach considered by members of the socio-cultural coalition. Alternatives included adding sport to the list of EU activities outlined in Article 3 of the Treaty, adding sport to Article 151 (ex 128) dealing with cultural policy and the greater use of soft law measures by the member states. The next chapter examines these proposals in greater depth.

The eventual appearance of sport in the Amsterdam Treaty came as a surprise despite the prevailing political climate in which Amsterdam was negotiated. Following the traumatic ratification of the Maastricht Treaty, it was widely expected that the EU would adopt measures in the new Treaty that would attempt to bring Europe's citizen's closer to the EU. Sport was considered one such issue through which the EU could achieve this objective. Despite this, sport was not mentioned in draft versions of the Treaty and was not included on the formal agenda of the Reflection Group. It was reported that when challenged on the omission of sport in an early draft of the Treaty, Irish officials (at the time holding the Presidency) claimed that no member state had raised the issue (*European Voice* 1996). Furthermore, the Commission was also reluctant. Nevertheless, following the conclusion of the 1996/1997 intergovernmental conference process, the Heads of State and Government of the member states meeting in Amsterdam attached a non-binding Declaration to the Treaty. The Declaration read:

> The conference emphasises the social significance of sport, in particular its role in forging identity and bringing people together. The conference therefore calls on the bodies of the European Union to listen to sports associations when important questions affecting sport are at issue. In this connection, special consideration should be given to the particular characteristics of amateur sport.[24]

Through the Declaration, the EU has formally acknowledged the social and integrationist qualities of sport even though, as a soft law measure, it has not legally committed itself to supranational action and therefore expenditure. The EU has however given a commitment that sport is to be taken into account when other EU policies are being adopted. To facilitate this, the EU has also committed itself to consult with sporting bodies. This has had the effect of further formalising and institutionalising the relationship between sport and the EU. Nevertheless, the result disappointed those who wanted the EU to adopt more formal measures. However, although Declarations have no formal legal status in the EU, their significance must not be underestimated. Soft law refers to rules of conduct which, in principle have no legally binding force but which nevertheless may have a significant effect on policy development. Soft law has the potential to produce significant effects. First, it is not uncommon for soft law to be used as quasi-legal justification by EU institutions for the development of policy initiatives. The Amsterdam Declaration was subsequently referred to by all the EU institutions, including the ECJ, in connection with sporting activity. Soft law therefore has the potential to harden over time. Second, the use of soft law is often a tactic used by the European Council and Council of Ministers when they are unable to agree upon binding measures but nevertheless wish to place political pressure on the EU institutions for a change in policy direction. Soft law can be employed by the member states as an implied threat of taking further harder measures unless EU institutions change their approach. As such, it has offered some guidance as to the interpretation and scope of application of EU law.

The re-assertion of socio-cultural ideas: the birth of the new approach 1998–

The Amsterdam Declaration added impetus to the socio-cultural agenda whilst also equipping them with an additional institutional venue to exploit. Their agenda took giant strides after 1998. Out of the confusion and ambiguity of the *Bosman* ruling emerged (is emerging) a more holistic and co-ordinated approach to sports policy. This 'new approach' has been forged through an alliance between the member states and the Education and

Culture Directorate. The member states have responded to pressure for a change of approach promoted by the Parliament by piecing together a series of policy guidelines on sports policy through a combination of soft law measures. In addition to Treaty Declarations, soft law refers to Presidency Conclusions and intergovernmental political guidelines. The Education and Culture Directorate has responded to these soft law developments by establishing a framework for the development of a EU sports policy. At the heart of this framework lies a more broad-based definition of sport which has brought into the development of EU sports policy many ideas supported by the socio-cultural coalition.

Initial Council Presidency conclusions 1997–1998

Prior to the Amsterdam Declaration, it was rare for the European Council to discuss sport. Since Amsterdam, it is rare for the member states not to discuss it in some intergovernmental forum. Initially, following the Amsterdam Treaty, sport was discussed as a vehicle through which unemployment could be tackled. This was partly the concern of Luxembourg's Presidency in the second half of 1997 and reflected a desire to follow up the employment provisions contained within the Treaty.

The British Council Presidency in the first half of 1998 continued the theme of examining sport in conjunction with employment but expanded its scope to examine the wider issue of how sport in Europe could be used to combat social exclusion and regenerate communities. A paper was prepared on this issue and discussed at a troika meeting of EU Sports Ministers in Twickenham in April 1998. Present at the meeting were representatives from the British, Luxembourg and Austrian governments and two representatives from DG X of the European Commission (now the Education and Culture Directorate).

The meeting discussed two topics. The first was how to build on the Amsterdam Declaration on Sport. In this connection, the Ministers identified four important issues for the Commission to take into consideration. First, a clear distinction needs to be made between amateur and professional sport. Second, this needs to inform the debate on the relationship between employment and EU law, particularly given the nature of the (as then) unresolved *Deliège* case. Third, this also feeds into the issue of freedom of movement for sportspersons between EU member states. Finally, the Declaration has implications for EU funding to professional, as opposed to, amateur sport.

The second topic for discussion concerned the Commission's preparation of a Green Paper on Sport. The Commission anticipated the Paper to include a focus on the structure ('model') of European sport, the role and importance of television in sport, the social dimension of sport and, following the Commission's 'First Report on Local Employment and Development Initiatives', the relationship between sport and employment. The Ministers indicated a number of themes that they believed the Paper should address.

These included improved co-ordinating mechanisms between bodies involved in sport, measures designed to tackle social exclusion and unemployment and an examination of the way European law affects sports organisations throughout Europe.[25] In the event, the Green Paper idea was replaced with a Commission working paper and consultation exercise (see below).

In a wider forum at the Cardiff European Council meeting of 15/16 June 1998, sport was mentioned in the Presidency Conclusions. Under the heading of 'Bringing the Union Closer to the People', the European Council invited the Council and member states 'to consider ideas to promote more contacts between young people, e.g. through the internet, and the scope for tackling social exclusion among young people, including sport'.[26] The spirit of Adonnino had returned.

Commission working paper: 'The Development and Prospects for Community Action in the Field of Sport, September 1998'[29]

In addition to intergovernmental developments, 1998 also saw the emergence of a more co-ordinated Commission response to the Amsterdam Declaration. The main contribution made by the Education and Culture Directorate to the establishment of a EU sports policy has come in its capacity as the initiator of sporting proposals and consultation documents. In essence, it has attempted to steer a middle course between the post-*Bosman* forces of Single Market regulation and the socio-cultural agenda.

In September 1998 as part of its response to the Declaration on Sport annexed to the Treaty of Amsterdam, DG X published a Commission working paper entitled *'The Development and Prospects for Community Action in the Field of sport'*. The paper identified sport as performing an educational, a public health, a social, a cultural and a recreational function. Although the paper addressed the economic function of sport, it represents an attempt to advance socio-cultural goals. In this connection, the paper represents a continuation in thinking from the Adonnino, Larive and Pack reports.

The introduction to the paper tentatively raises the underlying problem facing the EU in relation to the sports sector. Whilst sport accounts for 3 per cent of world trade, one European in three is actively involved in a sport and there are 545,000 sports clubs in the Community. In other words, sport represents a significant element of the European economy, but it also performs a crucial social role in European society. The more sport, in particular professional sport, is practised as a truly economic activity, so general EU legislation will become applied to the sports sector.

The working paper identifies three major areas of EU activity that particularly affects sport. The first is freedom of movement. The application of Article 39 in the *Bosman* case is the clearest example of this relationship. The second area relates to competition policy and audio-visual policy. These areas have an impact on how sport is televised in Europe. The third area concerns the application of other general EU policies such as health, education, vocational training and the environment. The paper also stresses how sport can be used as a tool for combating social exclusion and a source of voluntary work in Europe.

In the second section of the working paper, a general review of EU institutional involvement in sport is provided. The activities of the Court, Commission, Parliament and Council have all had an affect on the operation of sport in Europe.

The third section examines the 'positive effects' of sport and some problems facing European Sport. The paper acknowledges the difficulties in attempting to define sport. In the paper, the Commission employs the Council of Europe's definition of sport contained in the European Sports Charter. This defines sport as 'all forms of physical activity which, through casual or organised participation, aim at expressing or improving physical fitness and mental well being, forming social relationships or obtaining results in competition at all levels'[28] The paper argues that sport performs an educational function, a public health function, a social function, a cultural function and a recreational functional. However, the paper then proceeds to define sport in economic terms as well. Sport sponsorship generates US$15 billion, the sale of television rights US$42 billion and ticket sales US$50 billion. Furthermore, the European share of sports trade is 36 per cent, second only to the USA with 42 per cent.[29] Faced with these twin definitions of sport, the working paper represented a first significant realisation that the EU must find a satisfactory way of regulating the economic dimension of sport through the application of general EU policy to the sports sector, whilst recognising and indeed harnessing the 'positive effects' of sport.

Before addressing the specifics of EU involvement in sport, the working paper reviewed some of the problems and challenges facing European sport. Three issues are covered; the risk of excessive commercialisation, the lack of protection for young people taking part in top-level competitions and the ineffectiveness of anti-doping measures. In relation to commercialisation, the International Olympic Committee's decision in the 1980s to remove the distinction between amateurs and professionals at the Olympic Games and to allow the Games to be commercially sponsored, was a significant move towards commercialising sport. Commercialisation can potentially break the solidarity between professional and amateur sport.

In the fourth section, the paper addressed the specifics of EU action in sport. In particular, the issue of the economic regulation of sport was dealt with. The paper identified three key relationships between the EU and the sports sector in this regard. The first is the relationship between sport and television. The second relates to sport and competition policy and the third concerns matters relating to the 'freedoms' enshrined in the Treaty.

Having reviewed how EU policies affect the operation of sport, the paper examined how sport can be applied to general policy as 'various Community policies are excellent instruments for demonstrating to sporting interests the additional benefits of Community action'[30] Using the Declaration in the Amsterdam Treaty as justification for greater targeted action in sport, the paper called for a strategy on sport. Areas targeted by the paper included; public health, protection of young workers, safety at sports facilities, standards for sports equipment, the free movement of sports equipment, veterinary regulations concerning animals in sport, scientific and technological research, tourism, taxation and sport, sport and the environment, education and vocational training and sport for people with disabilities.

The paper also argued that sport could be integrated into the EU's wider external relations 'policy'. In this connection, sport can either be used to put pressure on third countries in the form of sanctions, or be used to help support developing countries. In the case of the latter, the paper sees the Lomé Convention as an appropriate mechanism to achieve this aim.

The paper's conclusion confirms the dual approach embodied in the document. On the one hand the EU, and in particular the Commission, will continue to implement EU law whilst on the other, sport will be increasingly integrated into other EU policies. As the EU lacks a Treaty competence to formulate a sports policy, the latter approach may be used as a framework for a future EU policy in sport.

'The European Model of Sport', Commission Consultation Document, November 1998[31]

Following the working paper on sport released by DG X in September 1998, the Commission (DG X) published a consultation document on the same subject later in the same year. The document reveals that at the time of publication, the Commission had received 55 sports-related complaints. In accordance with the guidelines contained in the Declaration on Sport annexed to the Treaty of Amsterdam, the Commission stated that its central aim was to provide assistance to sports organisations seeking to re-frame sporting rules in line with EU law. To achieve this, the Commission published the consultation document as a mechanism through which the European sports sector could express their opinions on the nature of the rapidly developing relationship between sport and the EU. The results of this consultation exercise were to be used first to prepare for the European Conference on Sport (Assises Européennes du sport) held in May 1999 and second to identify more clearly the 'real' features of European sport and to preserve them.

The Commission used the exercise as a stock-taking measure. As the working paper identified, not only is sport practised as a significant economic activity, but sport possesses socio-cultural and integrationist qualities that may well be worth preserving. A framework flexible enough to accommodate both characteristics yet compatible with EU law thus was being prepared. The consultation document comprises three chapters. First, the document attempts to describe the organisation of sport in Europe. Second, the document reviews sport's economic context by examining the relationship between sport and television. Third, the document examines the social policy dimension to sport.

The chapter on the 'European Model of Sport' examined how sport in Western Europe has traditionally been organised on a 'mixed' model basis where the actions of governmental and non-governmental organisations have existed side by side. In addition, sport has operated in an environment dominated by public service television. Developments in broadcasting in the 1980s have fundamentally changed this environment. The document describes the model of sport in Europe as a 'pyramid structure'. This structure describes both the organisational and competitive dimensions to European sport. In organisational terms, the structure comprises European federations, national federations, regional federations and the clubs.

At the pinnacle of the pyramid exist the European federations. Usually, European federations will attempt to maintain their regulatory dominance by only permitting one national federation per country to be affiliated to it. Below the European federations lie the national sporting federations who are affiliated to the European federation. A national federation organises and regulates the sport in question within the national territory. The national federations represent their members within the European or international federation. In addition, they organise national championships. Below the national federations lie the regional federations who are responsible for organising regional championships or co-ordinating sport on a regional level. Underpinning the pyramid are the sports clubs. Dominating this level are amateur sports men and women and administrators who are unpaid. The sports clubs offer the opportunity to local people to become involved in sport. As such, the clubs perform an important social function.

The pyramid structure also describes the competitive balance in European sport. Movement up and down the pyramid is an essential part of sport in Europe. This is achieved through promotion and relegation. In many sports, qualification for European competitions is achieved through championship or cup performance. In essence therefore, the pyramid structure implies considerable interdependence between the levels. This 'open' model contrasts with the 'closed' procedures in the USA where championships are closed and sport is governed by many federations.

The European 'model' has emerged out of the traditional culture of amateurism in European sport whilst the US 'model' represents professionalism. In this respect, European sport has traditionally not been practised as an overtly economic activity whilst sport in the US has. However, this tradition is changing. Sport in Europe has been greatly internationalised and commercialised. This has led to a number of problems. First, due to the growing importance of negotiating television rights, sports federations have assumed the role of a commercial company. This may conflict with their role as a regulatory body. Second, clubs regulated by the federations are beginning to demand a greater share of television rights. This may in time lead to some clubs leaving the federation and establishing a breakaway structure. Third, a tension exists between the requirement of federations to act as commercial bodies whilst at the same time promoting grassroots sport. Fourth, the commercial developments in sport have resulted in sports organisations changing internal rules to accommodate EU competition law. Fifth, some investment companies have expressed an interest in purchasing football clubs. Federation rules regulating multiple ownership may conflict with EU competition rules. Finally, due to the rapid commercialisation of sport in Europe it is feared that only the commercially viable sports will survive.

Chapter 2 of the consultation document reviews the relationship between sport and television in Europe. Most of the issues raised in this connection have already been addressed elsewhere in this text. The chapter examines the importance of broadcasting rights to sports bodies and reviews some themes relating to this. First, who should own broadcasting rights, the federations or the clubs? Second, how should rights be sold, individually or collectively? Third, should rights be sold on an exclusive basis? Fourth, should television companies be able to purchase football clubs thus owning and exploiting broadcasting rights? Fifth, should some sports be broadcast on free-to-air television and, relating to this point, what is to be the future role of public television in Europe?

Chapter 3 examined the social dimension to sport. Six themes were identified. First, sport performs an educational function. In particular, sport promotes both competition and sense of fair play. Second, sport can be used as a means of social integration. In particular sport can act as a tool to promote more tolerant attitudes towards specific groups in European society such as ethnic minorities and the disabled. Third, sporting platforms can help promote an awareness of the environment. Fourth, sport is inextricably linked to public health as participation in sport is an important preventative weapon in the fight against ill health. Fifth, a major issue in European and world sport is doping. The document argues that the EU lacks competence to act in doping matters but action can be taken in the context of other policy areas (such as health) and in the forum of Justice and Home Affairs cooperation. Finally, sport plays a significant role in creating employment opportunities yet this needs to be balanced with the need to protect young participants in sport.

Both the working paper and the consultation document represent an attempt by the Commission to steer a middle course between Single Market and socio-cultural forces. Although competition rules are still to apply to the sports sector, a more soft touch approach is implied. At the same time, the socio-cultural dimensions of sport are being recognised through the integration of sport into other EU policies. As such, the Commission signalled a desire to develop a more broad-based approach to sport policy. This theme was continued by the member states at the end of 1999 and throughout 2000.

The Committee of Regions (COR) opinion on the Commission's report welcomed the broad thrust of the report, particularly the Commission's call to examine how the concerns of sport can be taken into account in the EU Treaty.[32] Without an EU commitment to the social dimension of sport, the COR argued that sports role in forging a people's Europe risks being overlooked. As such, 'the COR considers that a European policy for sport should be developed with greater emphasis on the vital cultural and socio-economic role of sport in Europe'.[33] Such a policy should involve introducing and developing 'by suitable changes to European legislation, a framework of conditions which will enable sport in European regional and local authority areas to fulfil its socially valuable tasks'.[34]

The Austrian Presidency (July–December 1998)
The Austrian Council Presidency continued discussions on the relationship between sport and the EU. Once again sport appeared in the Presidency Conclusions following the Vienna European Council meeting of 11/12 December 1998. Point XII read:

> Recalling the Declaration on Sport attached to the Treaty of Amsterdam and recognising the social role of sport, the European Council invites the Commission to submit a report to the Helsinki European Council with a view to safeguarding current sports structures and maintaining the social function of sport within the Community framework. The European Council underlines its concern at the extent and seriousness of doping in sports, which undermines the sporting ethic and endangers public health. It emphasises the need for mobilisation at European Union level and invites the member states to examine jointly with the Commission and international sports bodies possible measures to intensify the fight against this danger, in particular through better co-ordination of existing national measures.[35]

The Austrian Presidency broadened the scope of the discussion on sport to include an examination of ways sporting structures and the social dimension of sport could be safeguarded within the EU framework. This statement is significant in that the member states hinted that the EU should be adopting a more soft touch application of EU law to the sports sector. It is also possible that the member states were hinting at a possible future hardening of the Amsterdam Declaration. The onus was placed on the Commission to examine these issues via the presentation of a report on sport to the Helsinki European Council to be held in December 1999. In addition to the issue of sport and EU law, the Presidency Conclusions are also significant for the first real signs of a EU commitment to fighting doping in sport.

The first European Union Conference on Sport (the Assises), May 1999
Attached to the Commission consultation document, *The European Model of Sport*, were a series of questionnaires designed to canvass opinion on the future structure of European sport, the future relationship between sport and television and the social dimension of sport, including doping issues. The Commission used the 100 replies to prepare the first EU conference on sport.

The conference was held in Greece in May 1999. The decision to hold it stemmed from a decision taken at the November 1998 European Sports Forum. The Amsterdam Declaration invited the Commission to establish a dialogue between sports organisations and the EU institutions. At the December 1998 Vienna European Council, the member states reaffirmed this desire by requesting the Commission to submit a report to the December 1999 Helsinki European Council with a view to safeguarding current sports structures and maintaining the social function of sport within the EU framework. The convening of the conference represents the Commission's response to these requests. Although the Commission's working paper and the consultation document also form part of this strategy, they also represent an 'in-house' attempt by the Commission to review the relationship between sport and the EU.

The conference participants were drawn from a wide range of backgrounds.[36] The participants were divided into three main working parties each of which discussed one issue relating to sport. The three working parties were each presented with a discussion paper covering, *'The European Model of Sport, Including the Social Dimension of Sport'*, *'Relations Between Sport and Television'* and *'The Fight Against Doping in Sport'*.

The group discussing the 'European Model of Sport' drew a number of conclusions. First, they argued that sporting 'autonomy' should be safeguarded from economic and political influences and that a balance between these pressures needs establishing. Second, they argued that the federal structure of sport (described above) should be maintained and protected. As such, the participants wanted potentially restrictive rules deterring the formation of breakaway structures to be maintained. Third, the participants wished to see young sportspersons being afforded greater protection. In this connection, the participants invited bodies such as the EU to take sport into consideration in the fields of policies on social integration, anti-doping measures, anti-racism measures, environmental policy, public health policy, education policy and youth policy. Fourth, the participants re-affirmed the importance of equal opportunities in sport and the importance of sport for promoting the integration of disabled persons. Finally, the participants attempted to persuade the EU of the importance of supporting regional sport, particularly in Eastern Europe, the Mediterranean region and in developing countries.

The group examining the relationship between sport and television acknowledged the increased competition in the broadcasting sector but argued that the autonomy of sport should be maintained. In particular, they argued that sport should not be used by broadcasters simply to attract audiences, and broadcasters should not interfere or exercise control over the organisation and scheduling of sport. Many participants expressed opposition to attempts by media companies to acquire an interest in sports clubs. Furthermore, most of the participants expressed the view that the collective sale of sports rights by federations was the best system for ensuring effective redistribution and maintaining the solidarity of sport. Whilst the working group acknowledged the competition policy implications of long exclusive broadcasting contracts, they argued that the duration of such rights should be 'sufficient'. They concluded by suggesting that a single rule on this issue would not benefit sport given the wide variety of sporting disciplines. Finally, on the issue of public access to sports broadcasts, the working group acknowledged the public interest argument that was at the heart of Article 3a of the TWF Directive, but argued that a balance needed to be struck between the need to exploit the new commercial developments in the broadcasting sector and the need to guarantee public access to events on television.

The final working group examined the Commission discussion paper on the fight against doping in sport. The group argued that sports organisations, national governments and EU institutions should co-ordinate efforts in order to eliminate doping. In particular, the participants drew attention to the need for effective out-of-competition controls and the need for the harmonisation of lists of banned substances, procedures and penalties. It was also recommended that EU action in this field should be co-ordinated with that of the Council of Europe.

The German Presidency (January–June 1999)

The German Presidency convened an informal meeting of EU Sports Ministers to discuss the growing debate on the relationship between sport and the EU. Meeting in Paderborn (31 May–2 June 1999), the Ministers added to the Austrian Presidency's calls for more anti-doping measures in sport. In addition, they discussed the use of sport as a potential source of employment and the portrayal of sport for the disabled in the media. A discussion relating to sporting contacts with the Federal Republic of Yugoslavia and the provision of sport possibilities for refugees from Kosovo in the refugee camps in Albania and Macedonia also took place. The significant discussion related to the Amsterdam Declaration on Sport. In this connection the Ministers drew the following conclusions:

> So as to safeguard the ethics and the social significance of sport, the particular concerns of sport should be supported especially in the following areas:
>
> - the application of competition law and internal market rules;
> - the EU measures relating to sport and television;
> - Community actions in the field of sport;

- the assistance programmes of the EU, in order to achieve greater transparency as regards the taking into account of sports;
- in light of the interest that the EU attaches to the campaign of the member states and of the sports organisations relating to the protection of minor athletes, the training of young persons, the social significance and the solidarity functions of sport.

The Sport Ministers invite the European Commission to set up a working group composed of representatives of the member states of the EU and of the Commission, which is to work out how the concerns of sport can be taken into account in the EU Treaty. In doing so, the Working Group will consult sport organisations.[37]

The conclusions relating to the Declaration have a strong socio-cultural character. The member states once again expressed the view that the relationship between sport and the EU Treaty should be further clarified without expressing a view as to how this should be achieved. Once again, the Ministers expected the Commission to propose such measures. However, the conclusions firmly indicate that the member states wish to see EU sports policy develop in a socio-cultural direction, be that in the way of a more sympathetic application of EU law to sport or through more formal Treaty measures. These conclusions have given considerable impetus to those socio-cultural actors who want the EU to adopt more formal Treaty measures in order to 'protect' sport from EU law.

The Finnish Presidency (July–December 1999)
In launching the priorities for the six-month term of office, the Finnish Presidency, in addition to carrying on discussions concerning anti-doping measures in sport, expressed the desire to, 'carry on the discussion on the status of sports in Community law, emphasising the social significance of sports and the need to take the special characteristics of sports into account in the application of legislation'.[38]

The Sports Directors of the EU member states met in Helsinki on the 18–20 October 1999 to discuss the sports-related Presidency priorities. Again, the conclusions of the meeting reflect a desire on the part of the member states to see the EU adopt a more holistic approach to sport. This naturally involves the EU promoting and safeguarding the socio-cultural dimension of sport in addition to recognising the economic dimension of sport. The Directors concluded, 'sport is an important resource that promotes people's well-being and health, the cultural dimension and social cohesion. Therefore, sport in its social significance should be seen as a broad-based sector'.[39] The Directors also discussed the establishment of the World Anti-Doping Agency (WADA), the use of sport for the social integration of young people, the use of sport as a source of employment, the use of sport as a civic activity promoting democracy in order to implement the Northern Dimension strategy of the EU, the use of sporting sanctions as a tool of foreign policy, the use of sport as a means of bringing the EU closer to EU citizens and mechanisms for improving the dialogue between the EU and the sports world. Following the meeting of the Directors, the Ministers for Sport met informally on 25 October in Vierumäki. At this meeting the Ministers agreed on the participation in the World Anti-Doping Agency for a two-year transitional period. Also at the meeting, the Commission submitted the Helsinki report on sport, a report requested by the member states during the Austrian Presidency.

The Helsinki report on sport, December 1999[40]

The conclusions of the May 1999 Conference on Sport were used by the Commission to respond to the member states request, made at the December 1998 Vienna European Council that the Commission should 'submit a report to the Helsinki European Council with a view to safeguarding current sports structures and maintaining the social function of sport within the Community framework'. Accordingly, in December 1999 the Commission submitted the Helsinki Report on Sport to the member states meeting in Finland. The bulk of the report is contained within three sections.

In the first section, the report claimed that the 'the development of sport in Europe risks weakening its educational and social function'.[41] In particular, the report claimed that the 'European approach' to sport has recently been affected by several important developments. These developments include the growth in the popularity of sport, the increasing internationalisation of sport and the unprecedented development of the economic dimension of sport. The advantages of these developments for the European economy are considerable. The number of jobs created directly or indirectly by the sports industry has risen by 60 per cent in the past ten years to reach nearly two million. However, the above developments have also led to some 'tensions'. First, doping may be a bi-product of increased competition stemming from commercial developments. Second, commercialism may be squeezing traditional sporting principles out of sport. In particular, the social function of sport is being threatened. Third, commercial pressures may lead to the current single structure for sport being fragmented as some participants seek a more lucrative future in breakaway leagues. This may jeopardise financial solidarity between professional and amateur sport. Finally, the above developments are putting an increasingly physical and mental strain on young sports people, thus risking their subsequent switch to alternative employment.

The second part of the report argued that 'the Community, its member states and the sporting movement need to reaffirm and strengthen the educational and social function of sport'.[42] In this connection the report makes two sets of recommendations. First, in relation to enhancing the educational role of sport, the report suggests that EU educational and training programmes could focus on (1) improving the position of sport and physical education at school through Community programmes; (2) promoting the subsequent switch to other employment and future integration on to the labour market of sportsmen and women; (3) promoting convergence between the training systems for sports workers in each member state.[43] Second, concerning doping in sport, the report outlines the measures adopted by the Commission in relation to anti-doping policy. Doping issues have been referred to the European Group on Ethics and a World Anti-Doping Agency has been established, following co-operation with the Olympic movement. Measures to improve legislative co-ordination with national anti-doping measures have also been explored.

The final section of the report, 'Clarifying the Legal Environment of Sport', examined the thorny issue of the relationship between sport and EU law. The report examined how the commercialisation of the sports sector has contributed to an increase in the number of conflicts involving EU law. These conflicts have ranged from disputes concerning the sale of television rights to issues of club ownership and geographical location. Quoting the conclusions of the first EU Conference on Sport organised by the Commission held in Olympia in May 1999, the paper argued that 'sport must be able to assimilate the new commercial framework in which it must develop, without at the same time losing its identity and autonomy, which underpin the functions it performs in the social, cultural, health and educational areas'.[44]

To enable the sports world to achieve this, the report identified a need for a 'new approach' for dealing with sports-related issues in the EU. As the report explains, 'this new approach involves preserving the traditional values of sport, while at the same time assimilating a changing economic and legal environment'.[45] Action at three levels was recommended.

At the *Community level*, central to this 'legal environment', is the application of EU competition law. The report argues that 'the application of Treaty's competition rules to the sports sector must take account of the specific characteristics of sport, especially the interdependence between sporting activity and the economic activity that it generates, the principle of equal opportunities and the uncertainty of results'.[46] In this connection, the report provided examples of (1) practices which do not come under the competition rules, (2) practices that are, in principle, prohibited by the competition rules and (3) practices likely to be exempted from the competition rules. Nevertheless, the report did not confront the issue of how the special characteristics of sport could be more widely safeguarded in the absence of a Treaty base for sport. At the *national level*, the report proposed measures designed to protect the national single structure 'model' of sporting organisation. In particular, the report suggests that 'one way of safeguarding the national federal structures could be to provide for them to be recognised by law in each member state of the Union'.[47] Finally, at the *level of sporting organisations*, the report suggested that sporting federations should more clearly define their 'missions and statutes'. This recommendation clearly places the emphasis on the federations to define the particular characteristics of sport and the measures they themselves have taken to protect and nurture such characteristics. Where sporting operations have a commercial dimension, the report argues that such operations must be 'founded on the principles of transparency and balanced access to the market, effective and proven redistribution and clarification of contracts, while prominence is given to the specific nature of sport'. Furthermore, regulatory measures should be 'objectively justified, non-discriminatory, necessary and proportional'[48] If sporting rules conform to these 'tests', they should not conflict with Treaty provisions.

At the heart of the Helsinki report on sport lies the concept of 'partnership', a concept widely employed by EU officials. In this context partnership means the knitting together of the macro (EU institutions), meso (member states) and micro (sub-national groups and non-state actors) levels of activity to ensure a more structured and co-ordinated approach to sport. Simultaneously of course, partnership also draws a wide range of actors into the regional integration process and serves to legitimise EU involvement in policy areas. The report clearly links commercialisation with the 'juridification' of sport. As sporting operations practice increasingly on a commercial basis, so EU law seeps into the internal laws of sport. The clearest example of this, other than the *Bosman* ruling is the application of EU competition law to the sports sector. The danger is that the 'special characteristics' of sport become squeezed between these commercial and legal developments. The paper makes clear that action at EU level alone will be insufficient to protect current structures and the social function of sport. Hence a 'partnership' approach is recommended.

In their response to the Helsinki report, the Parliament's Committee on Culture, Youth, the Media and Sport broadly supported the Commission.[49] In particular, the so-called Mennea report welcomed the Commission's focus on the social dimension of sport and their desire to clarify the legal environment within which sport operates in the EU. The report argues that the principles established in the *Bosman* ruling should be considered part of this legal environment and as such should not be undermined. The report therefore represents a continuation of Parliamentary thinking regarding the importance of extending the right of free movement to all EU citizens. Nevertheless, the report argues that the Amsterdam Declaration should be replaced with a Treaty Article for sport. Mennea supports the Pack recommendation of linking sport with cultural policy.

The road to Nice and beyond

Discussions on the fight against doping in sport and the social dimension of sport were continued by the Portuguese Presidency in the first half of 2000. The Sports Directors met in Lisbon in May in preparation for the informal meeting of Sports Ministers held on 10 May. At this meeting the Ministers recommended five developments in the field of EU sports policy. First, the establishment of an informal working group with the aim of proposing to the member states forms of participation with the WADA. Second, the Ministers argued that, 'the specific aspects of sport, namely its social dimension, should be taken into consideration in the implementation of Community policies'.[50] Third, the Ministers recommended 'the creation of a joint working group with representatives of the EU and the Commission, charged with studying the harmonisation of the specific aspects of sport within the Treaty of the Union'.[51] In a footnote below this passage it was noted that the United Kingdom had refused to approve the establishment of a working group for the inclusion of a new paragraph in the Treaty. Fourth, the Ministers recommended the creation of training and exchange programmes for young sportspersons and, finally, the Ministers recommended the creation of a sports information network between member states that would act as a mechanism for the dissemination of information. Following the Santa Maria da Feira European Council meeting, the Presidency Conclusions relating to sport read, 'the European Council requests the Commission and the Council to take account of the specific characteristics of sport in Europe and its social function in managing common policies'.[52]

The Portuguese discussions took place within the context of an on-going IGC process. The Amsterdam Treaty was designed to prepare the EU for the necessary deepening that was to take place prior to the successful widening of the organisation. In the event, the summit postponed many of the difficult decisions relating to the institutional reform of the EU. As a result, throughout much of 1999 and the first half of 2000, the EU embarked upon another IGC process in preparation for another revision to the Treaty (agreed December 2000 in Nice). This process has provided the socio-cultural coalition with another opportunity to push for more formal measures concerning the Treaty status of sport. In particular, the current debate on the Treaty status of sport has been heavily influenced by the debate within European football on how to mitigate the deleterious effects of *Bosman*. The Parliament once again emerged as an important forum through which such demands have been articulated.

Twenty national associations met at a joint FIFA/UEFA conference in Amsterdam in March 2000 to discuss the possibility of persuading the EU to adopt a protocol for sport within the newly revised Treaty. In April 2000, a FIFA/UEFA delegation floated the idea before the before the Parliament and met with the troika of EU Sports Ministers in Lisbon, Portugal. It was reported that FIFA/UEFA wanted sport to be granted a 'special status' within the Treaty. The meeting with the troika yielded two conclusions. First, a working committee was established by the Portuguese Presidency to discuss the proposal. Following the meeting, the Portuguese Minister for Sport remarked that there was a 'need to safeguard sport, notably soccer, from the perverseness that has emerged from the (Bosman) ruling'.[53] Second, the Ministers committed themselves to examining the merits of a protocol for sport being adopted in the newly revised Treaty and that this issue would be discussed at the meeting of all 15 member state Sports Ministers in May 2000.[54] A sporting protocol, if adopted could allow sport a derogation from certain aspects of EU law without the need to re-write the provisions on free movement and competition law. At this meeting, UEFA President claimed that the protocol idea had met with *'understanding'* from MEP's.[55]

The negotiation of the Nice Treaty, gave the French Presidency (June–December 2000) the opportunity to present their sports-related ideas to a wider forum whilst offering the European Council an opportunity to formally respond to the Helsinki report on Sport. In particular, the French Presidency expressed the desire that the conclusions of the working group should form the basis of discussions at the 9th European Sports Forum held in Lille on 26 and 27 October 2000 and that the conclusions of this meeting would lead to the adoption of 'significant' steps by the Nice European Council on 7 and 8 December 2000.

In the event, at Nice the protocol approach advocated by UEFA and FIFA was rejected by the member states in favour of a further Declaration on Sport presented as a Presidency Conclusion. The Declaration, reproduced in full below, is significant in that the member states offered some guidance as to the immediate resolution of (as then) pending disputes (notably the transfer issue) whilst also laying down some signposts for the longer-term future of EU involvement in sport. The Declaration read:

DECLARATION ON THE SPECIFIC CHARACTERISTICS OF SPORT AND ITS SOCIAL FUNCTION IN EUROPE, OF WHICH ACCOUNT SHOULD BE TAKEN IN IMPLEMENTING COMMON POLICIES

Presidency Conclusions, Nice European Council Meeting, 7, 8, 9 December 2000

1 The European Council has noted the report on sport submitted to it by the European Commission in Helsinki in December 1999 with a view to safeguarding current sports structures and maintaining the social function of sport within the European Union. Sporting organisations and the member states have a primary responsibility in the conduct of sporting affairs. Even though not having any direct powers in this area, the Community must, in its action under the various Treaty provisions, take account of the social, educational and cultural functions inherent in sport and making it special, in order that the code of ethics and the solidarity essential to the preservation of its social role may be respected and nurtured.

2 The European Council hopes in particular that the cohesion and ties of solidarity binding the practice of sports at every level, fair competition and both the moral and material interests and the physical integrity of those involved in the practice of sport, especially minors, may be preserved.

Amateur sport and sport for all

3 Sport is a human activity resting on fundamental social, educational and cultural values. It is a factor making for integration, involvement in social life, tolerance, acceptance of differences and playing by the rules.

4 Sporting activity should be accessible to every man and woman, with due regard for individual aspirations and abilities, throughout the whole gamut of organised or individual competitive or recreational sports.

5 For the physically or mentally disabled, the practice of physical and sporting activities provides a particularly favourable opening for the development of individual talent, rehabilitation, social integration and solidarity and, as such, should be encouraged. In this connection, the European Council welcomes the valuable and exemplary contribution made by the Paralympic Games in Sydney.

6 The member states encourage voluntary services in sport, by means of measures providing appropriate protection for and acknowledging the economic and social role of volunteers, with the support, where necessary, of the Community in the framework of its powers in this area.

Role of sports federations

7 The European Council stresses its support for the independence of sports organisations and their right to organise themselves through appropriate associative structures. It recognises that, with due regard for national and Community legislation and on the basis of a democratic and transparent method of operation, it is the task of sporting organisations to organise and promote their particular sports, particularly as regards the specifically sporting rules applicable and the make-up of national teams, in the way which they think best reflects their objectives.

8 It notes that sports federations have a central role in ensuring the essential solidarity between the various levels of sporting practice, from recreational to top-level sport, which co-exist there; they provide the possibility of access to sports for the public at large, human and financial support for amateur sports, promotion of equal access to every level of sporting activity for men and women alike, youth training, health protection and measures to combat doping, acts of violence and racist or xenophobic occurrences.

9 These social functions entail special responsibilities for federations and provide the basis for the recognition of their competence in organising competitions.

10 While taking account of developments in the world of sport, federations must continue to be the key feature of a form of organisation providing a guarantee of sporting cohesion and participatory democracy.

Preservation of sports training policies

11 Training policies for young sportsmen and -women are the life blood of sport, national teams and top-level involvement in sport and must be encouraged. Sports federations, where appropriate in tandem with the public authorities, are justified in taking the action needed to preserve the training capacity of clubs affiliated to them and to ensure the quality of

such training, with due regard for national and Community legislation and practices.

Protection of young sportsmen and -women

12 The European Council underlines the benefits of sport for young people and urges the need for special heed to be paid, in particular by sporting organisations, to the education and vocational training of top young sportsmen and -women, in order that their vocational integration is not jeopardised because of their sporting careers, to their psychological balance and family ties and to their health, in particular the prevention of doping. It appreciates the contribution of associations and organisations which minister to these requirements in their training work and thus make a valuable contribution socially.

13 The European Council expresses concern about commercial transactions targeting minors in sport, including those from third countries, inasmuch as they do not comply with existing labour legislation or endanger the health and welfare of young sportsmen and -women. It calls on sporting organisations and the member states to investigate and monitor such practices and, where necessary, to consider appropriate measures.

Economic context of sport and solidarity

14 In the view of the European Council, single ownership or financial control of more than one sports club entering the same competition in the same sport may jeopardise fair competition. Where necessary, sports federations are encouraged to introduce arrangements for overseeing the management of clubs.

15 The sale of television broadcasting rights is one of the greatest sources of income today for certain sports. The European Council thinks that moves to encourage the mutualisation of part of the revenue from such sales, at the appropriate levels, are beneficial to the principle of solidarity between all levels and areas of sport.

Transfers

16 The European Council is keenly supportive of dialogue on the transfer system between the sports movement, in particular the football authorities, organisations representing professional sportsmen and -women, the Community and the member states, with due regard for the specific requirements of sport, subject to compliance with Community law.

17 The Community institutions and the member states are requested to continue examining their policies, in compliance with the Treaty and in accordance with their respective powers, in the light of these general principles.[56]

Through the Declaration, the member states continued to insist on the special place of sport with the EU's legal framework without committing themselves to formal legal means to secure this. This point was picked up on by the Parliament's Draft Opinion of the Committee on Culture, Youth, Education, the Media and Sport for the Committee on Constitutional Affairs on the Nice Treaty.[57] In the draft opinion the Parliament remarked:

the Committee has always emphasised the important health, educational and social aspects to sport; and has consistently called for the introduction of a legal basis making possible Community action in the field of sport . . . The Amsterdam Treaty included a Declaration on Sport and the Treaty of Nice includes an Annex (Annex IV) on sport: neither of these, however, constitutes a legal basis for Community action.' In this connection the Committee 'regrets that its long-standing appeal for the inclusion in the Treaty of a legal basis for Community action in the field of sport has once again been rejected; and calls for the creation of such a legal base in any future revision of the Treaty'.[58]

Presidency follow-up discussions on sport took place throughout 2001 and 2002. In a series of meetings throughout the first half of 2001, the Swedish Presidency conducted a review of attitudes towards the Nice Declaration and carried on discussions on the fight against doping and the operation of WADA. These issues were continued by the Belgian Presidency in the second half of 2001. In October 2001, the Commission presented a proposal for the establishment of the European Year of Education through sport (2004).[59] This issue along with the question of the implementation of the Declaration and doping are now the key sports-related issues in the EU. However, also in 2004, the EU is committed to a revision of the Treaty. This is likely to be the fourth major sporting issue to appear on the Presidency's agenda.

The 10th annual European Sports Forum meeting in Brussels in October 2001 provided a forum for a review of EU sports policy at a crucial time for the sports world. The Forum established four working groups: Implementation of the Nice Declaration, Fight Against Doping, Social Economy, Sport for Disabled People. The discussion paper prepared for the Nice Declaration working group identified the following as key issues:[60]

- The place of sports federations in the organisation of sport today. Should they have an exclusive role? Should other forms of organisation of sport be examined? Should other structures independent of the federations have a role to play in the organisation of sport and competitions?
- Internal organisation of the sports organisations. How do they or should they take account of the new economic environment? Seek transparency and more democracy? Ensure that all categories of members are represented in the ruling bodies?
- Does not the emergence and success of international and European championships jeopardise the national base of sports' organisation? Is the national framework sometimes not too narrow for the organisation of certain championships? What should be done in the light of these developments?
- How should television rights be managed? How can the rights of each club and the principle of solidarity at the heart of federal organisations be reconciled? What are the national and Community approaches to this?

- How should the professionalisation of sport and its ever-increasing economic impact be analysed? Is this a favourable, unavoidable trend? Should it be brought under control? How? Where does voluntary activity fit into this context?
- Is there a Community-level social dialogue between the various partners involved in sport? Should it be supported? What should it be seeking to achieve?
- Protection of young people. What dangers lurk for young people? How can they be protected? Who should be responsible for implementing this protection? The federations? The public authorities? How?
- What place should sport have in Community policies? A specific place? Better consideration within other policies?

In the Nice working group's conclusions, the participants welcomed the political involvement of the members states through the release of the Nice Declaration.[61] Describing the Declaration as a 'breakthrough', the EU was urged to follow up the Declaration through the promotion of the ethical and social values of sport. The group also welcomed the outcome of competition law cases following the Declaration. The group noted that the sports-related cases had 'been dealt with in a way which respects Community law and the uniqueness of sport, and in line with the spirit advocated by the Nice Declaration'.[62] However, the group expressed the view that whilst the autonomy of sport should be respected, sport should be more closely integrated into a range of EU policies.

Comment

In attempting to challenge the dominance of the market-based approach of the ECJ and Competition Policy Directorate in order to redefine sport as a more social pursuit, the socio-cultural actors have encountered a number of difficulties. First, the EU has enshrined its market-based definition of sport in law. ECJ jurisprudence clearly links EU law to the practice of sport. Second, the EU lacks a Treaty base for sport. This limits the ability of the socio-cultural coalition to address sporting issues in non-Single Market policy venues. Third, the socio-cultural coalition is a coalition of convenience. It lacks unanimous agreement on policy strategy. Despite having access to numerous institutional venues, this lack of cohesion forecloses many legislative venues. As a result of these constraints, the activity of the socio-cultural coalition has been largely confined to the use of soft law. Although soft law is not legally binding it does still carry weight in the EU.

European Parliament initiatives   The European Parliament's sporting initiatives are consistent with the people's Europe project. However, the Parliament has not attempted to overturn the *Bosman* ruling because the establishment of a people's Europe requires discriminatory practices in sport to be abolished. As such, whilst both the Larive and Pack reports seek to establish a more socio-cultural definition of sport, they also support EU action to prohibit restrictive practises in sport. Due to the lack of a Treaty base for sport, the Parliament has attempted to assert its agenda through essentially *ad hoc* ventures into sports policy. In particular, the Parliament has used its budgetary, legislative and scrutiny powers to press for more EU involvement in sport. The Parliament's exploitation of its budgetary powers to keep the sports budgetary line afloat and its exploitation of legislative powers to revise the Television Without Frontiers Directive represent the most effective use of its formal powers.

Member state initiatives   Member state involvement in sports policy intensified post-*Bosman* following concerns raised by some governments on the direction of sports policy. The member states responded by establishing political guidelines for the future direction of sports policy. The most significant of these guidelines was the Amsterdam Treaty's Declaration on Sport. Previously at Milan in 1985 and at Maastricht in 1992, the member states had recognised the importance of social and cultural measures to the foundations of European integration. The Maastricht Treaty contained provisions on social, cultural and tourism policy. The inclusion of sport within the Treaty at Amsterdam was therefore a natural progression, particularly given the problematic ratification of the Maastricht Treaty and the subsequent desire on the part of the member states to bring Europe closer to the citizens. The Amsterdam Declaration has proved important, not only in guiding the application of EU law to sport, but also in progressively hardening sports policy. The contribution of soft law to policy development is an area frequently overlooked by researchers, yet one almost always in evidence in the history of the establishment of a new policy sector. Following Amsterdam, sports policy developed from a narrow examination of the relationship between sport and employment (2nd half 1997) to the adoption and implementation of the Nice Declaration on Sport (2nd half of 2002). The relative freedom of the Council Presidency to push individual agendas is significant in this respect (Kirchner 1992). Furthermore, the troika system allows for the preceding Presidency's agenda to be continued by the successor whilst also being coupled with the agenda of the successor Presidency.

Commission initiatives   The Commission's response to member state promptings has also come largely in the form of policy papers. Using its right of policy initiative, the Education and Culture Directorate has pieced together a series of measures, which, when taken together, represent a 'new approach' to sports policy. The two 1998 policy papers, '*The development and prospects for Community action in the field of sport*', and '*The European model of sport*' were used to prepare for the first EU conference on sport, held in Greece in May 1999. The conclusions of this exercise were used by the Commission to respond to the member states request, made at the December 1998 Vienna European Council that the Commission should write the *Helsinki report on sport*. This report states the current state of play.

Despite the predominance of soft law as a tactic with which to influence the definition of sport in the EU, the activities of the socio-cultural coalition have had some practical effects. Above all, the sports policy subsystem has been politicised. Previously dominated by legal norms, the subsystem has become penetrated by essentially political arguments concerning the social significance of sport. This politicisation has been aided by the high political salience of sport in Europe. Sport is an issue carrying very high public interest. Politicisation is an essential pre-requisite for policy change.

Policy change is evident within the sports policy subsystem. The key consequence of subsystem politicisation has been a change in the regulatory conditions within which sport operates. In other words the regulation of sport in the EU has been politicised. This politicisation of sports regulation has resulted in a drift from a Single Market model of sports regulation towards a socio-cultural model. Single Market regulation refers to regulation designed to protect and enhance the four fundamental freedoms. Socio-cultural regulation refers to a more sympathetic/soft touch application of this logic in which the specific and possibly unique characteristics of the sector are taken into consideration. The ECJ rulings in *Deliège* and *Lehtonen* and the Competition Directorate's post-Amsterdam approach for dealing with sport illustrates the extent to which political arguments have influenced the application of the EU law to sport. As such, these rulings/decisions are significant in that they mark the birth of an area of EU law called 'EU sports law'. It is to this issue that the final chapter now turns.

Notes

1 COM (84) 446 Final, A People's Europe, reports from the ad hoc Committee.
2 Ibid., para. 5.9.
3 A5-0133/2002b, 'Report on the division of competences between the European Union and the Member States' (2001/2024(INI)), Committee on Constitutional Affairs, 24/04/02. Rapporteur: Alain Lamassoure, pp. 18–19.
4 A-0415/88, 'Report for the Committee on Legal Affairs and Citizen's Rights, on the freedom of movement of professional footballers in the Community', 03/89. Rapporteur: J. Van Raay.
5 A3-0326/94/ Part A (27/4/94) Part B (29/4/94), 'Report on the European Community and Sport', Rapporteur: Mrs J. Larive.
6 A1-53/84, 'Sport and the Community' (Rapporteur: Mr Bord MEP); A2-32/87, 'Women in Sport' (Rapporteur: Mrs d'Ancona MEP); A2-70/85 and A2-215/87, 'Vandalism and Violence in Sport' (Rapporteur: Mrs Larive MEP); A2-282/88, 'Sport in the European Community and a People's Europe' (Rapporteur: Mrs Larive MEP).

7   B3-1909/90, 'Motion for a Resolution of 8/11/90 on the Protection of Popular Sporting Traditions in Europe', Rapporteur: Mrs Ewing.

8   B3-0862/91, 'Motion for a Resolution of 10/6/91 on the Need to Reappraise the EC's Sports Policy', Rapporteur: Mrs Banotti.

9   B3-1512/91, 'Motion for a Resolution of 15/10/91 on Professional Boxing', Rapporteur: Mr Díaz.

10 B3-1725/91, 'Motion for a Resolution of 12/11/91 on a Common Logo for Athletes from the 12 Member States Taking Part in the Next Olympic Games', Rapporteur: Mrs Muscardini.

11 B3-0456/92, 'Motion for a Resolution of 15/4/92 on Legislation to Outlaw Symbols Which Incite Violence in Sport', Rapporteur: Mr Abeilhe *et al.*

12 B3-0714/92, 'Motion for a Resolution of 1/6/92 on the Safety of Sports Installations', Rapporteur: Mrs Muscardini.

13 A4-0197/97. 'Report on the Role of the European Union in the Field of Sport', 28/5/97. Rapporteur: Mrs D. Pack

14 Ibid., para. A.

15 Ibid., para. B.

16 Ibid., para. I.

17 Ibid., section B, Explanatory statement.

18 See Case C-155/73, *Italy* v. *Sacchi* [1974] ECR 409 and Case C-52/79, *Procureur du Roi* v. *Debau*ve [1980] ECR 833.

19 See *Sacchi* and Case C-260/89, *ERT* v. *DEP* [1991] ECR I-2925. Also Case C-353/89, *Commission* v. *Netherlands* [1991] ECR I-4069. Case C-148/91, *Vereniging Veronica* v. *Commissariaat voor de Media* [1993] ECR I-487. Case C-23/93, *TV10 SA* v. *Commissariaat voor de Media* [1994] ECR I-4795.

20 Com (84) 300, 'On the Establishment of the Common Market Broadcasting, especially by Satellite and Cable', 1984.

21 Article 251 (ex 189b).

22 European Parliament reference: A4-346/96.

23 Article 3a Directive 97/36/EC.

24 Declaration 29, Treaty of Amsterdam amending the Treaty on European Union, the Treaties establishing the European Communities and certain related Acts, 1997.

25 Chamberlain, P. (1998), UK Presidency of the European Union. Troika Meeting of EU Sports Ministers, Twickenham Stadium, 2 April 1998. Sport and Recreation Division, 8/4/98.

26 British Presidency Conclusions (15–16/6/98), Cardiff European Council.

27 'Development and Prospects for Community Activity in the Field of Sport', Commission Staff Working Paper, Directorate General X, 29/09/98.

28 Ibid., para. 3.1.

29 Ibid., para. 3.1.

30 Ibid., para. 4.2.

31 'The European model of sport'. Consultation Document of DG X. 1998.

32 OJ C 374, 23/12/99, Opinion of the Committee of the Regions on 'The European Model of Sport'.

33 Ibid., para. 4.4.

34 Ibid., para. 4.2.

35 Austrian Presidency Conclusions (11–12/12/98), The Vienna European Council Presidency Conclusions.

36 For more on these participants, see Chapter 3 on the composition of the sports policy subsystem.

37 German Presidency Conclusions (31/5–2/6 99), Conclusions of the German European Council Presidency on the Occasion of the Informal Meeting of the Sport Ministers of the European Union – 'the Paderborn Conclusion'.

38 Finnish Ministry of Education (1999), Priorities: Ministry of Education, Finnish EU Presidency Website.

39 Finnish Presidency Conclusions (18–20/10/99), Sports Directors Meeting. Conclusions of the Presidency.

40 Com (1999) 644, 'Report from the Commission to the European Council with a view to safeguarding sports structures and maintaining the social significance of sport within the Community framework: the Helsinki report on sport', 1/12/99.

41 Ibid., para. 2.

42 Ibid., para. 3.

43 Ibid., para. 3.1.

44 Ibid., para. 4.

45 Ibid., para. 4.2.

46 Ibid., para. 4.2.1.

47 Ibid., para. 4.2.2.

48 Ibid., para. 4.2.3.

49 A5-0208/2000, 'Report on the Commission Report to the European Council with a View to Safeguarding Current Sports Structures and Maintaining the Social Function of Sport within the Community Framework – The Helsinki Report on Sport', The Mennea report, 18/07/00.

50 Conclusions of the Informal Council of Ministers of Sport of the European Union, Lisbon, 10/5/00.

51 Ibid.

52 Portuguese Presidency Conclusions (19–20/6/00), Presidency Conclusions, Santa Maria da Feira European Council.

53 BBC Online, 17/3/00.

54 'FIFA and UEFA to Intensify Dialogue with EU', UEFA News Release, 1/3/00. 'UEFA to Intensify Dialogue with European Parliament', UEFA News Release, 13/4/00. 'UEFA Chief Executive Hopeful EU Will Introduce New Measures', UEFA News Release, 13/4/00.

55 BBC Online, 12/4/00.

56 'Declaration on the Specific Characteristics of Sport and its Social Function in Europe, of Which Account Should be Taken in Implementing Common Policies', Presidency Conclusions, Nice European Council Meeting, 7, 8, 9 December 2000.

57 PE 286.761, 'Draft Opinion of the Committee on Culture, Youth, Education, the Media and Sport for the Committee on Constitutional Affairs on the Treaty of Nice and the Future of the European Union', 23/03/01, Draftsman: Barbara O'Toole.

58 PE 286.761, pp. 4–6.

59 Com (2001) 584 final, 'Proposal for a Decision of the European Parliament and of the Council Establishing the European Year of Education through Sport 2004'.

60　10th European Sports Forum. Framework document for working group discussions on the implementation of the Nice Declaration. Non-paper. 17/18 October 2001.

61　10th European Sports Forum. Conclusions of the working group on the follow up to the Nice Declaration. 17–18/10/01.

62　Ibid., para. 3.

7

The future of EU
sports law and policy

A central objective of this text was to place some order on the seemingly random and *ad hoc* impulses of EU activity in the sports sector. The book claims that today's EU sports policy has developed out of a policy tension within the EU. The tension between the Single Market regulatory impulses of EU activity in sport and the EU's political policy objectives for sport has contributed to the birth of a EU *sports policy* defined by the construction of the *separate territories* approach. In other words a distinct legal approach to sport has emerged. This implies the birth of *EU sports law*, which has had the result of shifting the nature of sports regulation towards a *socio-cultural* model of regulation. EU interventions in sport do not simply reflect a desire to correct market distortions or restrictions. Judicial intervention is sensitive to the requirements of current EU sports policy. As such, it is no longer appropriate to refer to the EU's regulation of sport as an example of *sport and the law*. Rather, by defining separate territories of sporting autonomy and judicial intervention, the EU has constructed a discrete body of law relating specifically to sport, hence the term *sports law*.

Why is the distinction between sport and the law and sports law important? On the face of it this may appear another one of those semantic and essentially pointless distinctions that is of academic interest only. Analysing the relationship between these concepts is however fundamental for understanding the future direction of EU sports policy. Academics, legal practitioners and sports administrators can trawl through EU case law and sports-related policy papers in order to form a view of where the relationship between sport and the EU currently stands. Although a rather time-consuming exercise, it is nonetheless a worthwhile exercise. However, in order to understand how the relationship between sport and the EU emerged and in what direction EU sports law and policy is heading, some further analysis is required.

Theoretical contributions

As explained in Chapter 2, an obvious gap in the sports law literature is the lack of theoretical investigation. This poses some problems for the credibility of the sports law thesis. Not only will a lack of theoretical underpinning inhibit the development of sports law as an academic discipline, it also leaves more practical questions about the future either unexplored or directionless. The concept of sports law is in its infancy. The sub-branch of EU sports law is even more nascent. The search for theory is therefore inhibited by a lack case law.

The prudent or more cautious could make a case for taking further time to reflect on developments in the EU. The task of attempting to construct an approach offering insights into the sports law phenomenon is not however a premature exercise. First, although not vast, sufficient empirical material exists to allow for the construction of ideas. The small amount of 'hard' law since 1999 combined with the proliferation in 'soft' law is sufficient to identify the emergence of EU sports law and policy. Second, EU involvement in new sectors offers political scientists and lawyers an excellent opportunity to test and refine existing theories of European integration. Third, if it is accepted that the EU's approach to sports regulation has changed in favour of a socio-cultural model, then it must remain a possibility for the future that the approach will change again. Greater theoretical investigation will illuminate the possible future contours of EU sports law and policy. Finally, the debate on the relationship between sport and the EU is a current one. The way in which the EU deals with sport tells us much about the type of organisation the EU wants to be. A major constitutional review of the EU's activities is currently under way with a view to further Treaty revision in 2004.[1] Sports location within the EU's constitutional structure post-2004 will be dependent on the activities of the two advocacy coalitions working within the sports policy subsystem. The sports policy subsystem is not a non-neutral arena existing simply to process inputs into outputs in an apolitical manner. Rather activity within it will determine sports future legal and constitutional status. The need to construct better empirical and theoretical understandings of the subsystem is therefore paramount.

The main theoretical contribution advanced in this book is the need for subsystem analysis. The approach presented here rejects the notion of monolithic EU institutions slugging it out between themselves for control over policy. Rather, it is argued that the EU is best characterised as a multi-level organisation in which a myriad of policy-specific subsystems exist. Activity within subsystems determines the nature of the policy output. The analysis therefore centres on the nature of the subsystem. If a better understanding of the subsystem can be developed, more accurate hypotheses about the future direction of policy can be advanced. Subsystem analysis requires two focuses. First, the actors within the subsystem need identifying and their belief systems specifying. Second, the institutional resources at the disposal of the actors need identifying.

Actors

The actors within the sports policy subsystem are organised into two advocacy coalitions. The belief system of the Single Market coalition is imbued with the logic of negative integration and Single Market regulation. In other words, the manner in which law is applied to sport should not allow the principles of the four freedoms to be undermined. The belief system of the socio-cultural coalition is held together by the logic of positive integration and a commitment to the socio-cultural model of sports regulation. Sport possesses social and cultural characteristics which necessitates a soft touch application of law. Furthermore, the market-based definition of sport adopted by the Single Market regulators conflicts with the socio-cultural coalition's concern to develop a people's Europe. Membership of the two advocacy coalitions is wide. The term 'actor' refers to those who are actively involved in the policy debate. This includes EU institutions either acting as discrete entities such as the ECJ, the Commission or the Parliament, or as individual components within institutions such as individual Directorates General within the Commission, individual committees within the Parliament and individual Presidencies within the context of intergovernmental forums. However, as previously explained, the term 'actor' should not be confused with 'institution'. The ECJ, Commission and Parliament are considered to be actors within the subsystem. The institutionalist element of the otherwise actor-centred approach stems not from their mere involvement within the subsystem as actors, but from the characteristics they bring to the subsystem. Institutions not only bring formal policy instruments and procedures to the subsystem, they also bring informal, cultural and normative resources to it (see below).

The Single Market coalition, consisting primarily of the ECJ and the Competition Policy Directorate, do not pursue a specific sports-related agenda. Their policy interest in sport is regulatory. Their key concern is for the protection of the four freedoms. The socio-cultural coalition was formed with particular sporting goals in mind. The key actors include the Parliament, the Education and Culture Directorate, the member states and a wide range of sports bodies. However, the coalition is a coalition of convenience given the differences within the secondary aspects of the belief system. In particular, strategic differences exist over (1) the extent to which sport should seek protection from EU law; (2) the method of achieving protection; and (3) the wider (and more controversial) issue of the desirability of a legally rooted common EU sports policy.

Institutional resources

The ability of the rival advocacy coalitions to achieve policy results consistent with their belief system depends on the extent to which they are institutionally well resourced. In other words, do they possess the ability to re-direct policy? Coalitions seek to re-direct policy through the exploitation of institutional venues – hence the need for an actor-centred brand of institutionalism. If actors are unsuccessful in one venue, a well-resourced coalition will go venue shopping in another. The term institutional venue refers not only to the formal administrative, legal and political dimensions of institutions, but also the informal arenas of political systems such as informal rules, norms, symbols, beliefs and codes of conduct.

The Single Market coalition is well resourced. Their belief system is strongly rooted, both legally and culturally, within the Treaty. Legally, the logic of negative integration is underpinned by the EU's legal system, particularly the provisions relating to the four freedoms and competition policy. The ECJ and the Commission also have a strong role in implementing and enforcing these provisions. Furthermore, the principles of direct applicability, direct effect and supremacy, combined with the preliminary reference procedure (Article 234) and the Commission's complaints procedure, creates a strong link between EU law and national law. Culturally, the SEM project has established a strong ideological commitment to guaranteeing the four freedoms. The extent to which the Single Market coalition is institutionally powerful equips them with the means through which they could undermine the deep and policy core belief system of the socio-cultural coalition. For example, the ruling in *Bosman* struck at the heart of the socio-cultural coalition's belief system.

The socio-cultural advocacy coalition is a coalition of convenience. This restricts their ability to act as a cohesive force but it does allow them to exploit a wider range of institutional venues. In particular, the coalition has exploited (1) the right of policy initiative within the Education and Culture Directorate; (2) the Parliament's legislative, scrutiny and budgetary powers; (3) the primary and secondary law-making functions of member states; (4) soft law including Treaty Declarations, Presidency Conclusions, political guidelines and Commission policy papers; (5) Council Presidency agenda setting; (6) the use of formal sports forums/sports conferences such as the European Sports Forum and the EU Conference on Sport; (7) the strength of positive (socio-cultural) integration post-Maastricht; and (8) related policy subsystems such as the health, audio-visual, education and youth. The involvement of the member states within the coalition has been significant. This has equipped the coalition with the power of political pressure and Treaty revision. Accordingly, the socio-cultural coalition also possesses the ability to adopt measures which could undermine the deep and policy core belief system of the Single Market regulators. A revision to the Treaty granting sport an exemption from EU law would undermine the uniform application of the four freedoms and create a precedent for further claims of special treatment by a range of commercial sectors. In circumstances where both coalitions possess the ability to undermine the belief system of their rival, coalition mediation is likely (see below).

Empirical contributions

The tension between the EU's regulatory and political policy ambitions for sport has driven the development of today's EU sports policy. This policy is not however legally rooted in the Treaty. In other words, sport is not mentioned in the legally binding chapters of the Treaty. As such, EU sports policy lacks a legislative framework even though the development of one remains a possibility for the future (see below). The defining characteristic of modern EU sports policy is judicial not legislative. The construction of separate territories and hence EU sports law is at the heart of the EU's policy towards sport. This allows both the regulatory and political policy strands of EU sporting activity to co-exist. The above analysis, focusing on subsystem politics, actors and institutional resources allows us to piece together the relationship between these themes and establish a methodology for understanding how changes in EU sports law will affect the future direction of EU sports policy and *vice versa*.

Sport and EU law: Single Market sports regulation

Within national legal systems established general legal principles deriving from criminal law, contract law, the law of torts, public law, administrative law, property law, competition law, company law and fiscal law have gradually impinged upon the operation of sport. This process of juridification appears to be closely associated with the commercialisation of sport, although the relationship between sport and the law has a long history. Issues such as public order and sport, drugs and sport, safety in sport, disciplinary measures in sport, conduct in sport and wider issues relating to restraint of trade and anti-competitive behaviour in sport are today common features of the national legislative and judicial landscape. The internationalisation of sporting competition and finance combined with the development of the EU has internationalised juridification. Article 3 of the EU's founding Treaty specified that the activities of the Community shall include 'an internal market characterised by the abolition, as between member states, of the obstacles to the free movement of goods, persons, services and capital' and 'a system ensuring that competition in the internal market is not distorted'. Further Treaty Articles elaborated these goals, as did the passing of secondary legislation and the case law decision making of the ECJ. Although the Treaty did not refer to sport with the list of Community activities contained in Article 3, the consequences of sports commercialisation became felt as EU provisions on the free movement of persons, services and competition law became applied to sport. The ECJ rulings in *Walrave, Donà, Heylens* and *Bosman* firmly established sports relationship to EU law whenever it was practised as an economic activity. The cases involved the application of established legal principles to sporting situations. As such, the rulings, based on a Single Market model of regulation, did not create a discrete area of sports law.

The politics of sports regulation: re-asserting socio-cultural values
The relationship between *sport and EU law* has been forged through the strength of negative integration within the EU's constitutional structure. Observing the first decade of European integration, Pinder argued that the 'free trade ideology is firmly built into the system, but the planning ethic is no more than a possibility for the future' (Pinder 1968: 98). In other words, the socio-cultural dimension to European integration was considered a secondary goal to that of securing economic integration. As Featherstone observes, this economic path to integration has undermined popular support for the integration project (Featherstone 1994). The sheer existence of the Adonnino report was a formal acknowledgment by the EU that it had neglected the social and cultural dimensions of European integration. The growing legitimacy crisis within the EU would, unless addressed, fundamentally undermine the market-based achievements of integration. The people's Europe project was an attempt by the EU to address this issue by 'reconnecting' with its citizens.

The 1986 Single European Act and subsequent Single European Market project significantly advanced economic integration and laid the foundations for the birth of the single European currency. The 1992 Maastricht Treaty was a turning point for the EU. The completion of the SEM and the collapse of Communism offered the EU an opportunity to push for the launch of the single currency. However, the legitimacy question had not been tackled, potentially calling into question the viability of major EU projects such as the launching of a new currency. The Treaty adopted a series of measures designed to confront the legitimacy question. The Treaty expanded its range of social and cultural activities by granting a new legal base for culture, education, public health and consumer protection. Existing policies with a social expression such as environmental and cohesion policy were strengthened. The concept of European citizenship was created and the powers of the directly elected Parliament were increased. The name of the organisation also changed – from European Community to European Union. The name change reflected a shift in emphasis away from a *Community* established on economic foundations to a *Union* underpinned by social values. In short, Maastricht represented an attempt to change the cultural context of integration.

The Maastricht ratification crisis demonstrated the extent to which the EU's attempt to connect with its citizens had failed. The 1997 Amsterdam Treaty again re-visited the socio-cultural context of integration. However, wracked with division over the extent to which the EU needed reforming in preparation for enlargement, the EU adopted a cautious approach. Provisions on openness, employment, the image of EU, respect for human rights, the simplification of the Treaty, bringing the EU closer to the people, sex equality, environmental protection and anti-discrimination measures were agreed. The Declaration on Sport was also annexed to the Treaty. More concrete decisions on institutional reform were delayed until the 2000 Nice Treaty.

Treaty revisions have altered the cultural context of integration. The list of activities contained within Article 3 now extends beyond the scope of negative integration. The Treaty also contains a commitment to promote positive integration. In this connection, Article 3 includes activities of a more social and cultural nature, even though sport is not explicitly mentioned. The relationship between sport and the EU has been affected by the forces of negative and positive integration – the twin engines of European integration. The imbalance in favour of negative integration contributed to the emergence of a specific sports policy subsystem within the EU. In particular, the formation of the socio-cultural coalition with specific political sports policy objectives linked to the Adonnino agenda has greatly influenced the nature of EU involvement in sport. Since *Bosman* members of the socio-cultural advocacy coalition have used a variety of legal, semi-legal and non-legal measures to challenge the essentially economic and market-based definition of sport adopted by the Single Market coalition. By co-opting institutionally powerful members (such as the member states) into the socio-cultural coalition, it has been able to exploit a growing range of institutional venues in order to seek re-definition. In circumstances where two advocacy coalitions operating within the subsystem are both institutionally privileged, mediation is likely. The result of this mediation has seen the birth of a discrete area of sports law operating within the context of a more holistic EU sports policy.

EU sports law and policy

The *Bosman* ruling was a turning point for sport. It led to the creation of the sports policy subsystem. Actors unhappy at the economic Single Market approach the ECJ adopted in relation to sport, co-ordinated their activity to seek greater protection for sport from the application of EU law. As each coalition possessed the ability to undermine each other other's deep and policy core belief systems, coalition mediation took place. Past experience, perceptions of future losses and the cultural norm within the EU of mutual adjustment facilitated mediation. In other words, the unsatisfactory prospect of potential coalition confrontation led to a learning process taking place within the subsystem. The Education and Culture Directorate emerged as a key venue through which mediation between the two advocacy coalitions has occurred. In 1999, the Commission organised the first EU Conference on Sport to complement the annual European Sports Forum. The Directorate has also been active in elaborating the general policy of the member states in the form of policy papers. The Helsinki report on Sport represents the Commission's current position and the birth of a *de facto* if not *de jure* EU sports policy. From within the mediation and learning process has emerged compromise between the coalitions. The goal of mediation was to find grounds for compromise without undermining the deep and policy core beliefs of both coalitions. As such, compromise has taken place within the secondary aspects of the coalitions belief systems. Coalition compromise has resulted in the following developments.

First, coalition compromise has resulted in the birth of a more co-ordinated EU sports policy located within secondary aspects of both coalitions belief systems. It is not a policy which is legislatively rooted. In other words there is no Article or protocol on sport within the Treaty. This move is resisted by the Single Market coalition as it would undermine their deep and policy core beliefs. Therefore sports policy is still essentially regulatory in nature. Although the socio-cultural aspects of sport can be harnessed to implement other policy goals in the EU, the lack of a Treaty base for sport inhibits the development of a redistributive strand in sports policy. Disagreement over the merits of this development exist within the socio-cultural coalition.

Second, the cornerstone of EU sports policy is the separate territories concept. Separate territories refers to the creation of spheres of jurisdiction for sports bodies and the law. One territory is sporting autonomy. Within this territory the EU will either not intervene judicially or accept justifications for exemptions from the application of law. The other territory is judicial intervention. Within this territory, EU law will continue to be applied.

Third, the development of the separate territories approach marks the birth of EU sports law. As Beloff *et al.* argue, 'the cornerstone of what could be called the founding principles of sports law is the definition of respective territories of the courts and the bodies which govern sport' (Beloff *et al.* 1999: 4). The construction of separate territories necessitates sport being treated differently to other sectors, another defining characteristic of sports law. Even though historically both the ECJ and the Commission have acknowledged the special characteristics of sport in their case law, EU sports law is a very recent phenomenon.

Finally, the above developments have had practical effects on the nature of EU sports regulation. Previously based on the Single Market model, the separate territories approach has introduced greater socio-cultural values into the approach. Again, this new approach to sports regulation is confined to the secondary aspects of the coalitions belief systems. Nevertheless, by compromising in this area both coalitions are protecting the fundamentals of their deep and policy core beliefs.

The above developments are the product of activity within the sports policy subsystem – hence the need for subsystem analysis. Four strands of EU activity illustrate how the construction of this approach has occurred.

Bureaucratic measures   The activities of the Education and Culture Directorate have been instrumental in elaborating the policy objectives of the member states and establishing an embryonic separate territories framework. By establishing dialogue with the sports world through the organising of the first EU Conference on Sport in 1999 and managing the annual meeting of the European Sports Forum, the Commission has been able to prepare the Helsinki report on Sport for the member states. The paper argued that 'sport must be able to assimilate the new commercial framework in which it must develop, without at the same time losing its identity and autonomy, which underpin the functions it performs in the social, cultural, health and educational areas'.[2] The concept of separate territories has therefore received Commission approval.

Legislative measures   Separate territories has also received legislative and quasi-legislative attention. The Parliament's revision of the Television Without Frontiers Directive represents the most formal attempt to have sport treated differently to other sectors. By permitting the establishment of protected national lists, the Directive has granted sport an exception from the general principle of free movement of services in trans-frontier broadcasting.[3] Member state activity in the legislative field has been confined to soft law. The Declaration on Sport annexed to the Amsterdam Treaty and subsequent soft law measures culminating in the Nice Declaration on Sport demonstrate the member state's desire to see the separate territories concept more widely employed. The Nice Declaration argued that 'even though not having any direct powers in this area, the Community must, in its action under the various Treaty provisions, take account of the social, educational and cultural functions inherent in sport and making it special, in order that the code of ethics and the solidarity essential to the preservation of its social role may be respected and nurtured'. The Declaration represents the clearest indication yet from the member states that the rules of sport bodies which are designed to maintain a competitive balance between participants should be treated differently by EU law to similar restrictions in other sectors. Until the member states have had time to observe the impact of the separate territories approach, they have shied away from adopting harder measures.

ECJ jurisprudence   The ECJ's involvement in the construction of the separate territories concept is potentially most significant. The ECJ has in previous sports related case law acknowledged the social significance of sport. For instance in *Bosman* the ECJ argued that 'in view of the considerable social importance of sporting activities and in particular football in the Community, the aims of maintaining a balance between clubs by preserving a certain degree of equality and uncertainty as to results and of encouraging the recruitment and training of young players must be accepted as legitimate'.[4] Nevertheless, the rulings in *Deliège* and *Lehtonen* mark a more substantial application of the view expressed in *Bosman*. In *Bosman*, the ECJ defined the operation of the international transfer system for football and the use of nationality quotas in sport as falling within the EU judicial territory. In *Deliège* and *Lehtonen* the ECJ has identified selection criteria and transfer windows as falling within the territory of sporting autonomy. In essence *Deliège* and *Lehtonen* establish that the rules which sports bodies retain competence over concern those which are inherent in the conduct and/or organisation of sporting events. Despite the limitations to the rulings examined in Chapter 4, they do open up the possibility for sports bodies to connect sporting interest arguments with public interest justifications. This was the conclusion of the Advocate General in *Lehtonen*. If sports bodies can be successful in this connection, this could act as a vehicle for the expansion of the sporting autonomy territory and the contraction of the judicial intervention territory.

Commission quasi-jurisprudence　　The concept of separate territories is also beginning to establish itself in the field of competition law. The February 1999 paper on the application of competition rules to sport was the Commission's first significant exploration of the separate territories approach.[5] The paper has informed subsequent Commission analyses of alleged restrictive practices in sport. A review of the case law within sports exploitation, contest and supply markets illustrates the development of the separate territories approach within competition law. The *exploitation market* concerns the collective sale of sports rights, exclusive contracts, the purchase of sports rights, the transmission of the rights, ticketing practices and merchandising arrangements. The Commission's general approach to the exploitation market has been two-fold. First, it has generally held that sports rules are covered by the scope of Article 81 and 82. Second, it has however been willing to recognise the specificity of sport by informally clearing or formally exempting such rules. The *contest market* refers to the organisation of the sporting contest. The Commission has been sympathetic to rules which seek to maintain the single structure model of sport and rules restricting multiple club ownership and club relocation. In the Formula One case the Commission separated the FIA's regulatory and commercial functions. Commission investigations into sport's *supply market* have essentially concentrated on the operation of the international transfer system for football. The Commission initially made it clear that it was not prepared to accept alternatives to the transfer system that compromised EU law. However, the March 2001 settlement on transfers reflects a more sympathetic approach to sport. The Commission has accepted the argument that restrictions on player mobility and restrictions on the ability of clubs to employ players without obstruction can be justified in terms of maintaining a competitive balance between participants. The Commission has therefore acknowledged the specificity of sport within the context of EU competition law and further defined the separate territories concept.

Taken as a whole, the body of 'hard' sports law reviewed above does not amount to a great deal – hence the need to refer to the 'birth' of EU sports law and policy. Nevertheless, a system of law governing the practice of sport is emerging in the EU of which the use of soft law is a particular feature. Within the context of mediation between coalitions, the use of soft law allows both coalitions to protect their deep and policy core belief systems. For the Single Market coalition, soft law does not legally challenge entrenched Treaty principles. Harder measures such as the use of Treaty exemptions for sport runs the risk of undermining the fundamentals of their belief system. For the socio-cultural coalition, soft law, although less satisfactory, allows for the construction of the separate territories approach which, if defined favourably, can safeguard sports autonomy. Of course, the use of soft law by the EU is not without its critics (Kinsella and Daly 2001).

The future of EU sports law and policy

Current EU sports policy based on the separate territories concept is therefore located within the secondary aspects of the coalitions belief systems. Is this reconciliation between coalitions and hence current EU sports policy sustainable? Might EU sports policy break out of the confines of the mediated approach? The answer lies not only in the extent to which the separate territories approach has satisfied and will continue to satisfy the objectives of both coalitions but also the feasibility of the coalitions exploiting further institutional venues in order to affect further policy change. The separate territories approach allows the socio-cultural coalition to claim some special status for sport within the Treaty framework without compromising the line of reasoning developed by the Single Market coalition in relation to the economic status of the sector. As such, the separate territories approach has the potential to satisfy the objectives of both coalitions. However, whilst the current approach offers a degree of short-term stability, is more strategic thinking required?

First, due to the predominance of soft law, the separate territories approach is not fully enshrined in law. As such, the definition of the separate territories is fluid. This leaves the regulatory environment within which the socio-cultural coalition operates confusing and prone to legal challenge. Even if the Commission employs the exemption criteria more widely to the sports sector, the ECJ still remains a venue for litigation. Competition law exemptions will still need to satisfy the requirements of Article 39. The separate territories approach is therefore legally fragile and susceptible to being undermined. This may encourage members of the socio-cultural coalition to venue shop for a hardening of the separate territories approach. In this connection tactical differences within their secondary aspects of their belief system may yet hamper them (see below).

Second, does the case-by-case approach satisfy the Single Market coalition's (in particular the Commission's) desire to reduce the number of sports-related cases coming before them? Only by providing clear guidelines on exemptions can the Commission hope to avoid the resource sapping case-load that has burdened it throughout the late 1990s.

The future of sports law and policy is likely to be influenced by developments external and internal to the EU. Externally, a change in the economic status of sport will affect the policy debate. Just as *Bosman* was influenced by (and indeed promoted) the commercialisation of sport, a downturn in the economic wealth of sport could strengthen public interest and solidarity arguments for the expansion of the sports autonomy territory. However, the post-ITV Digital financial crisis within the English Football League does not seem to have advanced these arguments. The case for a Division One break-away is increasingly being made which, if successful, would undermine the concept of solidarity between all members of the Football League.

Within the context of the EU, the forthcoming 2004 intergovernmental conference offers the socio-cultural coalition a possible venue for harder measures to be entrenched within a new Treaty. The year 2004 is likely to be influenced by the staging of major sporting events in Europe. The Olympic Games are to be held in Greece and the football European Championships will also be staged. Furthermore, 2004 is due to be declared European Year of Education Through Sport, thus giving sport a high profile during the IGC discussions.[6] Following the Year of Education through Sport initiative, the Commission intends to prepare a proposal implementing a December 1999 Council resolution on education and sport.[7] In previous reports, the EU has identified the excessive commercialisation of sport as an actual and potential threat to sports social, cultural and educational values.[8] The socio-cultural coalition therefore has a strong case in arguing that current sporting rules which are designed to maintain a competitive balance within the sector but which *prima facie* contravene EU law require a greater level of protection than that offered by the current approach. In this connection, the separate territories approach could develop in a number of directions.

The option closely related to the status quo is for the Commission to make greater use of the individual exemption procedure outlined in Article 81(3). The current soft law approach could harden with the adoption of formal decisions to close cases. Failing that, guidance in the form of notices could provide further guidelines to sport. For the Commission, this approach would help reduce its sports-related caseload whilst also lessening the threat of the member states adopting harder Treaty measures – an option traditionally resisted by the Commission. For the socio-cultural coalition, the use of individual exemptions offers the potential for sport to incrementally gain a partial exemption from EU law through the expansion of the sporting autonomy territory.

The second option would be for the member states to use soft law to place added pressure on the ECJ and the Commission to extend the sporting autonomy territory within the separate territories approach. In particular, the member states could strengthen the Amsterdam Declaration through the use of Presidency Conclusions at the end of European Council summits or through a new Declaration annexed to a revised Treaty. As with the first option, this relatively uncontroversial move is likely to be favoured as it not only offers the socio-cultural coalition the most realistic prospect of progress but it also allows the Single Market coalition scope to compromise with socio-cultural actors without undermining the fundamental principles on which the Single European Market is based.

A third option would be for the Commission to issue a block exemption Regulation for sport which would exempt particular sporting practices from the application of Article 81. For such a move to be effective sufficient case law experience must first be gained and a wide consultation process established. As this is a very lengthy process, the establishment of such a Regulation is therefore a longer-term possibility. For some 'moderate' socio-cultural actors (particularly the sports governing bodies) this option is favoured as it offers sport's specific characteristics legal protection from the application of competition law. It is however an option unlikely to be sanctioned by the Competition Policy Directorate. Previously the Commission has argued that such an exemption is *'unnecessary, undesirable and unjustified'* (Schaub 1998). Furthermore, wide consensus on the need for block exemptions is preferred by the Commission. Such consensus is absent. However, precedents for block exemptions do exist and potentially such exemptions, if carefully conceived, can reduce the number of individual exemption requests. The under-resourced Commission would welcome any significant reduction. The longer-term prospect of a block exemption for sport should therefore not be discounted. As EU sports law develops, so a line of reasoning on sport will emerge which could potentially persuade the Commission to explore the feasibility of an exemption.

Fourth, the member states could attach a protocol on sport to the Treaty. The EU has adopted such protocols to: (1) address specific member state concerns (as with the social protocol); (2) to provide exemptions to Treaty principles (as with the Danish Second Homes protocol); or (3) to limit the effects of a Court ruling (as with the Barber protocol). Clearly, all three instances pose problems. In the first instance a precedent for a more flexible *a la carte* Europe is set. In the second instance, a precedent is set for allowing a range of industries to claim 'special status'. In the third, a potentially undemocratic precedent is established whereby member states interfere in Court rulings. The protocol approach is supported by the moderates within the socio-cultural advocacy coalition and has gathered some support within member state capitals. A joint FIFA/UEFA task force examined the protocol proposal. UEFA Chief Executive, Gerhard Aigner explained, 'we are not seeking to change EU law by having the Bosman ruling repealed but what we do want is a sporting protocol to the European Treaty which would allow the EU to apply certain exemptions in sport'.[9] UEFA's support for a sports protocol was further elaborated in their brochure, 'A Vision for European Sport:

The Case for a Sports Protocol' (Blackshaw 2002). UEFA sees a protocol as a method of legally rooting the expansion of the sporting autonomy territory whilst maintaining distance from the Treaty. An Article for Sport would entail much greater supranational involvement in sport. However, the protocol option is not favoured by the Single Market coalition. The Commission is concerned that such a move would undermine the legal foundations of the Single Market. It is uncertain whether the member states could muster the required unanimous support for such a move.

Fifth, sport could be added to the list of EU activities outlined in Article 3 of the Treaty. Article 308 of the Treaty states that, 'if action by the Community should prove necessary to attain, in the course of the operation of the market, one of the objectives of the Community and this Treaty has not provided the necessary powers, the Council shall, acting unanimously on a proposal from the Commission and after consulting the European Parliament, take the appropriate measures'. Combining Article 3 with this 'catch-all' Article would permit action by the EU in sports matters if it was felt appropriate for the attainment of one of the objectives of the Treaty.

The sixth option involves the member states placing limits on the freedom of movement for workers (sportsmen and women) by amending Articles 39, 43 and 49. In addition, partial or full exemptions from the Treaty's Competition Policy provisions could be established by amending Articles 81 and 82. Both options are resisted by the Single Market coalition as they would undermine their deep and policy core beliefs. Furthermore, the many socio-cultural actors, including the Parliament, are reluctant to restrict the free movement of sports men and women. The rights afforded to EU citizens are seen as universal rights. The chances of success are therefore limited.

The seventh option involves including sport within the remit of Cultural policy (Article 151). The assumption underlying this approach is that sport can be equated with culture, even though this analogy was rejected by the ECJ in *Bosman*.[10] Furthermore, sport could be incorporated within Article 149 on Education, Vocational Training and Youth. Whilst this option has some maximalist support, it fails to address the sports specific concerns of the socio-cultural coalition. The cultural option is traditionally supported by the Parliament.

A related eighth option would be for the member states to create a new protective Article for Sport in a revised Treaty. Not all members of the socio-cultural coalition agree on this option. The maximalists favour the development of a common sports policy through the establishment of a legal base for sport (although see option seven). An Article for sport would not only shape and stabilise the legal environment in which sport operates, it would also provide a legal base for the development of sports funding programmes. These programmes could assist in the implementation of maximalist policy goals whilst providing sports bodies with an alternative source of income. The moderates do not support the development of a common sports policy but do wish to see the legal environment clarified through the adoption of a Treaty protocol on sport which would place a legal obligation on the EU to recognise the specificity of sport within its legal framework. Finally, the minimalists (particularly the Governments of Britain, Sweden and Denmark) do not see a greater role for the EU in sport as Treaty incorporation for sport would contradict the EU's claims of subsidiarity. Sufficient flexibility exists within the EU's legal framework for the EU to recognise the specificity of sport. As options seven and eight require Treaty revision, they require the unanimous support of the member states. This is a significant hurdle.

A ninth option lies within the wording of Article 86(2) of the Treaty. Article 86(2) potentially allows for an exemption from Treaty principles if undertakings entrusted with the operation of services of *general economic interest* or having the character of a *revenue-producing monopoly* can demonstrate that the application of the competition rules would obstruct the performance of tasks assigned to it. The prospects of such a move are however remote. Member states would have to take legal steps to create these entrusted sporting undertakings, as undertakings created by private initiative would be excluded. It is not only unlikely that member states would be willing to take such a step, it is also unlikely that sports organisations would see this move as desirable.

Finally, parallels can be drawn with the experience of sports treatment under US law. The debate concerning the application of competition rules to sport has also taken place in the USA. In the USA, two arguments have been advanced to support sports claim for an exemption from competition law. The rule of reason approach 'is based on the assumption that the efficiency promoting effects of certain agreements (amateur, junior sport, solidarity, competitive balance) are more important than the possible competitive distorting effects of the restrictions that arise from the agreement or behaviour'.[11] The rule of reason approach does not sit comfortably with EU competition law as the Commission can achieve the balance between pro- and anti-competitive rules through the exemption criteria. The second argument concerns the so-called single entity theory. This theory rests on the assumption that sport is a single economic entity. This means that anti-competitive measures may be tolerated within the sector. In the USA the US soccer federation has succeeded with this classification (Gray 2000: 281, Cairns 2002: 74). The *Danish Co-operatives* case provides a European parallel of sorts. Here an agricultural co-operative was permitted to prohibit their members from participating in alternative agricultural co-operatives as the restriction benefited competition. The logic of the single entity has not, as yet, been transferred to sport. In the view of Egger and Stix-Hackl, 'although sporting contests cannot be carried out by one club alone, but only by several clubs, nevertheless there is no 'single entity'. This particularity of football sport does not change the fact the individual clubs are undertakings. That the clubs are not to be regarded as a unit is shown precisely by their behaviour in connection with transfers of players, where the different interests of the individual clubs are especially clearly visible. It follows from the independence of the clubs that there is thus no question of 'internal' competition within a group of undertakings' (Egger and Stix-Hackl 2002: 86).

Conclusions

The application of the actor-centred institutional methodology employed throughout this text allows the researcher to judge with greater, although not total, certainty the future direction in which EU sports law and policy will develop. The methodology has asserted the need for subsystem analysis. By identifying actors and their belief systems and the institutional resources available to them, the researcher can better understand coalition strategy and the chances of strategic success. The Single Market coalition and the socio-cultural coalition are relatively evenly matched in terms of institutional resources. The socio-cultural coalition is however hampered by the diversity of opinion within the coalition. Nevertheless, both coalitions possess the institutional resources to undermine each other's deep and policy core belief systems.

Deeply embedded within the EU is the institutional norm of mediation. As a diverse multi-competence, multi-national and multi-level organisation, the EU has developed channels for mediation. However, unlike as is commonly portrayed in the media, the EU is not simply a venue in which all beliefs are sacrificed. The methodology employed in this text indicates the extent to which the coalitions will compromise. It has been claimed that the coalitions will seek to protect their deep and policy core beliefs above anything else. To fundamentally compromise these beliefs would be to call in question their reason for existing. Nevertheless, some under-resourced coalitions may be faced with having to accept compromise in their deep and policy core belief system. In the case of the sports policy subsystem, both coalitions are well resourced. As such, it is to the secondary aspects of their belief systems that the analysis must turn. The future direction of policy is likely to be confined to this field.

In the case of sport, the mediation resulted in the construction of the separate territories approach, an essential characteristic of EU sports policy. In order to protect their deep and policy core beliefs, both coalitions accepted the tactic of defining a territory of sporting autonomy and a territory of legal intervention. This distinct legal approach to sport marks the birth of EU sports law. The separate territories approach is quite a simple concept. The rules of sport are either sporting in nature and as such are not in breach of EU law (either falling outside the scope of EU law or are able to be justified and as such exempted from it) or they are commercial in nature and could potentially fall foul of EU law. However, as the book has already discussed, the precise definition of what constitutes sporting rules and commercial rules is problematic. Nevertheless, the future of EU sports law will be concerned with exactly this definitional issue. Where will the boundaries of the separate territories lie?

The ten policy options outlined above tend to stress strategies to expand the sporting autonomy territory. However, as has been demonstrated above, the socio-cultural coalition is a coalition of convenience. It lacks a cohesive approach to sport. Whilst the diversity of the coalition allows for the greater potential for venue exploitation, it also poses practical problems of co-ordinated action. The lack of consensus over Treaty incorporation for sport illustrates such divisions. It is therefore possible that the separate territories approach can be undermined through the contraction of the sporting autonomy territory and the expansion of the territory for judicial intervention. However, in the short to medium term, the sporting autonomy territory is unlikely to contract. By accepting the principle of separate territories, the Single Market coalition has in effect sanctioned the modest expansion of the sporting autonomy territory.

As changes in EU sports law are likely to be confined to the secondary aspects of the coalitions belief systems, only options one and two are likely to be pursued in the short to medium term. The Commission is therefore likely to continue to make use of the negative clearance and individual exemption criteria outlined in Articles 81 and 82. This allows the Commission to respond to socio-cultural pressure for an acknowledgement of sports special characteristics whilst not undermining the concept of free competition in the Single Market. Such case law will allow for greater clarity over the definition of the separate territories, although the likely continued use of soft law may undermine this. The member states are also likely to confirm their desire to see the sporting autonomy territory expanded. Again, soft law in the form of Presidency Conclusions or Treaty Declarations is likely to be the preferred option. Such an approach does not fundamentally challenge the deep and policy core beliefs of the Single Market coalition and it avoids the problematic question of how to secure consensus within the socio-cultural coalition over the relationship between sport and the Treaty. Member state soft law is also likely to guide the jurisprudence of the ECJ without the need to take Treaty bound measures. The ECJ's role is crucial to the development of EU sports law. Recent ECJ case law has contributed to the separate territories approach by making a distinction between sports rules which are inherent to the game and rules which are of a commercial nature. With further political pressure, the 'sporting' justification argument may develop into a 'public interest' justification. Finally, soft law could be used as justification for sport to be integrated into a range of other EU activities as a way of safeguarding the special characteristics of sport and promoting wider socio-cultural policy goals. The Commission has identified doping and youth activities as two such areas in which sport plays a significant role (see below).[12] By recognising the social, cultural, educational and health qualities of sport, the EU can implement sports policy goals in these neighbouring subsystems. This can be achieved without the problematic option of developing a fully fledged common sports policy.

The tactic of dispersing sports policy within neighbouring subsystems is however problematic. As illustrated above (and below), maximalist members of the socio-cultural coalition argue that a sports policy unattached to the Treaty leaves the legal environment uncertain. In addition, it does not grant sport a specific budgetary line. Any extension of the EU's involvement in sports policy must therefore be carefully conceived. In *UK* v. *Commission*, the ECJ held that each budget item must have a legal base.[13] This ruling resulted in the Commission abandoning its sports-related Eurathlon programme. Subsequent developments in sports policy requiring a budgetary line have had to navigate within the EU's rigorous budgetary rules. On these grounds, the Commission's 2002 call for proposals concerning the development of a Community policy in the field of sport appears legally fragile.[14] However, it relates to *preparatory measures* falling within the meaning of the Interinstitutional Agreement on legal bases and the implementation of the budget.[15] This agreement stipulates that any budgetary initiative must be supported by a 'basic act' of secondary legislation. As sport is not legally rooted in the Treaty, the EU has not passed sports specific legislation and as such the basic act requirement has not been fulfilled. The soft law initiatives which have characterised much of the development of EU sports policy are not considered 'basic acts'. However, appropriations relating to preparatory measures intended to prepare proposals with a view to the adoption of future Community actions are permitted subject to certain limitations. These preparatory measures must still however fall within the competence of the EU.[16] The Commission has interpreted this as justification for their call for preparatory measures concerning how sport relates to doping and youth activities. Should this activity fail to gain a legal base within three years, the funding would however have to cease. The budgetary 'rules of the game' therefore place further limits on the future scope of EU sports policy. Nevertheless, the extent to which the EU has acquired a greater socio-cultural expression in its policy remit since Maastricht means that sport now sits more comfortably within the EU's policy architecture.

Effectively, an expanded separate territories approach affords sports organising bodies considerable influence over the sport which they organise. Previously this power has not been exercised wisely – hence the juridification of sport. As Weatherill observes, it has been the choices made by sport that has driven juridification, not the EU (Weatherill 2000b). The Helsinki report on sport has already made a plea for reform at the level of the sports organisations. In particular, the report suggested that sporting federations should more clearly define their 'missions and statutes' in order to demonstrate that they themselves have taken measures to protect and nurture those special characteristics of sport that they are asking the EU to protect. Sports bodies need to address a number of issues. First, the rights of players need greater protection within the constitutions of sports bodies. This also refers to their ability to appeal the decisions of sports bodies. Not all sportsmen and women conform to the multi-millionaire stereotype. Without such protection, the EU will continue to be regarded as a venue for legal redress. Second, sports bodies need to demonstrate a greater commitment to solidarity in sport. By doing so, sport can rely more satisfactorily on the sporting justifications argument when issues of a commercial nature are being examined. Finally, the interests of fans should be safeguarded. Although sports bodies have an obligation to maximise the commercial potential of sport, the extent of permitted commercialisation should be proportionate to the requirements of the solidarity function of the sports bodies. As Foster argues, 'without these minimum conditions for limited autonomy, sports federations should expect further legal regulation to ensure that sport as a business is still run partly for the love of the game and not just for the love of money' (Foster 2000a: 64). Above all, sport should finally recognise that the EU is remarkably receptive to claims of special treatment. Working within the sports policy subsystem has allowed sports governing bodies to make these claims more coherently. It has also alerted sport to what is and what is not possible. Subsystem analysis demonstrates that currently the mediated approach taking place within the secondary aspects of both coalition's belief systems offers sport the best venue for protecting sports rules. This acceptance requires sport to abandon the rather feeble 'we know best' claim. It requires a psychological jump on the part of both sport and the EU institutions to acknowledge that increasingly the ECJ and the Commission are emerging as a supranational sports regulator – not in the sense of establishing a legislative framework for sport but as a clearing-house for sports rules. It is arguable that the EU's role as a sports regulator extends beyond even that of a clearing-house for sports rules. Although the Helsinki report's 'model of sport' cannot be imposed on sport, measures adopted by sport which undermine its principles are unlikely to be cleared by the EU. Although all parties reject the desirability of a supranational sports regulator, it is surely difficult to argue that current EU sports policy is not based on this reality.

The trend towards supranational sports regulation may in future be complicated by the Commission's proposal to amend the procedures for applying competition law.[17] This will undoubtedly affect the future definition of the separate territories. The proposal to devolve the exemption system outlined in Article 81(3) to national courts and national competition authorities will draw into the sports policy subsystem many more actors. Although the current separate territories landscape will inform their judgements, the lack of hard law within the subsystem and the lingering shadow of *Bosman* casts doubt on the longer-term viability of separate territories in its current form. Although private enforcement of competition law is not new, the wider involvement of national authorities could result in increased venue shopping from litigants. Any contraction in the territory of sports autonomy as a result of the involvement of national regulatory authorities is likely to lead to further venue shopping by the socio-cultural coalition as well. As further subsystem activity remains a possibility for the future, the construction of the separate territories approach may not therefore establish a settled legal environment for sport. Law will undoubtedly play a prominent feature within the sports policy subsystem in the future. However, as Weatherill concludes these issues should not mask the central question which involves 'the short sightedness of (some) clubs in pursuing commercialisation without adequate respect for the nature and purpose of sport in society' (Weatherill 2000b). Although sport has so often been portrayed as a victim of European integration, it has been sports own actions (or lack of them) which has driven the internationalisation of sports law.

Notes

1 The Convention is currently gathering opinion on possible Treaty change. The Nice Treaty committed the EU to a further intergovernmental conference in 2004.

2 Para. 4. Com (1999) 644, 'Report from the Commission to the European Council with a View to Safeguarding Sports Structures and Maintaining the Social Significance of Sport within the Community Framework: The Helsinki Report on Sport', 1/12/99.

3 Although other events of major importance to society can also be listed and protected.

4 Para. 106. Case C-415/93, *Union Royale Belge Sociétés de Football Association and others* v. *Bosman* [1995] ECR I-4291.

5 DN: IP/99/133, 'Commission Debates Application of Its Competition Rules to Sport', 24/02/99.

6 COM (2001) 584 Final, 'Proposal for a Decision of the European Parliament and of the Council Establishing the European Year of Education Through Sport', 16/10/01.

7 OJ C 8 12/01/00.

8 'Development and Prospects for Community Activity in the Field of Sport', Commission Staff Working Paper, Directorate General X, 29/09/98. 'The European Model of Sport'. Consultation Document of DG X. 1998. COM (2001) 584 Final, 'Proposal for a Decision of the European Parliament and of the Council establishing the European Year of Education through Sport', 16/10/01.

9 UEFA News Release 13/4/00.

10 Para. 78. Case C-415/93, *Union Royale Belge Sociétés de Football Association and others* v. *Bosman* [1995] ECR I-4291.

11 'The balance between the game and the money', Final Report. Study commissioned by the Netherlands' Ministry of Health, Welfare and Sports Directorate. Re-produced in Caiger and Gardiner (2000).

12 See 'Preparatory Measures for a Community Policy in the Field of Sport', Call for proposals. DG EAC No. 33/02. See also COM (2001) 584 Final, 'Proposal for a Decision of the European Parliament and of the Council Establishing the European Year of Education through Sport, 16/10/01.
13 Case C-106/96, *UK* v. *Commission* ECR I-02729.
14 See note 12.
15 OJ C 344, 12/11/98. Subsequently replaced by OJ C 172/1, 18/06/99 (Interinstitutional Agreement of 06/05/99).
16 For a full review of the potential legal bases relating to sporting actions see Commission document 'Community Aid Programmes'. Available online at: http://europa.eu.int/comm/sport/doc/ecom/actions_comm_en.pdf
17 See COM (2000) 582 Final, 'Proposal for a Council Regulation on the Implementation of the Rules on Competition Laid Down in Articles 81 and 82 of the Treaty and amending Regulations (EEC) No. 1017/68, (EEC) No. 2988/74, (EEC) No. 4056/86 and (EEC) No. 3975/87. ('Regulation Implementing Articles 81 and 82 of the Treaty'), 27/09/00.

Appendix 1: The *Bosman* ruling

Judgment of the Court of 15 December 1995.

Union Royale Belge des Sociétés de Football Association ASBL v. *Jean-Marc Bosman, Royal club Liégeois SA* v. *Jean-Marc Bosman and others and Union des Associations Européennes de Football (UEFA)* v. *Jean-Marc Bosman.*

Reference for a preliminary ruling: Cour d'Appel de Liège – Belgium. Freedom of movement for workers – Competition rules applicable to undertakings – Professional footballers – Sporting rules on the transfer of players requiring the new club to pay a fee to the old club – Limitation of the number of players having the nationality of other Member States who may be fielded in a match.

Case C-415/93.
European Court reports 1995, *page I-4921.*

Judgment

(1)   By judgment of 1 October 1993, received at the Court on 6 October 1993, the Cour d'Appel (Appeal Court), Liège, referred to the Court for a preliminary ruling under Article 177 of the EEC Treaty a set of questions on the interpretation of Articles 48, 85 and 86 of that Treaty.

(2)   Those questions were raised in various proceedings between (i) Union Royale Belge des Sociétés de Football Association ASBL ('URBSFA') and Mr Bosman, (ii) Royal Club Liégois SA ('RC Liège') and Mr Bosman, SA d'Économie Mixte Sportive de l'Union Sportive du Littoral de Dunkerque ('US Dunkerque'), URBSFA and Union des Associations Européennes de Football (UEFA) ('UEFA') and, (iii) UEFA and Mr Bosman.

The rules governing the organization of football

(3)   Association football, commonly known as 'football', professional or amateur, is practised as an organized sport in clubs which belong to national associations or federations in each of the Member States. Only in the United Kingdom are

there more than one (in fact, four) national associations, for England, Wales, Scotland and Northern Ireland respectively. URBSFA is the Belgian national association. Also dependent on the national associations are other secondary or subsidiary associations responsible for organizing football in certain sectors or regions. The associations hold national championships, organized in divisions depending on the sporting status of the participating clubs.

(4)   The national associations are members of the Fédération Internationale de Football Association ('FIFA'), an association governed by Swiss law, which organizes football at world level. FIFA is divided into confederations for each continent, whose regulations require its approval. The confederation for Europe is UEFA, also an association governed by Swiss law. Its members are the national associations of some 50 countries, including in particular those of the Member States which, under the UEFA Statutes, have undertaken to comply with those Statutes and with the regulations and decisions of UEFA.

(5)   Each football match organized under the auspices of a national association must be played between two clubs which are members of that association or of secondary or subsidiary associations affiliated to it. The team fielded by each club consists of players who are registered by the national association to play for that club. Every professional player must be registered as such with his national association and is entered as the present or former employee of a specific club.

Transfer rules   *Belgium Association*

(6)   The 1983 URBSFA federal rules, applicable at the time of the events giving rise to the different actions in the main proceedings, distinguish between three types of relationship: affiliation of a player to the federation, affiliation to a club, and registration of entitlement to play for a club, which is necessary for a player to be able to participate in official competitions. A transfer is defined as the transaction by which a player affiliated to an association obtains a change of club affiliation. If the transfer is temporary, the player continues to be affiliated to his club but is registered as entitled to play for another club.

(7)   Under the same rules, all professional players' contracts, which have a term of between one and five years, run to 30 June. Before the expiry of the contract, and by 26 April at the latest, the club must offer the player a new contract, failing which he is considered to be an amateur for transfer purposes and thereby falls under a different section of the rules. The player is free to accept or refuse that offer.

(8)   If he refuses, he is placed on a list of players available, between 1 and 31 May, for 'compulsory' transfer, without the agreement of the club of affiliation but subject to payment to that club by the new club of a compensation fee for 'training', calculated by multiplying the player's gross annual income by a factor varying from 14 to 2 depending on the player's age. *may have been more complicated than this*

(9)   1 June marks the opening of the period for 'free' transfers, with the agreement of both clubs and the player, in particular as to the amount of the transfer fee which the new club must pay to the old club, subject to penalties which may include striking off the new club for debt.

(10)   If no transfer takes place, the player's club of affiliation must offer him a new contract for one season on the same terms as that offered prior to 26 April. If the player refuses, the club has a period until 1 August in which it may suspend him,

failing which he is reclassified as an amateur. A player who persistently refuses to sign the contracts offered by his club may obtain a transfer as an amateur, without his club's agreement, after not playing for two seasons.

(11)   The UEFA and FIFA regulations are not directly applicable to players but are included in the rules of the national associations, which alone have the power to enforce them and to regulate relations between clubs and players.

(12)   UEFA, URBSFA and RC Liège stated before the national court that the provisions applicable at the material time to transfers between clubs in different Member States or clubs belonging to different national associations within the same Member State were contained in a document entitled 'Principles of Cooperation between Member Associations of UEFA and their Clubs', approved by the UEFA Executive Committee on 24 May 1990 and in force from 1 July 1990.

(13)   That document provides that at the expiry of the contract the player is free to enter into a new contract with the club of his choice. That club must immediately notify the old club which in turn is to notify the national association, which must issue an international clearance certificate. However, the former club is entitled to receive from the new club compensation for training and development, to be fixed, failing agreement, by a board of experts set up within UEFA using a scale of multiplying factors, from 12 to 1 depending on the player's age, to be applied to the player's gross income, up to a maximum of SFR 5 000 000.

(14)   The document stipulates that the business relationships between the two clubs in respect of the compensation fee for training and development are to exert no influence on the activity of the player, who is to be free to play for his new club. However, if the new club does not immediately pay the fee to the old club, the UEFA Control and Disciplinary Committee is to deal with the matter and notify its decision to the national association concerned, which may also impose penalties on the debtor club.

(15)   The national court considers that in the case with which the main proceedings are concerned URBSFA and RC Liège applied not the UEFA but the FIFA regulations.

(16)   At the material time, the FIFA regulations provided in particular that a professional player could not leave the national association to which he was affiliated so long as he was bound by his contract and by the rules of his club and his national association, no matter how harsh their terms might be. An international transfer could not take place unless the former national association issued a transfer certificate acknowledging that all financial commitments, including any transfer fee, had been settled.

(17)   After the events which gave rise to the main proceedings, UEFA opened negotiations with the Commission of the European Communities. In April 1991, it undertook in particular to incorporate in every professional player's contract a clause permitting him, at the expiry of the contract, to enter into a new contract with the club of his choice and to play for that club immediately. Provisions to that effect were incorporated in the Principles of Cooperation between Member Associations of UEFA and their Clubs adopted in December 1991 and in force from 1 July 1992.

(18)   In April 1991, FIFA adopted new Regulations governing the Status and Transfer of Football Players. That document, as amended in December 1991 and December 1993, provides that a player may enter into a contract with a new club

NOT NEW.

where the contract between him and his club has expired, has been rescinded or is to expire within six months. AMENDED 'GLOBAL' AGREEMENT : extension?

(19)   Special rules are laid down for 'non-amateur' players, defined as players who have received, in respect of participation in or an activity connected with football, remuneration in excess of the actual expenses incurred in the course of such participation, unless they have reacquired amateur status.

(20)   Where a non-amateur player, or a player who assumes non-amateur status within three years of his transfer, is transferred, his former club is entitled to a compensation fee for development or training, the amount of which is to be agreed upon between the two clubs. In the event of disagreement, the dispute is to be submitted to FIFA or the relevant confederation.

(21)   Those rules have been supplemented by UEFA regulations 'governing the fixing of a transfer fee', adopted in June 1993 and in force since 1 August 1993, which replace the 1991 'Principles of Cooperation between Member Associations of UEFA and their Clubs'. The new rules retain the principle that the business relationship between the two clubs are to exert no influence on the sporting activity of the player, who is to be free to play for the club with which he has signed the new contract. In the event of disagreement between the clubs concerned, it is for the appropriate UEFA board of experts to determine the amount of the compensation fee for training or development. For non-amateur players, the calculation of the fee is based on the player's gross income in the last 12 months or on the fixed annual income guaranteed in the new contract, increased by 20% for players who have played at least twice in the senior national representative team for their country and multiplied by a factor of between 12 and 0 depending on age.

✓ earliest 6 months before hand.

(22)   It appears from documents produced to the Court by UEFA that rules in force in other Member States also contain provisions requiring the new club, when a player is transferred between two clubs within the same national association, to pay the former club, on terms laid down in the rules in question, a compensation fee for transfer, training or development.

(23)   In Spain and France, payment of compensation may only be required if the player transferred is under 25 years of age or if his former club is the one with which he signed his first professional contract, as the case may be. In Greece, although no compensation is explicitly payable by the new club, the contract between the club and the player may make the player's departure dependent on the payment of an amount which, according to UEFA, is in fact most commonly paid by the new club.

DIFFERENT WHY

(24)   The rules applicable in that regard may derive from the national legislation, from the regulations of the national football associations or from the terms of collective agreements.

3\ *Nationality clauses*

not will : the national association } NOT ⎯ UEFA introduced rules ⎯ FIFA

(25)   From the 1960s onwards, many national football associations introduced rules ('nationality clauses') restricting the extent to which foreign players could be recruited or fielded in a match. For the purposes of those clauses, nationality is defined in relation to whether the player can be qualified to play in a country's national or representative team.

(26)   In 1978, UEFA gave an undertaking to Mr Davignon, a Member of the Commission of the European Communities, that it would remove the limitations on

✗

the number of contracts entered into by each club with players from other Member States and would set the number of such players who may participate in any one match at two, that limit not being applicable to players established for over five years in the Member State in question.

(27)   In 1991, following further discussions with Mr Bangemann, a Vice-President of the Commission, UEFA adopted the '3 + 2' rule permitting each national association to limit to three the number of foreign players whom a club may field in any first division match in their national championships, plus two players who have played in the country of the relevant national association for an uninterrupted period of five years, including three years as a junior. The same limitation also applies to UEFA matches in competitions for club teams.

Facts of the cases before the national court

(28)   Mr Bosman, a professional footballer of Belgian nationality, was employed from 1988 by RC Liège, a Belgian first division club, under a contract expiring on 30 June 1990, which assured him an average monthly salary of BFR 120 000, including bonuses.

(29)   On 21 April 1990, RC Liège offered Mr Bosman a new contract for one season, reducing his pay to BFR 30 000, the minimum permitted by the URBSFA federal rules. Mr Bosman refused to sign and was put on the transfer list. The compensation fee for training was set, in accordance with the said rules, at BFR 11 743 000.

(30)   Since no club showed an interest in a compulsory transfer, Mr Bosman made contact with US Dunkerque, a club in the French second division, which led to his being engaged for a monthly salary in the region of BFR 100 000 plus a signing-on bonus of some BFR 900 000.

(31)   On 27 July 1990, a contract was also concluded between RC Liège and US Dunkerque for the temporary transfer of Mr Bosman for one year, against payment by US Dunkerque to RC Liège of a compensation fee of BFR 1 200 000 payable on receipt by the Fédération Française de Football ('FFF') of the transfer certificate issued by URBSFA. The contract also gave US Dunkerque an irrevocable option for full transfer of the player for BFR 4 800 000.

(32)   Both contracts, between US Dunkerque and RC Liège and between US Dunkerque and Mr Bosman, were however subject to the suspensive condition that the transfer certificate must be sent by URBSFA to FFF in time for the first match of the season, which was to be held on 2 August 1990.

(33)   RC Liège, which had doubts as to US Dunkerque's solvency, did not ask URBSFA to send the said certificate to FFF. As a result, neither contract took effect. On 31 July 1990, RC Liège also suspended Mr Bosman, thereby preventing him from playing for the entire season.

(34)   On 8 August 1990, Mr Bosman brought an action against RC Liège before the Tribunal de Première Instance (Court of First Instance), Liège. Concurrently with that action, he applied for an interlocutory decision ordering RC Liège and URBSFA to pay him an advance of BFR 100 000 per month until he found a new employer, restraining the defendants from impeding his engagement, in particular by requiring payment of a sum of money, and referring a question to the Court of Justice for a preliminary ruling.

(35) By order of 9 November 1990, the judge hearing the interlocutory application ordered RC Liège and URBSFA to pay Mr Bosman an advance of BFR 30 000 per month and to refrain from impeding Mr Bosman's engagement. He also referred to the Court for a preliminary ruling a question (in Case C-340/90) on the interpretation of Article 48 in relation to the rules governing transfers of professional players ('transfer rules').

(36) In the meantime, Mr Bosman had been signed up by the French second-division club Saint-Quentin in October 1990, on condition that his interlocutory application succeeded. His contract was terminated, however, at the end of the first season. In February 1992, Mr Bosman signed a new contract with the French club Saint-Denis de la Réunion, which was also terminated. After looking for further offers in Belgium and France, Mr Bosman was finally signed up by Olympic de Charleroi, a Belgian third-division club.

(37) According to the national court, there is strong circumstantial evidence to support the view that, notwithstanding the 'free' status conferred on him by the interlocutory order, Mr Bosman has been boycotted by all the European clubs which might have engaged him.

(38) On 28 May 1991, the Cour d'Appel, Liège, revoked the interlocutory decision of the Tribunal de Première Instance in so far as it referred a question to the Court of Justice for a preliminary ruling. But it upheld the order against RC Liège to pay monthly advances to Mr Bosman and enjoined RC Liège and URBSFA to make Mr Bosman available to any club which wished to use his services, without it being possible to require payment of any compensation fee. By order of 19 June 1991, Case C-340/90 was removed from the register of the Court of Justice.

(39) On 3 June 1991, URBSFA, which, contrary to the situation in the interlocutory proceedings, had not been cited as a party in the main action before the Tribunal de Première Instance, intervened voluntarily in that action. On 20 August 1991, Mr Bosman issued a writ with a view to joining UEFA to the proceedings which he had brought against RC Liège and URBSFA and bringing proceedings directly against it on the basis of its responsibility in drafting the rules as a result of which he had suffered damage. On 5 December 1991, US Dunkerque was joined as a third party by RC Liège, in order to be indemnified against any order which might be made against it. On 15 October and 27 December 1991 respectively, Union Nationale des Footballeurs Professionnels ('UNFP'), a French professional footballers' union, and Vereniging van Contractspelers ('VVCS'), an association governed by Netherlands law, intervened voluntarily in the proceedings.

(40) In new pleadings lodged on 9 April 1992, Mr Bosman amended his initial claim against RC Liège, brought a new preventive action against URBSFA and elaborated his claim against UEFA. In those proceedings, he sought a declaration that the transfer rules and nationality clauses were not applicable to him and an order, on the basis of their wrongful conduct at the time of the failure of his transfer to US Dunkerque, against RC Liège, URBSFA and UEFA to pay him BFR 11 368 350 in respect of the damage suffered by him from 1 August 1990 until the end of his career and BFR 11 743 000 in respect of loss of earnings since the beginning of his career as a result of the application of the transfer rules. He also applied for a question to be referred to the Court of Justice for a preliminary ruling.

(41) By judgment of 11 June 1992, the Tribunal de Première Instance held that it had jurisdiction to entertain the main actions. It also held admissible Mr Bosman's

claims against RC Liège, URBSFA and UEFA seeking, in particular, a declaration that the transfer rules and nationality clauses were not applicable to him and orders penalizing the conduct of those three organizations. But it dismissed RC Liège's application to join US Dunkerque as a third party and indemnifier, since no evidence of fault in the latter's performance of its obligations had been adduced. Finally, finding that the examination of Mr Bosman's claims against UEFA and URBSFA involved considering the compatibility of the transfer rules with the Treaty, it made a reference to the Court of Justice for a preliminary ruling on the interpretation of Articles 48, 85 and 86 of the Treaty (Case C-269/92).

(42) URBSFA, RC Liège and UEFA appealed against that decision. Since those appeals had suspensive effect, the procedure before the Court of Justice was suspended. By order of 8 December 1993, Case C-269/92 was finally removed from the register following the new judgment of the Cour d'Appel, Liège, out of which the present proceedings arise.

(43) No appeal was brought against UNFP or VVCS, who did not seek to intervene again on appeal.

$ Grounds continued under DOC.NUM: 693J0415.1

(44) In its judgment ordering the reference, the Cour d'Appel upheld the judgment under appeal in so far as it held that the Tribunal de Première Instance had jurisdiction, that the actions were admissible and that an assessment of Mr Bosman's claims against UEFA and the URBSFA involved a review of the lawfulness of the transfer rules. It also considered that a review of the lawfulness of the nationality clauses was necessary, since Mr Bosman's claim in their regard was based on Article 18 of the Belgian Judicial Code, which permits actions 'with a view to preventing the infringement of a seriously threatened right', and Mr Bosman had adduced factual evidence suggesting that the damage which he fears . . . that the application of those clauses may impede his career . . . will in fact occur.

(45) The national court considered in particular that Article 48 of the Treaty could, like Article 30, prohibit not only discrimination but also non-discriminatory barriers to freedom of movement for workers if they could not be justified by imperative requirements.

(46) With regard to Article 85 of the Treaty, it considered that the FIFA, UEFA and URBSFA regulations might constitute decisions of associations of undertakings by which the clubs restrict competition between themselves for players. Transfer fees were dissuasive and tended to depress the level of professional sportsmen's pay. In addition, the nationality clauses prohibited foreign players' services from being obtained over a certain quota. Finally, trade between Member States was affected, in particular by the restriction of players' mobility.

(47) Furthermore, the Cour d'Appel thought that URBSFA, or the football clubs collectively, might be in a dominant position, within the meaning of Article 86 of the Treaty and that the restrictions on competition mentioned in connection with Article 85 might constitute abuses prohibited by Article 86.

(48) The Cour d'Appel dismissed UEFA's request that it ask the Court of Justice whether the reply to the question submitted on transfers would be different if the system permitted a player to play freely for his new club even where that club had not paid the transfer fee to the old club. It noted in particular that, because of the

threat of severe penalties for clubs not paying the transfer fee, a player's ability to play for his new club remained dependent on the business relationships between the clubs.

(49)   In view of the foregoing, the Cour d'Appel decided to stay the proceedings and refer the following questions to the Court of Justice for a preliminary ruling: 'Are Articles 48, 85 and 86 of the Treaty of Rome of 25 March 1957 to be interpreted as:

(i)   prohibiting a football club from requiring and receiving payment of a sum of money upon the engagement of one of its players who has come to the end of his contract by a new employing club;

ii   prohibiting the national and international sporting associations or federations from including in their respective regulations provisions restricting access of foreign players from the European Community to the competitions which they organize?'

(50)   On 3 June 1994, URBSFA applied to the Belgian Cour de Cassation (Court of Cassation) for review of the Cour d'Appel's judgment, requesting that the judgment be extended to apply jointly to RC Liège, UEFA and US Dunkerque. By letter of 6 October 1994, the Procureur Général (Principal Crown Counsel) to the Cour de Cassation informed the Court of Justice that the appeal did not have suspensive effect in this case.

(51)   By judgment of 30 March 1995, the Cour de Cassation dismissed the appeal and held that as a result the request for a declaration that the judgment be extended was otiose. The Cour de Cassation has forwarded a copy of that judgment to the Court of Justice.

The request for measures of inquiry

(52)   By letter lodged at the Court Registry on 16 November 1995, UEFA requested the Court to order a measure of inquiry under Article 60 of the Rules of Procedure, with a view to obtaining fuller information on the role played by transfer fees in the financing of small or medium-sized football clubs, the machinery governing the distribution of income within the existing football structures and the presence or absence of alternative machinery if the system of transfer fees were to disappear.

(53)   After hearing again the views of the Advocate General, the Court considers that that application must be dismissed. It was made at a time when, in accordance with Article 59(2) of the Rules of Procedure, the oral procedure was closed. The Court has held (see Case 77/70 *Prelle* v. *Commission* [1971] ECR 561, paragraph 7) that such an application can be admitted only if it relates to facts which may have a decisive influence and which the party concerned could not put forward before the close of the oral procedure.

(54)   In this case, it is sufficient to hold that UEFA could have submitted its request before the close of the oral procedure. Moreover, the question whether the aim of maintaining a balance in financial and competitive terms, and in particular that of ensuring the financing of smaller clubs, can be achieved by other means such as a redistribution of a portion of football takings was raised, in particular by Mr Bosman in his written observations.

Jurisdiction of the Court to give a preliminary ruling on the questions submitted

(55)   The Court's jurisdiction to give a ruling on all or part of the questions submitted by the national court has been challenged, on various grounds, by URBSFA, by UEFA, by some of the governments which have submitted observations and, during the written procedure, by the Commission.

(56)   First, UEFA and URBSFA have claimed that the main actions are procedural devices designed to obtain a preliminary ruling from the Court on questions which meet no objective need for the purpose of settling the cases. The UEFA regulations were not applied when Mr Bosman's transfer to US Dunkerque fell through; if they had been applied, that transfer would not have been dependent on the payment of a transfer fee and could thus have taken place. The interpretation of Community law requested by the national court thus bears no relation to the actual facts of the cases in the main proceedings or their purpose and, in accordance with consistent case law, the Court has no jurisdiction to rule on the questions submitted.

(57)   Secondly URBSFA, UEFA, the Danish, French and Italian Governments and, in its written observations, the Commission have claimed that the questions relating to nationality clauses has no connection with the disputes, which concern only the application of the transfer rules. The impediments to his career which Mr Bosman claims arise out of those clauses are purely hypothetical and do not justify a preliminary ruling by the Court on the interpretation of the Treaty in that regard.

(58)   Thirdly, URBSFA and UEFA pointed out at the hearing that, according to the judgment of the Cour de Cassation of 30 March 1995, the Cour d'Appel did not accept as admissible Mr Bosman's claims for a declaration that the nationality clauses in the URBSFA regulations were not applicable to him. Consequently, the issues in the main proceedings do not relate to the application of nationality clauses and the Court should not rule on the questions submitted on that point. The French Government concurred in that conclusion, subject however to verification of the scope of the judgment of the Cour de Cassation.

(59)   As to those submissions, it is to be remembered that, in the context of the cooperation between the Court of Justice and the national courts provided for by Article 177 of the Treaty, it is solely for the national court before which the dispute has been brought, and which must assume responsibility for the subsequent judicial decision, to determine in the light of the particular circumstances of the case both the need for a preliminary ruling in order to enable it to deliver judgment and the relevance of the questions which it submits to the Court. Consequently, where the questions submitted by the national court concern the interpretation of Community law, the Court of Justice is, in principle, bound to give a ruling (see, inter alia, Case C-125/94 *Aprile* v. *Amministrazione delle Finanze dello Stato* [1995] ECR I-0000, paragraphs 16 and 17).

(60)   Nevertheless, the Court has taken the view that, in order to determine whether it has jurisdiction, it should examine the conditions in which the case was referred to it by the national court. The spirit of cooperation which must prevail in the preliminary-ruling procedure requires the national court, for its part, to have regard to the function entrusted to the Court of Justice, which is to assist in the administration of justice in the Member States and not to deliver advisory opinions on general or hypothetical questions (see, inter alia, Case C-83/91 *Meilicke* v. *ADV/ORGA* [1992] ECR I-4871, paragraph 25).

Why football & not gov?

(61) That is why the Court has held that it has no jurisdiction to give a preliminary ruling on a question submitted by a national court where it is quite obvious that the interpretation of Community law sought by that court bears no relation to the actual facts of the main action or its purpose (see, inter alia, Case C-143/94 *Furlanis* v. *ANAS* [1995] ECR I-0000, paragraph 12) or where the problem is hypothetical and the Court does not have before it the factual or legal material necessary to give a useful answer to the questions submitted to it (see, inter alia, Meilicke, cited above, paragraph 32).

(62) In the present case, the issues in the main proceedings, taken as a whole, are not hypothetical and the national court has provided this Court with a clear statement of the surrounding facts, the rules in question and the grounds on which it believes that a decision on the questions submitted is necessary to enable it to give judgment.

(63) Furthermore, even if, as URBSFA and UEFA contend, the UEFA regulations were not applied when Mr Bosman's transfer to US Dunkerque fell through, they are still in issue in the preventive actions brought by Mr Bosman against URBSFA and UEFA (see paragraph 40 above) and the Court's interpretation as to the compatibility with Community law of the transfer system set up by the UEFA regulations may be useful to the national court.

(64) With regard more particularly to the questions concerning nationality clauses, it appears that the relevant heads of claim have been held admissible in the main proceedings on the basis of a national procedural provision permitting an action to be brought, albeit for declaratory purposes only, to prevent the infringement of a right which is seriously threatened. As is clear from its judgment, the national court considered that application of the nationality clauses could indeed impede Mr Bosman's career by reducing his chances of being employed or fielded in a match by a club from another Member State. It concluded that Mr Bosman's claims for a declaration that those nationality clauses were not applicable to him met the conditions laid down by the said provision.

(65) It is not for this Court, in the context of these proceedings, to call that assessment in question. Although the main actions seek a declaratory remedy and, having the aim of preventing infringement of a right under threat, must necessarily be based on hypotheses which are, by their nature, uncertain, such actions are none the less permitted under national law, as interpreted by the referring court. Consequently, the questions submitted by that court meet an objective need for the purpose of settling disputes properly brought before it.

(66) Finally, the judgment of the Cour de Cassation of 30 March 1995 does not suggest that the nationality clauses are extraneous to the issues in the main proceedings. That court held only that URBSFA's appeal against the judgment of the Cour d'Appel rested on a misinterpretation of that judgment. In its appeal, URBSFA had claimed that that court had held inadmissible a claim by Mr Bosman for a declaration that the nationality clauses contained in its regulations were not applicable to him. However, it would appear from the judgment of the Cour de Cassation that, according to the Cour d'Appel, Mr Bosman's claim sought to prevent impediments to his career likely to arise from the application not of the nationality clauses in the URBSFA regulations, which concerned players with a nationality other than Belgian, but of the similar clauses in the regulations of UEFA and the other national associations which are members of it, which could concern him as a player with Belgian

nationality. Consequently, it does not appear from the judgment of the Cour de Cassation that those latter nationality clauses are extraneous to the main proceedings.

(67)   It follows from the foregoing that the Court has jurisdiction to rule on the questions submitted by the Cour d'Appel, Liège.

Interpretation of Article 48 of the Treaty with regard to the transfer rules

(68)   By its first question, the national court seeks in substance to ascertain whether Article 48 of the Treaty precludes the application of rules laid down by sporting associations, under which a professional footballer who is a national of one Member State may not, on the expiry of his contract with a club, be employed by a club of another Member State unless the latter club has paid to the former a transfer, training or development fee. ·cross border compensation

Application of Article 48 to rules laid down by sporting associations

(69)   It is first necessary to consider certain arguments which have been put forward on the question of the application of Article 48 to rules laid down by sporting associations.

(70)   URBSFA argued that only the major European clubs may be regarded as undertakings, whereas clubs such as RC Liège carry on an economic activity only to a negligible extent. Furthermore, the question submitted by the national court on the transfer rules does not concern the employment relationships between players and clubs but the business relationships between clubs and the consequences of freedom to affiliate to a sporting federation. Article 48 of the Treaty is accordingly not applicable to a case such as that in issue in the main proceedings.

(71)   UEFA argued, inter alia, that the Community authorities have always respected the autonomy of sport, that it is extremely difficult to distinguish between the economic and the sporting aspects of football and that a decision of the Court concerning the situation of professional players might call in question the organization of football as a whole. For that reason, even if Article 48 of the Treaty were to apply to professional players, a degree of flexibility would be essential because of the particular nature of the sport. √

(72)   The German Government stressed, first, that in most cases a sport such as football is not an economic activity. It further submitted that sport in general has points of similarity with culture and pointed out that, under Article 128(1) of the EC Treaty, the Community must respect the national and regional diversity of the cultures of the Member States. Finally, referring to the freedom of association and autonomy enjoyed by sporting federations under national law, it concluded that, by virtue of the principle of subsidiarity, taken as a general principle, intervention by public, and particularly Community, authorities in this area must be confined to what is strictly necessary. √

(73)   In response to those arguments, it is to be remembered that, having regard to the objectives of the Community, sport is subject to Community law only in so far as it constitutes an economic activity within the meaning of Article 2 of the Treaty (see Case 36/74 *Walrave* v. *Union Cycliste Internationale* [1974] ECR 1405, paragraph 4). This applies to the activities of professional or semi-professional footballers,

where they are in gainful employment or provide a remunerated service (see Case 13/76 *Donà* v. *Mantero* [1976] ECR 1333, paragraph 12).

(74)   It is not necessary, for the purposes of the application of the Community provisions on freedom of movement for workers, for the employer to be an undertaking; all that is required is the existence of, or the intention to create, an employment relationship.

(75)   Application of Article 48 of the Treaty is not precluded by the fact that the transfer rules govern the business relationships between clubs rather than the employment relationships between clubs and players. The fact that the employing clubs must pay fees on recruiting a player from another club affects the players' opportunities for finding employment and the terms under which such employment is offered.

(76)   As regards the difficulty of severing the economic aspects from the sporting aspects of football, the Court has held (in Donà, cited above, paragraphs 14 and 15) that the provisions of Community law concerning freedom of movement of persons and of provision of services do not preclude rules or practices justified on non-economic grounds which relate to the particular nature and context of certain matches. It stressed, however, that such a restriction on the scope of the provisions in question must remain limited to its proper objective. It cannot, therefore, be relied upon to exclude the whole of a sporting activity from the scope of the Treaty.

(77)   With regard to the possible consequences of this judgment on the organization of football as a whole, it has consistently been held that, although the practical consequences of any judicial decision must be weighed carefully, this cannot go so far as to diminish the objective character of the law and compromise its application on the ground of the possible repercussions of a judicial decision. At the very most, such repercussions might be taken into consideration when determining whether exceptionally to limit the temporal effect of a judgment (see, inter alia, Case C-163/90 *Administration des Douanes* v. *Legros and Others* [1992] ECR I-4625, paragraph 30).

(78)   The argument based on points of alleged similarity between sport and culture cannot be accepted, since the question submitted by the national court does not relate to the conditions under which Community powers of limited extent, such as those based on Article 128(1), may be exercised but on the scope of the freedom of movement of workers guaranteed by Article 48, which is a fundamental freedom in the Community system (see, inter alia, Case C-19/92 *Kraus* v. *Land Baden-Wuerttemberg* [1993] ECR I-1663, paragraph 16).

(79)   As regards the arguments based on the principle of freedom of association, it must be recognized that this principle, enshrined in Article 11 of the European Convention for the Protection of Human Rights and Fundamental Freedoms and resulting from the constitutional traditions common to the Member States, is one of the fundamental rights which, as the Court has consistently held and as is reaffirmed in the preamble to the Single European Act and in Article F(2) of the Treaty on European Union, are protected in the Community legal order.

(80)   However, the rules laid down by sporting associations to which the national court refers cannot be seen as necessary to ensure enjoyment of that freedom by those associations, by the clubs or by their players, nor can they be seen as an inevitable result thereof. SO NON PREDICTED + EXTENDED.

(81)   Finally, the principle of subsidiarity, as interpreted by the German Government to the effect that intervention by public authorities, and particularly Community authorities, in the area in question must be confined to what is strictly necessary, cannot lead to a situation in which the freedom of private associations to adopt sporting rules restricts the exercise of rights conferred on individuals by the Treaty.

(82)   Once the objections concerning the application of Article 48 of the Treaty to sporting activities such as those of professional footballers are out of the way, it is to be remembered that, as the Court held in paragraph 17 of its judgment in Walrave, cited above, Article 48 not only applies to the action of public authorities but extends also to rules of any other nature aimed at regulating gainful employment in a collective manner.

(83)   The Court has held that the abolition as between Member States of obstacles to freedom of movement for persons and to freedom to provide services would be compromised if the abolition of State barriers could be neutralized by obstacles resulting from the exercise of their legal autonomy by associations or organizations not governed by public law (see Walrave, cited above, paragraph 18).

(84)   It has further observed that working conditions in the different Member States are governed sometimes by provisions laid down by law or regulation and sometimes by agreements and other acts concluded or adopted by private persons. Accordingly, if the scope of Article 48 of the Treaty were confined to acts of a public authority there would be a risk of creating inequality in its application (see Walrave, cited above, paragraph 19). That risk is all the more obvious in a case such as that in the main proceedings in this case in that, as has been stressed in paragraph 24 above, the transfer rules have been laid down by different bodies or in different ways in each Member State.

(85)   UEFA objects that such an interpretation makes Article 48 of the Treaty more restrictive in relation to individuals than in relation to Member States, which are alone in being able to rely on limitations justified on grounds of public policy, public security or public health.

(86)   That argument is based on a false premises. There is nothing to preclude individuals from relying on justifications on grounds of public policy, public security or public health. Neither the scope nor the content of those grounds of justification is in any way affected by the public or private nature of the rules in question.

(87)   Article 48 of the Treaty therefore applies to rules laid down by sporting associations such as URBSFA, FIFA or UEFA, which determine the terms on which professional sportsmen can engage in gainful employment.

(d) *Whether the situation envisaged by the national court is of a purely internal nature*

(88)   UEFA considers that the disputes pending before the national court concern a purely internal Belgian situation which falls outside the ambit of Article 48 of the Treaty. They concern a Belgian player whose transfer fell through because of the conduct of a Belgian club and a Belgian association.

(89)   It is true that, according to consistent case law (see, inter alia, Case 175/78 *Regina* v. *Saunders* [1979] ECR 1129, paragraph 11; Case 180/83 *Moser* v. *Land Baden-Wuerttemberg* [1984] ECR 2539, paragraph 15; Case C-332/90 *Steen* v. *Deutsche Bundespost* [1992] ECR I-341, paragraph 9; and Case C-19/92 Kraus,

cited above, paragraph 15), the provisions of the Treaty concerning the free movement of workers, and particularly Article 48, cannot be applied to situations which are wholly internal to a Member State, in other words where there is no factor connecting them to any of the situations envisaged by Community law.

(90) However, it is clear from the findings of fact made by the national court that Mr Bosman had entered into a contract of employment with a club in another Member State with a view to exercising gainful employment in that State. By so doing, as he has rightly pointed out, he accepted an offer of employment actually made, within the meaning of Article 48(3)(a).

(91) Since the situation in issue in the main proceedings cannot be classified as purely internal, the argument put forward by UEFA must be dismissed.

Existence of an obstacle to freedom of movement for workers

(92) It is thus necessary to consider whether the transfer rules form an obstacle to freedom of movement for workers prohibited by Article 48 of the Treaty.

(93) As the Court has repeatedly held, freedom of movement for workers is one of the fundamental principles of the Community and the Treaty provisions guaranteeing that freedom have had direct effect since the end of the transitional period.

(94) The Court has also held that the provisions of the Treaty relating to freedom of movement for persons are intended to facilitate the pursuit by Community citizens of occupational activities of all kinds throughout the Community, and preclude measures which might place Community citizens at a disadvantage when they wish to pursue an economic activity in the territory of another Member State (see Case 143/87 *Stanton* v. *INASTI* [1988] ECR 3877, paragraph 13, and Case C-370/90 *The Queen* v. *Immigration Appeal Tribunal and Surinder Singh* [1992] ECR I-4265, paragraph 16).

(95) In that context, nationals of Member States have in particular the right, which they derive directly from the Treaty, to leave their country of origin to enter the territory of another Member State and reside there in order there to pursue an economic activity (see, inter alia, Case C-363/89 *Roux* v. *Belgium* [1991] ECR I-273, paragraph 9, and Singh, cited above, paragraph 17).

(96) Provisions which preclude or deter a national of a Member State from leaving his country of origin in order to exercise his right to freedom of movement therefore constitute an obstacle to that freedom even if they apply without regard to the nationality of the workers concerned (see also Case C-10/90 *Masgio* v. *Bundesknappschaft* [1991] ECR I-1119, paragraphs 18 and 19).

(97) The Court has also stated, in Case 81/87 *The Queen* v. *H.M. Treasury and Commissioners of Inland Revenue ex parte Daily Mail and General Trust plc* [1988] ECR 5483, paragraph 16, that even though the Treaty provisions relating to freedom of establishment are directed mainly to ensuring that foreign nationals and companies are treated in the host Member State in the same way as nationals of that State, they also prohibit the Member State of origin from hindering the establishment in another Member State of one of its nationals or of a company incorporated under its legislation which comes within the definition contained in Article 58. The rights guaranteed by Article 52 et seq. of the Treaty would be rendered meaningless if the Member State of origin could prohibit undertakings from leaving in order to establish themselves in another Member State. The same considerations apply, in relation

to Article 48 of the Treaty, with regard to rules which impede the freedom of movement of nationals of one Member State wishing to engage in gainful employment in another Member State.

(98)   It is true that the transfer rules in issue in the main proceedings apply also to transfers of players between clubs belonging to different national associations within the same Member State and that similar rules govern transfers between clubs belonging to the same national association.

(99)   However, as has been pointed out by Mr Bosman, by the Danish Government and by the Advocate General in points 209 and 210 of his Opinion, those rules are likely to restrict the freedom of movement of players who wish to pursue their activity in another Member State by preventing or deterring them from leaving the clubs to which they belong even after the expiry of their contracts of employment with those clubs.

(100)   Since they provide that a professional footballer may not pursue his activity with a new club established in another Member State unless it has paid his former club a transfer fee agreed upon between the two clubs or determined in accordance with the regulations of the sporting associations, the said rules constitute an obstacle to freedom of movement for workers.

(101)   As the national court has rightly pointed out, that finding is not affected by the fact that the transfer rules adopted by UEFA in 1990 stipulate that the business relationship between the two clubs is to exert no influence on the activity of the player, who is to be free to play for his new club. The new club must still pay the fee in issue, under pain of penalties which may include its being struck off for debt, which prevents it just as effectively from signing up a player from a club in another Member State without paying that fee.

(102)   Nor is that conclusion negated by the case law of the Court cited by URBSFA and UEFA, to the effect that Article 30 of the Treaty does not apply to measures which restrict or prohibit certain selling arrangements so long as they apply to all relevant traders operating within the national territory and so long as they affect in the same manner, in law and in fact, the marketing of domestic products and of those from other Member States (see Joined Cases C-267/91 and C-268/91 Keck and Mithouard [1993] ECR I-6097, paragraph 16).

(103)   It is sufficient to note that, although the rules in issue in the main proceedings apply also to transfers between clubs belonging to different national associations within the same Member State and are similar to those governing transfers between clubs belonging to the same national association, they still directly affect players' access to the employment market in other Member States and are thus capable of impeding freedom of movement for workers. They cannot, thus, be deemed comparable to the rules on selling arrangements for goods which in Keck and Mithouard were held to fall outside the ambit of Article 30 of the Treaty (see also, with regard to freedom to provide services, Case C-384/93 *Alpine Investments* v *Minister van Financiën* [1995] ECR I-1141, paragraphs 36 to 38).

(104)   Consequently, the transfer rules constitute an obstacle to freedom of movement for workers prohibited in principle by Article 48 of the Treaty. It could only be otherwise if those rules pursued a legitimate aim compatible with the Treaty and were justified by pressing reasons of public interest. But even if that were so, application of those rules would still have to be such as to ensure achievement of the aim in question and not go beyond what is necessary for that purpose (see, inter alia,

the judgment in Kraus, cited above, paragraph 32, and Case C-55/94 *Gebhard* [1995] ECR I-0000, paragraph 37).

Existence of justifications

(105)   First, URBSFA, UEFA and the French and Italian Governments have submitted that the transfer rules are justified by the need to maintain a financial and competitive balance between clubs and to support the search for talent and the training of young players.

(106)   In view of the considerable social importance of sporting activities and in particular football in the Community, the aims of maintaining a balance between clubs by preserving a certain degree of equality and uncertainty as to results and of encouraging the recruitment and training of young players must be accepted as legitimate.

(107)   As regards the first of those aims, Mr Bosman has rightly pointed out that the application of the transfer rules is not an adequate means of maintaining financial and competitive balance in the world of football. Those rules neither preclude the richest clubs from securing the services of the best players nor prevent the availability of financial resources from being a decisive factor in competitive sport, thus considerably altering the balance between clubs.

(108)   As regards the second aim, it must be accepted that the prospect of receiving transfer, development or training fees is indeed likely to encourage football clubs to seek new talent and train young players.

(109)   However, because it is impossible to predict the sporting future of young players with any certainty and because only a limited number of such players go on to play professionally, those fees are by nature contingent and uncertain and are in any event unrelated to the actual cost borne by clubs of training both future professional players and those who will never play professionally. The prospect of receiving such fees cannot, therefore, be either a decisive factor in encouraging recruitment and training of young players or an adequate means of financing such activities, particularly in the case of smaller clubs.

(110)   Furthermore, as the Advocate General has pointed out in point 226 et seq. of his Opinion, the same aims can be achieved at least as efficiently by other means which do not impede freedom of movement for workers.

(111)   It has also been argued that the transfer rules are necessary to safeguard the worldwide organization of football.

(112)   However, the present proceedings concern application of those rules within the Community and not the relations between the national associations of the Member States and those of non-member countries. In any event, application of different rules to transfers between clubs belonging to national associations within the Community and to transfers between such clubs and those affiliated to the national associations of non-member countries is unlikely to pose any particular difficulties. As is clear from paragraphs 22 and 23 above, the rules which have so far governed transfers within the national associations of certain Member States are different from those which apply at the international level.

(113)   Finally, the argument that the rules in question are necessary to compensate clubs for the expenses which they have had to incur in paying fees on recruiting their players cannot be accepted, since it seeks to justify the maintenance of obstacles

to freedom of movement for workers simply on the ground that such obstacles were able to exist in the past.

(114)   The answer to the first question must therefore be that Article 48 of the Treaty precludes the application of rules laid down by sporting associations, under which a professional footballer who is a national of one Member State may not, on the expiry of his contract with a club, be employed by a club of another Member State unless the latter club has paid to the former club a transfer, training or development fee.

(3) Interpretation of Article 48 of the Treaty with regard to the nationality clauses

(115)   By its second question, the national court seeks in substance to ascertain whether Article 48 of the Treaty precludes the application of rules laid down by sporting associations, under which, in matches in competitions which they organize, football clubs may field only a limited number of professional players who are nationals of other Member States.

(4) Existence of an obstacle to freedom of movement for workers

(116)   As the Court has held in paragraph 87 above, Article 48 of the Treaty applies to rules laid down by sporting associations which determine the conditions under which professional sports players may engage in gainful employment. It must therefore be considered whether the nationality clauses constitute an obstacle to freedom of movement for workers, prohibited by Article 48.

(117)   Article 48(2) expressly provides that freedom of movement for workers entails the abolition of any discrimination based on nationality between workers of the Member States as regards employment, remuneration and conditions of work and employment.

(118)   That provision has been implemented, in particular, by Article 4 of Regulation (EEC) No 1612/68 of the Council of 15 October 1968 on freedom of movement for workers within the Community (OJ, English Special Edition, 1968(II), p. 475), under which provisions laid down by law, regulation or administrative action of the Member States which restrict by number or percentage the employment of foreign nationals in any undertaking, branch of activity or region, or at a national level, are not to apply to nationals of the other Member States.

(119)   The same principle applies to clauses contained in the regulations of sporting associations which restrict the right of nationals of other Member States to take part, as professional players, in football matches (see the judgment in Donà, cited above, paragraph 19).

(120)   The fact that those clauses concern not the employment of such players, on which there is no restriction, but the extent to which their clubs may field them in official matches is irrelevant. In so far as participation in such matches is the essential purpose of a professional player's activity, a rule which restricts that participation obviously also restricts the chances of employment of the player concerned.

⒖Existence of justifications

(121)   The existence of an obstacle having thus been established, it must be considered whether that obstacle may be justified in the light of Article 48 of the Treaty.

(122)   URBSFA, UEFA and the German, French and Italian Governments argued that the nationality clauses are justified on non-economic grounds, concerning only the sport as such. *sport a non-economic entity.*

(123)   First, they argued, those clauses serve to maintain the traditional link between each club and its country, a factor of great importance in enabling the public to identify with its favourite team and ensuring that clubs taking part in international competitions effectively represent their countries.

(124)   Secondly, those clauses are necessary to create a sufficient pool of national players to provide the national teams with top players to field in all team positions.

(125)   Thirdly, they help to maintain a competitive balance between clubs by preventing the richest clubs from appropriating the services of the best players.

(126)   Finally, UEFA points out that the '3+2' rule was drawn up in collaboration with the Commission and must be revised regularly to remain in line with the development of Community policy.

(127)   It must be recalled that in paragraphs 14 and 15 of its judgment in Donà, cited above, the Court held that the Treaty provisions concerning freedom of movement for persons do not prevent the adoption of rules or practices excluding foreign players from certain matches for reasons which are not of an economic nature, which relate to the particular nature and context of such matches and are thus of sporting interest only, such as, for example, matches between national teams from different countries. It stressed, however, that that restriction on the scope of the provisions in question must remain limited to its proper objective.

(128)   Here, the nationality clauses do not concern specific matches between teams representing their countries but apply to all official matches between clubs and thus to the essence of the activity of professional players.

(129)   In those circumstances, the nationality clauses cannot be deemed to be in accordance with Article 48 of the Treaty, otherwise that Article would be deprived of its practical effect and the fundamental right of free access to employment which the Treaty confers individually on each worker in the Community rendered nugatory (on this last point, see Case 222/86 UNECTEF v. *Heylens and Others* [1987] ECR 4097, paragraph 14).

(130)   None of the arguments put forward by the sporting associations and by the governments which have submitted observations detracts from that conclusion.

(131)   First, a football club's links with the Member State in which it is established cannot be regarded as any more inherent in its sporting activity than its links with its locality, town, region or, in the case of the United Kingdom, the territory covered by each of the four associations. Even though national championships are played between clubs from different regions, towns or localities, there is no rule restricting the right of clubs to field players from other regions, towns or localities in such matches. *Good point*

(132)   In international competitions, moreover, participation is limited to clubs which have achieved certain results in competition in their respective countries, without any particular significance being attached to the nationalities of their players.

(133)   Secondly, whilst national teams must be made up of players having the nationality of the relevant country, those players need not necessarily be registered to play for clubs in that country. Indeed, under the rules of the sporting associations, foreign players must be allowed by their clubs to play for their country's national team in certain matches.

(134)   Furthermore, although freedom of movement for workers, by opening up the employment market in one Member State to nationals of the other Member States, has the effect of reducing workers' chances of finding employment within the Member State of which they are nationals, it also, by the same token, offers them new prospects of employment in other Member States. Such considerations obviously apply also to professional footballers.

(135)   Thirdly, although it has been argued that the nationality clauses prevent the richest clubs from engaging the best foreign players, those clauses are not sufficient to achieve the aim of maintaining a competitive balance, since there are no rules limiting the possibility for such clubs to recruit the best national players, thus undermining that balance to just the same extent.

(136)   Finally, as regards the argument based on the Commission's participation in the drafting of the '3+2' rule, it must be pointed out that, except where such powers are expressly conferred upon it, the Commission may not give guarantees concerning the compatibility of specific practices with the Treaty (see also Joined Cases 142/80 and 143/80 *Amministrazione delle Finanze dello Stato* v. *Essevi and Salengo* [1981] ECR 1413, paragraph 16). In no circumstances does it have the power to authorize practices which are contrary to the Treaty.

(137)   It follows from the foregoing that Article 48 of the Treaty precludes the application of rules laid down by sporting associations under which, in matches in competitions which they organize, football clubs may field only a limited number of professional players who are nationals of other Member States.

Interpretation of Articles 85 and 86 of the Treaty

(138)   Since both types of rule to which the national court's question refer are contrary to Article 48, it is not necessary to rule on the interpretation of Articles 85 and 86 of the Treaty.

The temporal effects of this judgment

(139)   In their written and oral observations, UEFA and URBSFA have drawn the Court's attention to the serious consequences which might ensue from its judgment for the organization of football as a whole if it were to consider the transfer rules and nationality clauses to be incompatible with the Treaty.

(140)   Mr Bosman, whilst observing that such a solution is not indispensable, has suggested that the Court could limit the temporal effects of its judgment in so far as it concerns the transfer rules.

(141)   It has consistently been held that the interpretation which the Court, in the exercise of the jurisdiction conferred upon it by Article 177 of the Treaty, gives to a rule of Community law clarifies and where necessary defines the meaning and scope of that rule as it must be, or ought to have been, understood and applied from the time of its coming into force. It follows that the rule as thus interpreted can, and

must, be applied by the courts even to legal relationships arising and established before the judgment ruling on the request for interpretation, provided that in other respects the conditions for bringing before the courts having jurisdiction an action relating to the application of that rule are satisfied (see, inter alia, Case 24/86 *Blaizot* v. *University of Liège and Others* [1988] ECR 379, paragraph 27).

(142)   It is only exceptionally that the Court may, in application of the general principle of legal certainty inherent in the Community legal order, be moved to restrict the opportunity for any person concerned to rely upon the provision as thus interpreted with a view to calling in question legal relationships established in good faith. Such a restriction may be allowed only by the Court, in the actual judgment ruling upon the interpretation sought (see, inter alia, the judgments in Blaizot, cited above, paragraph 28, and Legros, cited above, paragraph 30).

(143)   In the present case, the specific features of the rules laid down by the sporting associations for transfers of players between clubs of different Member States, together with the fact that the same or similar rules applied to transfers both between clubs belonging to the same national association and between clubs belonging to different national associations within the same Member State, may have caused uncertainty as to whether those rules were compatible with Community law.

(144)   In such circumstances, overriding considerations of legal certainty militate against calling in question legal situations whose effects have already been exhausted. An exception must, however, be made in favour of persons who may have taken timely steps to safeguard their rights. Finally, limitation of the effects of the said interpretation can be allowed only in respect of compensation fees for transfer, training or development which have already been paid on, or are still payable under an obligation which arose before, the date of this judgment.

(145)   It must therefore be held that the direct effect of Article 48 of the Treaty cannot be relied upon in support of claims relating to a fee in respect of transfer, training or development which has already been paid on, or is still payable under an obligation which arose before, the date of this judgment, except by those who have brought court proceedings or raised an equivalent claim under the applicable national law before that date.

(146)   With regard to nationality clauses, however, there are no grounds for a temporal limitation of the effects of this judgment. In the light of the Walrave and Donà judgments, it was not reasonable for those concerned to consider that the discrimination resulting from those clauses was compatible with Article 48 of the Treaty.

Costs

(147)   The costs incurred by the Danish, French, German and Italian Governments and the Commission of the European Communities, which have submitted observations to the Court, are not recoverable. Since these proceedings are, for the parties to the main proceedings, a step in the action pending before the national court, the decision on costs is a matter for that court.

On those grounds,
THE COURT,
in answer to the questions referred to it by the Cour d'Appel, Liège, by judgment of
1 October 1993, hereby rules:

(1)   Article 48 of the EEC Treaty precludes the application of rules laid down by
sporting associations, under which a professional footballer who is a national of one
Member State may not, on the expiry of his contract with a club, be employed by a
club of another Member State unless the latter club has paid to the former club a
transfer, training or development fee.

(2)   Article 48 of the EEC Treaty precludes the application of rules laid down by
sporting associations under which, in matches in competitions which they organize,
football clubs may field only a limited number of professional players who are
nationals of other Member States.

(3)   The direct effect of Article 48 of the EEC Treaty cannot be relied upon in
support of claims relating to a fee in respect of transfer, training or development
which has already been paid on, or is still payable under an obligation which arose
before, the date of this judgment, except by those who have brought court proceedings or raised an equivalent claim under the applicable national law before that date.

Appendix 2: The Helsinki report on sport

Commission of the European Communities

Brussels, 10.12.1999

COM (1999) 644 final

Report from the Commission to the European Council with a view to safeguarding current sports structures and maintaining the social function of sport within the Community framework – *The Helsinki report on sport.*

1 Introduction

'Recalling the Declaration on Sport attached to the Treaty of Amsterdam and recognising the social role of sport', the European Council, meeting in Vienna on 11 and 12 December 1998, invited 'the Commission to submit a report to the Helsinki European Council with a view to safeguarding current sports structures and maintaining the social function of sport within the Community framework'. This report by the Commission is the response to the European Council's invitation.

Following this invitation and in accordance with the Amsterdam Declaration, numerous consultations were held (Olympic movement, sporting federations, sports industries, media, governments and Community institutions), especially at the 'European Union Conference on Sport' organised in Olympia from 20 to 23 May 1999. Sport is one of the areas of activity that most concerns and brings together the citizens of the European Union, irrespective of age and social origin. More than half of them regularly do sport, either in one of the 700 000 clubs that exist in the Union or outside these clubs. Almost two million teachers, instructors and voluntary workers spend their working or leisure time organising sporting activities.

This social function of sport, which is in the general interest, has for some years been affected by the emergence of new phenomena which sometimes call into question the ethics of sport and the principles on which it is organised, be they violence in the stadiums, the increase in doping practices or the search for quick profits to the detriment of a more balanced development of sport.

This report gives pointers for reconciling the economic dimension of sport with its popular, educational, social and cultural dimensions.

2 The development of sport in Europe risks weakening its educational and social function

There are many common features in the ways in which sport is practised and organised in the Union, in spite of certain differences between the Member States, and there is therefore possible to talk of a European approach to sport based on common concepts and principles.

For several years, the European approach to sport has been affected by several phenomena:

- *the rise in the popularity of sport* in terms of the number of people doing and watching sport. A total of 37 billion television viewers watched the matches of the most recent football World Cup, which is nearly 600 million television viewers per match;
- *the internationalisation of sport*, with the increase in the number of international competitions. In 1999, 77 world championships and 102 European championships were organised in Europe;
- *the unprecedented development of the economic dimension of sport*, with, for example, the spectacular increase in television rights: the value of the television rights negotiated by the IOC has risen from USD 441 million in 1992 (Barcelona Olympic Games) to an expected USD 1.318 billion for the 2000 Olympic Games in Sydney.

These phenomena provide certain advantages for sport and society. Accordingly, the number of jobs created directly or indirectly by the sport industry has risen by 60% in the past ten years to reach nearly 2 million. It has to be recognised, however, that these phenomena may also cause tension.

One of the first signs of these developments is the overloading of sporting calendars, which, linked to the need to produce results under the pressure of sponsors, may be considered to be one of the causes of the expansion of doping.

A second consequence is the increase in the number of lucrative sporting events, which may end up promoting the commercial approach, to the detriment of sporting principles and the social function of sport.

A third symptom is the temptation for certain sporting operators and certain large clubs to leave the federations in order to derive the maximum benefit from the economic potential of sport for themselves alone. This tendency may jeopardise the principle of financial solidarity between professional and amateur sport and the system of promotion and relegation common to most federations.

Another consequence that has been observed is the hazardous future facing young people who are being led into top-level competitive sport at an increasingly early age, often with no other vocational training, with the resulting risks for their physical and mental health and their subsequent switch to other employment.

3 The Community, its Member States and the sporting movement need to reaffirm and strengthen the educational and social function of sport

The Declaration on Sport annexed to the Amsterdam Treaty 'emphasises the social significance of sport, in particular its role in forging identity and bringing people together'. Physical and sporting activities need to find their place in the education system of each Member State.

The values that they represent (equal opportunities, fair play, solidarity, etc.) must also be passed on by sports associations. Sport affects all social classes and age groups and is an essential tool for social integration and education.

3.1 Enhancing the educational role of sport

The Commission's White Paper on Education and Training[1] stresses that 'knowledge is defined as an acquired corpus of fundamental and technical knowledge and social skills' that concern 'relational skills, such as the ability to cooperate and work as part of a team, creativeness and the quest for quality', all of which are values conveyed by sport. With this in mind, Community action, within the context of its educational and training programmes, could focus on the following objectives:

- *improving* the position of sport and physical education at school through the Community programmes;
- *promoting* the subsequent switch to other employment and future integration onto the labour market of sportsmen and women;
- *promoting* convergence between the training systems for sports workers in each Member State.

Moreover, the Council of Europe rightly stressed that sport is also 'an ideal platform for social democracy'.[2] It is therefore important for the existing Community programmes to make use of sport in combating exclusion, inequalities, racism and xenophobia.

Furthermore, the violence that sometimes develops at sporting events is unacceptable. As part of the European Union's objective to provide its citizens with a high level of protection in an area of freedom, safety and justice, the responsible authorities will have to step up their cooperation in order to prevent this type of violence.

3.2 Joining forces to combat doping

The Vienna European Council also wished to underline 'its concern at the extent and seriousness of doping in sports'. It mentioned the need for mobilisation at European Union level and invited the Member States and the Commission 'to examine possible measures to intensify the fight against this danger', together with the sports bodies.

The measures implemented by the Commission,[3] in close cooperation with the Member States, have focused on three fronts:

- *Referring* this matter to the European Group on Ethics. The opinion issued by this Group suggests a number of avenues that could be explored by the State authorities and sporting organisations;
- *Cooperating* with the Olympic movement to create a world anti-doping agency and to make sure that it works independently and transparently;
- *Mobilising* Community instruments to supplement and strengthen the work already carried out by the Member States in the areas of research, public health, education and youth, but also cooperation, as provided for by the

third pillar. Further work needs to be done to improve legislative coordination.

However, this work will come to nothing unless the public authorities and the sporting organisations tackle the root causes of the rise in doping. The development of the fight against doping also depends on the general development of sport.

4 Clarifying the legal environment of sport

As underlined by the conclusions of the European Union Conference on Sport organised by the Commission in Olympia in May 1999, 'sport must be able to assimilate the new commercial framework in which it must develop, without at the same time losing its identity and autonomy, which underpin the functions it performs in the social, cultural, health and educational areas'.

While the Treaty contains no specific provisions on sport, the Community must nevertheless ensure that the initiatives taken by the national State authorities or sporting organisations comply with Community law, including competition law, and respect in particular the principles of the internal market (freedom of movement for workers, freedom of establishment and freedom to provide services, etc.).

In this respect, accompanying, coordination or interpretation measures at Community level might prove to be useful, for example in the area of the fight against doping. They would be designed to strengthen the legal certainty of sporting activities and their social function at Community level. However, as Community powers currently stand, there can be no question of large-scale intervention or support programmes or even of the implementation of a Community sports policy.

4.1 *The increase in the number of conflicts*

The economic developments observed in the area of sport and the responses of the various State authorities and sporting organisations to the problems that they raise do not go far enough to guarantee that the current structures of sport and its social function can be safeguarded. The increase in the number of court proceedings is the sign of growing tension.

- Certain clubs contest the collective sale of television rights. Several complaints have been submitted to national courts, and the judgments delivered at national level have come to differing conclusions. The question of the collective sale of such rights is also raised in certain cases pending before the Commission;
- the Bosman judgment, delivered by the Court of Justice in December 1995 on the basis of the principle of freedom of movement for workers, has had major repercussions on the organisation of sport in Europe. It has done much to eliminate certain abuses and to promote the mobility of sportsmen and women. However, the sporting federations – which, incidentally, have not set up a new alternative system to the one condemned by the Court – consider that it has widened the economic gap between clubs and between players and has caused problems for the training of young people in clubs. Certain clubs which have established training centres for professional

sportsmen and women have seen their best people leave, without them receiving any compensation for the investment they have made in training;

- there are differences in fiscal legislation, and hence in the taxation of professional sportsmen and women or of sporting clubs, within the European Union. This situation is a source of inequality between countries and clubs and contributes to the phenomenon of ever higher offers;
- several Member States of the European Union have recently announced measures to limit or manage the effects of the commercialisation of sport. While these measures obviously help to preserve the principles and social function of sport, they may increase the disparities between Member States of the European Union and cause problems in the area of Community law;
- certain complaints also concern the monopoly of federations on the organisation of sporting competitions, the ownership of several clubs by one person (multiple ownership), the rules on the geographical organisation of sport, the statutes of professional clubs and certain commercial operations carried out by the federations.

On the other hand, other measures have been taken at the Community level, in keeping with the principle of subsidiarity, which are strengthening the legal framework while preserving the 'common interest' dimension of sport. One example is the decision taken at the time of the 1997 revision of the 'Television without Frontiers' Directive. Under the terms of the revised text, the Member States may take measures, in keeping with Community law, to ensure that the general public has access to major sporting events.

4.2 The need for convergent endeavours

If it is advisable, as wished by the European Council, but also the European Parliament[4] and the Committee of the Regions,[5] to preserve the social function of sport, and therefore the current structures of the organisation of sport in Europe, there is a need for a new approach to questions of sport both at European Union level and in the Member States, in compliance with the Treaty, especially with the principle of subsidiarity, and the autonomy of sporting organisations.

This new approach involves preserving the traditional values of sport, while at the same time assimilating a changing economic and legal environment. It is designed to view sport globally and coherently. This overall vision assumes greater consultation between the various protagonists (sporting movement, Member States and European Community) at each level. It should lead to the clarification, at each level, of the legal framework for sports operators.

The European Union would have an essential part to play in implementing this new approach, given the increasing internationalisation of sport and the direct impact of Community policies on European sport.

4.2.1 The Community level

In terms of the economic activity that it generates, the sporting sector is subject to the rules of the EC Treaty, like the other sectors of the economy. The application of the Treaty's competition rules to the sporting sector must take account of the specific characteristics of sport, especially the interdependence between sporting activity and the economic activity that it generates, the principle of equal opportunities and the uncertainty of the results.

With a view to an improved definition of the legal environment, it is possible to give examples, without prejudice to the conclusions that the Commission could draw from the in-depth analysis of each case, of practices of sports organisations.

4.2.1.1 Practices which do not come under the competition rules   The regulations of sporting organisations drawing up rules without which a sport could not exist, or which are necessary for its organisation or for the organisation of competitions, might not be subject to the competition rules. The rules inherent to sport are, first and foremost, the 'rules of the game'. The aim of these rules is not to distort competition.

4.2.1.2 Practices that are, in principle, prohibited by the competition rules   These are restrictive practices in the economic activities generated by sport. They may concern, in particular, restrictions on parallel imports of sports products and the sale of entrance tickets to stadiums that discriminate between users who are resident in a particular Member State and those who live outside that Member State.

Sponsoring agreements that close a market by removing other suppliers for no objective reason are prohibited. The systems of international transfers based on arbitrarily calculated payments which bear no relation to training costs seem to have been prohibited, irrespective of the nationality of the player concerned.

Lastly, it is likely that there would be a ban on the practice of a sporting organisation using its regulatory power to exclude from the market, for no objective reason, any economic operator which, even though it complies with the justified quality or safety standards, has not been able to obtain a document from this organisation certifying to the quality or safety of its products.

4.2.1.3 Practices likely to be exempted from the competition rules
- The *Bosman* judgment mentioned above recognised as legitimate the objectives designed to maintain a balance between clubs, while preserving a degree of equality of opportunity and the uncertainty of the result, and to encourage the recruitment and training of young players. Consequently, it is likely that agreements between professional clubs or decisions by their associations that are really designed to achieve these two objectives would be exempted. The same would be true of a system of transfers or standard contracts based on objectively calculated payments that are related to the costs of training, or of an exclusive right, limited in duration and scope, to broadcast sporting events. It goes without saying that the other provisions of the Treaty must also be complied with in this area, especially those that guarantee freedom of movement for professional sportsmen and women;
- It is likely that short-term sponsoring agreements based on an invitation to tender and with clear and non-discriminatory selection criteria would be authorised;
- any exemptions granted in the case of the joint sale of broadcasting rights must take account of the benefits for consumers and of the proportional nature of the restriction on competition in relation to the legitimate objective pursued. In this context, there is also a need to examine the extent to which a link can be established between the joint sale of rights and

financial solidarity between professional and amateur sport, the objectives of the training of young sportsmen and women and those of promoting sporting activities among the population. However, with regard to the sale of exclusive rights to broadcast sporting events, it is likely that any exclusivity which, by its duration and/or scope, resulted in the closing of the market, would be prohibited.

4.2.2 *The national level*

The national State authorities also need to clarify the legal rules in order to safeguard the current structures and the social function of sport. One way of safeguarding the national federal structures could be to provide for them to be recognised by law in each Member State of the Union. Other ways of achieving this objective would be the partnership agreements between the State and the sporting federations and to grant the representative sporting federations a specific status which could be based on that of the professional associations. There is also a need to examine, in legal terms, the legal status of clubs, their purchase or the participation of commercial or financial groups in their equity.

4.2.3 *The level of sporting organisations*

In order to clarify the legal environment of sport, it is also necessary for the federations to make an effort to define their missions and statutes more precisely. The pyramid structure of the organisation of sport in Europe gives sporting federations a practical 'monopoly'. The existence of several federations in one discipline would risk causing major conflicts. Indeed, the organisation of national championships and the selection of national athletes and national teams for international competitions often require the existence of one umbrella organization bringing together all the sports associations and competitors of one discipline.

The federations should also perform tasks such as the promotion of amateur and professional sport and carry out a role of integration into society (young people, the disabled, etc.). Their statutes should explicitly state these missions. These responsibilities should be translated effectively into practice by financial mechanisms of internal solidarity and the structural and solidarity-based relationship between competitive sport and amateur sport. Operations with an economic dimension should be founded on the principles of transparency and balanced access to the market, effective and proven redistribution and clarification of contracts, while prominence is given to the 'specific nature of sport'.

It must be stressed that the basic freedoms guaranteed by the Treaty do not generally conflict with the regulatory measures of sports associations, provided that these measures are objectively justified, non-discriminatory, necessary and proportional.

There is also a need to find solutions, in partnership with the sporting federations, in order to develop alternatives to the transfer systems condemned by the Bosman judgment.

5 Conclusion

If the Commission is asked whether it can guarantee that the current development of sport will not jeopardise the current structures and social function of sport, its unequivocal answer is that it cannot. It is indeed important to remember that the Commission has no direct responsibility for sport under the Treaty.

In order to safeguard the current sports structures and maintain the social function of sport, there is a need for a new approach to questions of sport. The first step towards such a new approach is for the various protagonists involved to respect a common foundation of sporting principles:

- The European Union recognises the eminent role played by sport in European society and attaches the greatest importance to the maintenance of its functions of promoting social integration and education and making a contribution to public health and to the general interest function performed by the federations;
- The integrity and autonomy of sport must be preserved. The purchase of sporting clubs by commercial bodies (communication groups etc.) must, if permitted, be governed by clear rules, out of a concern for the preservation of sporting structures and ethics;
- The system of promotion and relegation is one of the characteristics of European sport. This system gives small or medium-sized clubs a better chance and rewards sporting merit;
- Doping and sport are diametrically opposed. There can be no let-up in the fight against doping;
- The 'trade' in young sportsmen and women must be combated. Each young sportsman or woman trained by a club for top-level competition must receive vocational training in addition to sports training.

On the basis of these principles, there is a need for a new partnership between the European institutions, the Member States and the sports organisations, all moving in the same direction, in order to encourage the promotion of sport in European society, while respecting sporting values, the autonomy of sporting organisations and the Treaty, especially the principle of subsidiarity.

Insufficient coordination between the protagonists of sport (federations, Member States and the European Community), all of them working in isolation, would risk thwarting the efforts to achieve these shared principles. However, the convergent efforts of the European Community, the Member States and the sporting federations could make an effective contribution to the promotion in Europe of sport that is true to its social role, while ensuring that its organisational aspects assimilate the new economic order.

Notes

1 'Teaching and Learning: Towards the Knowledge-based Society', Commission White Paper on Education and Training, OPOCE, Luxembourg, 1995.
2 'Social Cohesion and Sport', Clearing House, Sport Division of the Council of Europe, Committee for the Development of Sport, Strasbourg, March 1999.
3 'Community Support Plan in the Combat against Doping in Sport', COM (1999) 643 of 1/12/99.
4 'Resolution of the European Parliament on the Role of the European Union in the Field of Sport', OJ C 200, 30/6/97.
5 Opinion of the Committee of the Regions on 'The European Model of sport', CdR 37/99, 15/9/99.

References

Allison, L. (ed.) (1986), *The Politics of Sport*, Manchester: Manchester University Press.

Allison, L. (ed.) (1993), *The Changing Politics of Sport*, Manchester: Manchester University Press.

Almond, G. and Powell, G. (1988), *Comparative Politics Today: A World View*, Chicago: Scott, Foresman.

Armstrong, K. and Bulmer, S. (1998), *The Governance of the Single European Market*, Manchester: Manchester University Press.

Baumgartner, F.R. and Jones, B.D. (1991), Agenda Dynamics and Policy Subsystems, *The Journal of Politics*, 53(4): 1044–1074.

Bell, S. and McGillivray, D. (2000), *Environmental Law*, 5th edition, London: Blackstone Press.

Bell, A. and Turner-Kerr, P. (2002), The Place of Sport within the Rules of Community Law: Clarification from the ECJ? The *Deliège* and *Lehtonen* Cases, *European Competition Law Review*, 23(5): 256–260.

Beloff, M., Kerr, T. and Demetriou, M. (1999), *Sports Law*, Oxford: Hart Publishing.

Blackshaw, I. (2002), The Battle for a Sports Protocol Continues, *Sports Law Bulletin*, 5(1): 14–15.

Blanpain, R. and Inston, R. (1996), *The Bosman Case: The End of the Transfer System?* Leuven, Belgium: Peeters and Sweet and Maxwell.

Bulmer, S. (1994), Institutions and Policy Change in the European Communities: The Case of Merger Control, *Public Administration*, 72(3): 423–444.

Bulmer, S. (1998), New Institutionalism and the Governance of the Single European Market, *Journal of European Public Policy*, 5(3): 365–386.

Burley, A.M. and Mattli, W. (1993), Europe Before the Court: A Political Theory of Legal Integration, *International Organisation*, 47(1): 41–76.

Caiger, A. and Gardiner, S. (eds) (2000), *Professional Sport in the European Union, Regulation and Re-regulation*, The Hague, Netherlands: T.M.C. Asser Press.

Cairns, W. (2002), Sports Law Current Survey, *Sport and the Law Journal*, 10(1): 8–117.

Cashmore, E. (1996), *Making Sense of Sports*, 2nd edition London: Routledge.

Cobb, R.W. and Elder, C.D. (1972), *Participation in American Politics: The Dynamics of Agenda Building*, Baltimore: Johns Hopkins University Press.

Collins, R. (1994), *Broadcasting and Audio-Visual Policy in the European Single Market*, London: John Libby.

Commission of the European Communities (1996), *Information on the Bosman Case, Sport Info Europe*, DG X, Brussels.

Commission of the European Communities (1998), Broadcasting of Sports Events and Competition Law, *Competition Policy Newsletter*, No. 2, June.

Coopers and Lybrand (1995), *The Impact of European Union Activities on Sport*, Study for DG X of the European Commission.

Craig, P. and De Búrca, G. (1998), *EU Law. Text, Cases and Materials*, Oxford: Oxford University Press.

Cram, L. (1994), The European Commission as a Multi-Organisation: Social Policy and IT Policy in the EU, *Journal of European Public Policy*, 1(2): 195–217.

Cram, L. (1996), Integration Theory and the Study of the European Policy Process, in J. Richardson, *European Union: Power and Policy-Making*, London: Routledge.

Cram, L. (1997), *Policymaking in the EU*, London: Routledge.

Cram, L., Dinan, D. and Nugent, N. (eds) (1999), *Developments in the European Union*, Basingstoke: Macmillan Press.

Dahl, R. (1961), *Who Governs? Democracy and Power in an American City*, New Haven, Conn: Yale University Press.

Doern, B. and Wilks, S. (1996), *Comparative Competition Policy, National Institutions in a Global Market*, Oxford: Clarendon Press.

Duff, A. (1998), Scottish Update: A Brief Synopsis of Newsworthy Matters Concerning Football, Rugby and Others from 1997 to Date, *Sport and the Law Journal*, 6(3): 93–101.

Easton, D. (1965), *A Systems Analysis of Political Life*, New York: Wiley.

Egger, A. and Stix-Hackl, C. (2002), Sports and Competition Law: A Never-Ending Story? *European Competition Law Review*, 23(2): 81–91.

European Voice (1996), All Work and No Play in IGC Talks, 20 September.

Featherstone, K. (1994), Jean Monnet and the Democratic Deficit in the EU, *Journal of Common Market Studies*, 32(2): 149–170.

Fenger, M. and Klok. P.-J. (2001), Interdependency, Beliefs, and Coalition Behaviour: A Contribution to the Advocacy Coalition Framework, *Policy Sciences*, 34: 157–170.

FIFPRO (2001), 'Time for a New Approach. The International Player Transfer System', *FIFPRO Report to the European Commission*, 9 February.

Financial Times (1999a), Brussels to Probe Football Dispute, 7 January.

Financial Times (1999b), Football Owners Fight for Sporting Chance, 2 June.

Foster, K. (1993), 'Developments in Sporting Law', in L. Allison (ed.), *The Changing Politics of Sport*, Manchester: Manchester University Press.

Foster, K. (2000a), Can Sport be Regulated by Europe? An Analysis of Alternative Models, in A. Caiger and S. Gardiner (eds), *Professional Sport in the EU, Regulation and Re-regulation*, The Hague, Netherlands: T.M.C. Asser Press.

Foster, K. (2000b) How can Sport be Regulated?, in S. Greenfield and G. Osborn (eds), *Law and Sport in Contemporary Society*, London: Frank Cass.

Gardiner, S. (1997), 'Birth of a Legal Area: Sport and the Law or Sports Law?', *Sport and the Law Journal*, 5(2): 10–14.

Gardiner, S., Felix, A., James, M., Welch, R. and O'Leary, J. (1998), *Sports Law. Text and Materials*, London: Cavendish Publishing.

Gardiner, S., James, M., O'Leary, J., Welch, R., Blackshaw, I., Boyes, S. and Caiger, A. (2001), *Sports Law. Text and Materials*, London: Cavendish Publishing.

Garrett, G. and Weingast, B.R. (1993), Ideas, Interests and Institutions: Constructing the European Community's Internal Market, in J. Goldstein and R. O. Keohane (eds), *Ideas and Foreign Policy: Beliefs, Institutions and Political Change*, Ithaca: Cornell University Press.

Goyder, D. (1998), *EC Competition Law*, Oxford: Oxford University Press.

Gray, J. (2000), Regulation of Sports Leagues, Team, Athletes and Agents in the United States, in A. Caiger and S. Gardiner (eds), *Professional Sport in the EU, Regulation and Re-regulation*, The Hague, Netherlands: T.M.C. Asser Press.

Grayson, E. (1994), *Sport and the Law*, 2nd edition, London: Butterworth and Co.

Greenfield, S. and Osborn, G. (eds) (2000), *Law and Sport in Contemporary Society*, London: Frank Cass.

Greenfield, S. and Osborn, G. (2001), *Regulating Football. Commodification, Consumption and the Law*, London: Pluto Press.

Griffith-Jones, D. (1997), *Law and the Business of Sport*, London: Butterworths and Co.

Haas, E. (1957), *The Uniting of Europe*, Stanford: Stanford University Press.

Haas, E. (1961), International Integration: The European and Universal Process, *International Organisation*, 15(3): 366–392.

Haas, E. (1976), Turbulent Fields and the Theory of Regional Integration, *International Organisation*, 30: 173–212.

Harcourt, A. (1998), EU Media Ownership Regulation: Conflict over the Definition of Alternatives, *Journal of Common Market Studies*, 36(3): 369–389.

Henry, I. and Matthews, N. (1998), Sport, Policy and European Union: The Post-Maastricht Agenda, *Managing Leisure* 3: 1–17.

Hix, S. (1999), *The Political System of the European Union*, Basingstoke: Macmillan.

Hoffmann, S. (1965), The European Process at Atlantic Cross Purposes, *Journal of Common Market Studies*, (3): 85–101.

Hoffmann, S. (1966), Obstinate or Obsolete? The Fate of the Nation State and the Case of Western Europe, *Daedelus*, 95: 862–915.

Hogwood, B. and Gunn, L. (1984), *Policy Analysis for the Real World*, Oxford: Oxford University Press.

Hoskins, M. (1999), The Impact of the Free Movement Rules of the EC on Sports, Conference Paper, Sports: Competition Law and EC Law, University College London, Faculty of Law, 10 February.

Houlihan, B. (1997), *Sport Policy and Politics: A Comparative Analysis*, London: Routledge.

Humphreys, P. (1996), *Mass Media and Media Policy in Western Europe*, Manchester: Manchester University Press.

Jessop, R. (1990), *State Theory: Putting Capitalist States in Their Place*, University Park, Pennsylvania: The Pennsylvania State University Press.

Jessop, R. (draft, 2000), *Institutional (Re) Turns and the Strategic-Relational Approach*, Published by the Department of Sociology, Lancaster University at: www.comp.lancaster.ac.uk/sociology/soc046rj.html

Kent, P. (2001), *The Law of the European Union*, Harlow: Longman.

Kingdon, J. (1995), *Agendas, Alternatives and Public Policies*, New York: Harper Collins.

Kinsella, S. and Daly, K. (2001), European Competition Law and Sports, *Sports Law Bulletin*, 4(6): 7–13.

Kirchner, E. (1992), *Decision-Making in the European Community: The Council Presidency and European Integration*, Manchester: Manchester University Press.

Kiser, L. and Ostrom, E. (1982), The Three Worlds of Action, in E. Ostrom (ed.), *Strategies of Political Inquiry*, E. Beverly Hills: Sage.

Lindberg, L. and Scheingold, S. (1970), *Europe's Would Be Polity: Patterns of Change in the European Community*, New Jersey: Englewood Cliffs.

Lindberg, L. and Scheingold, S. (1971), *Regional Integration Theory and Research*, Cambridge, Mass: Harvard University Press.

Majone, G. (1996), *Regulating Europe*, London: Routledge.

March, J. and Olsen, J. (1984), The New Institutionalism: Organisational Factors in Political Life, *American Political Science Review*, 78, 734–749.

March, J. and Olsen, J. (1989), *Rediscovering Institutions: The Organisational Basis of Politics*, New York: The Free Press.

Marks, G., Hooghe, L. and Blank, K. (1996), European Integration from the 1980s: State-Centric v. Multi-Level Governance, *Journal of Common Market Studies*, 34(3): 341–378.

Marwell, G. and Oliver, P. (1993), *The Critical Mass in Collective Action: A Micro-Social Theory*, Cambridge: Cambridge University Press.

McCormick, J. (1999), *Understanding the European Union*: McArdle, D. (2000), *From Boot Money to Bosman: Football, Society and the Law*, London: Cavendish Publishing. *A Concise Introduction*, Basingstoke: Macmillan.

Miller, F. (1996), Beyond Bosman, *Sport and the Law Journal*, 4(3): 45–53.

Milward, A. (1992), *The European Rescue of the Nation State*, London: Routledge.

Milward, A., Lynch, F.M.B., Ranieri, R., Romero, F. and Sørensen, V. (1993), *The Frontier of National Sovereignty: History and Theory, 1945–92*, London: Routledge.

Mintrom, M. and Vergari, S. (1996), Advocacy Coalitions, Policy Entrepreneurs, and Policy Change, *Policy Studies Journal*, 24(3): 420–434.

Mitrany, D. (1943 [1966]), *A Working Peace System*, Chicago: Quadrangle.

Moe, T. (1990), Political Institutions: The Neglected Side of the Story, *Journal of Law, Economics and Organisation*, 6: 213–253.

Monnington, T. (1992), Politicians and Sport: Uses and Abuses, in L. Allison, (ed.), *The Changing Politics of Sport*, Manchester: Manchester University Press.

Moravcsik, A. (1991), Negotiating the Single European Act , in R. Keohane and S. Hoffmann (eds), *The New European Community: Decision Making and Institutional Change*, Boulder, CO: Westview Press, pp. 41–84.

Moravcsik, A. (1993), Preferences and Power in the European Community, *Journal of Common Market Studies*, 31(4), 473–524.

Moravcsik, A. (1995), Liberal Intergovernmentalism and Integration: A Rejoinder, *Journal of Common Market Studies*, 33(4): 611–628.

Morris, P.E. *et al.* (1996), EC Law and Professional Football: Bosman and its Implications, *Modern Law Review*, 59(6): pp. 893–918.

Muttimer, D. (1989), 1992 and the Political Integration of Europe, *Journal of European Integration*, 13(1): 75–101.

Nugent, N. (1994), *The Government and Politics of the European Union*, 3rd edition, Basingstoke: Macmillan.

O'Keefe, D. and Osbourne, P. (1996), The European Court Scores a Goal, *The International Journal of Comparative Labour Law and Industrial Relations*, 12(2): 111–130.

O'Leary, J. (ed.) (2000), *Drugs and Doping in Sport: Socio-Legal Perspectives*, London: Cavendish Publishing.

O'Neill, M. (1996), *The Politics of European Integration*, London: Routledge.

Olson, M. (1971), *The Logic of Collective Action: Public Goods and the Theory of Groups*, Cambridge, MA: Harvard University Press.

Ostrom, E. (1999), Institutional Rational Choice: An Assessment of the Institutional Analysis and Development Framework, in P. Sabatier (ed.), *Theories of the Policy Process*, Boulder, CO: Westview Press.

Parry, R. (1996), Switching on and Tuning in to Money in Sport. The Impact of Sponsorship and Television on Sport in the United Kingdom, Speech to the Annual Conference of the British Association for Sport and Law 1996, *Sport and the Law Journal*, 4(3): 19–45.

Parsons, W. (1995), *Public Policy. An Introduction to the Theory and Practice of Policy Analysis*, Aldershot: Edward Elgar.

Peters, B.G. (1996), Agenda Setting in the European Union, in J. Richardson, *European Union: Power and Policy-Making*, London: Routledge.

Peterson, J. (1995), Decision Making in the European Union: Towards a Framework for Analysis, *Journal of European Public Policy*, 2(1): 69–93.

Peterson, J. and Bomberg, E. (1999), *Decision-Making in the European Union*, Basingstoke: Macmillan.

Pierson, P. (1996), The Path to European Integration: A Historical Institutionalist Analysis, *Comparative Political Studies*, 29(2): 123–163

Pinder, J. (1968), Positive and Negative Integration. Some Problems of Economic Union in the EEC, *World Today*, 24: 88–110.

Pinder, J. (1993), The Single Market: A Step Towards Union, in J. Lodge (ed.), *The European Community and the Challenge of the Future*, 2nd edition, London: Pinter.

Pollack, M. (1994), Creeping Competence: The Expanding Agenda of the European Community, *Journal of Public Policy*, 14(2): 95–145.

Pollack, M. (1996), The New Institutionalism and EC Governance: The Promise and Limits of Institutional Analysis, *Governance: An International Journal of Policy and Administration*, 9(4): 429–458.

Pollack, M. (2000), The End of Creeping Competence? EU Policy-Making Since Maastricht, *Journal of Common Market Studies*, 38(3): 519–538.

Polsby, N. (1993), quoted in R. Hague *et al.*: *Comparative Government and Politics, an Introduction*, Basingstoke, London.

Pons, J.-F. (1999), Speech to the Fordham Corporate Law Institute's Twenty-Sixth Annual Conference on International Anti-Trust Law and Policy, New York, 14–15 October.

Radaelli, C. (1999a), *Technocracy in the European Union*, London: Longman.

Radaelli, C. (1999b), The Public Policy of the European Union: Whither Politics of Expertise?, *Journal of European Public Policy*, 6(5): 757–774.

Rasmussen, H. (1986), *On Law and Policy in the European Court of Justice: A Comparative Study in Judicial Policy-Making*, Dortrecht: M. Nijhoff.

Ratliff, J. (1998), EC Competition Law and Sport, *Sport and the Law Journal*, 6(3): 4–17.

Rhodes, R. (1988), *Beyond Westminster and Whitehall: The Sub-Central Governments of Britain*, London: Unwin Hyman.

Richardson, J. and Jordan, A.G. (1979), *Governing Under Pressure, the Policy Process in a Post-Parliamentary Democracy*, Oxford: Martin Robertson.

Richardson, J. (1996), *European Union: Power and Policy-Making*, London: Routledge.

Rochefort, D. and Cobb, R. (1994), *The Politics of Problem Definition, Shaping the Policy Agenda*, Lawrence, KA: University Press of Kansas.

Sabatier, P. (1988), An Advocacy Coalition Framework of Policy Change and the Role of Policy-Oriented Learning Therein, *Policy Sciences*, 21: 129–168.

Sabatier, P. (1991), Toward Better Theories of the Policy Process, *Political Science and Politics*, 24: 147–156.

Sabatier, P. (1998), The Advocacy Coalition Framework: Revisions and Relevance for Europe, *Journal of European Public Policy*, 5(1): 98–130.

Sabatier, P. (ed.) (1999), *Theories of the Policy Process*, Boulder CO: Westview Press.

Sandholtz, W. and Zysman, J. (1989), 1992: Recasting the European Bargain, *World Politics*, 42: 95–128.

Scharpf, F. (1988), The Joint Decision-Trap: Lessons From German Federalism and European Integration, *Public Administration*, 66(3): 239–278.

Scharpf, F. (1997), *Games Real Actors Play*, Oxford: Westview Press.

Schattschneider, E.E. (1960), *The Semi-Sovereign People*, New York: Holt, Rinehart and Winston.

Schaub, A. (1998), *EC Competition Policy and its Implications for the Sports Sector*, Speech delivered to the World Sports Forum, St Moritz, March.

Schlager, E. (1995), Policy Making and Collective Action: Defining Coalitions Within the Advocacy Coalition Framework, *Policy Sciences* 28: 243–270.

Spink, P. and Morris, P. (2000), The Battle for TV Rights in Professional Sport, in A. Caiger and S. Gardiner (eds), *Professional Sport in the EU: Regulation and Re-regulation*, The Hague, Netherlands: T.M.C. Asser Press.

Van den Brink, J.P. (2000a), EC Competition Law and the Regulation of Football: Part 1, *European Competition Law Review*, 8: 359–368.

Van den Brink, J.P. (2000b), EC Competition Law and the Regulation of Football: Part II, *European Competition Law Review*, 9: 420–427.

Van Miert, K. (1997), *Sport and Competition*, Speech by Commissioner Van Miert, 27 November.

Volcansek, M. (1992), The European Court of Justice: Supranational Policymaking, *West European Politics*, 15 (July): 109–121.

Weatherill, S. (1989), Discrimination on the Grounds of Nationality in Sport, *Yearbook of European Law*, 55(9): 55–92.

Weatherill, S. (2000a), 0033149875354: Fining the Organizers of the 1998 Football World Cup, *European Competition Law Review*, 21(6): 275–282.

Weatherill, S. (2000b), Resisting the Pressures of 'Americanisation': The Influence of European Community Law on the 'European Model of Sport', in S. Greenfield and G. Osborn (eds), *Law and Sport in Contemporary Society*, London: Frank Cass.

Weiler, J. (1981), The Community System: The Dual Character of Supranationalism, *Yearbook of European Law*, 1: 268–306.

Weiler, J.H.H. (1993), Journey to an unknown destination: a retrospective and prospective of the European Court of Justice in the arena of political integration, *Journal of Common Market Studies*, 31(4): 417–446.

Wincott, D. (1996), The Court of Justice and the European Policy Process in J. Richardson, *European Union. Power and Policy Making*, London: Routledge.

World Soccer (1997), The Revolution Will Be Televised, January.

Tables of statutes, cases, decisions and reports

European Union Secondary Legislation

Decisions of the European Court of Justice and Court of First Instance

Presidency Publications and Miscellaneous Member State Papers

Cases before the National Courts

Miscellaneous publications

Index